THE OFFICIAL New Print Shop HANDBOOK

THE OFFICIAL *New*
Print Shop
HANDBOOK

IDEAS, TIPS, AND DESIGNS FOR HOME, SCHOOL, AND PROFESSIONAL USE

MARY SCHENCK and RANDI BENTON

Foreword by Doug Carlston, President, Broderbund Software

BANTAM BOOKS

TORONTO · NEW YORK · LONDON · SYDNEY · AUCKLAND

THE OFFICIAL NEW PRINT SHOP HANDBOOK

A Bantam Book / August 1990

ISBN 0-553-34967-8

Published simultaneously in the United States and Canada

*Bantam Books are published by Bantam Books, a division of Bantam Doubleday Dell
Publishing Group, Inc. Its trademark, consisting of the words "Bantam Books" and
the portrayal of a rooster, is Registered in U.S. Patent and Trademark Office and in
other countries. Marca Registrada, Bantam Books, 666 Fifth Avenue, New York, New
York 10103*

PRINTED IN THE UNITED STATES OF AMERICA

0 9 8 7 6

To my parents — for always believing

RB

To my young daughter, Laura — who inspires me
with the spirit of adventure
and freshness she brings to all her endeavors

MS

Foreword

by Doug Carlston
President, Brøderbund Software

The initial success and phenomenal staying power of The Print Shop have delighted us all. The program and its successor, The New Print Shop, have sold over 2 million copies, with no sign of slowing down. It has been used in the home, and by schools and businesses to create greeting cards, signs, and banners for many uses, both ordinary and extraordinary. Our users have expressed themselves creatively in ways that inspired us to new levels of creativity ourselves.

The success of the first *Official Print Shop Handbook* proved beyond a doubt that Print Shop users were still eager for creative ways to get more power. Randi Benton and Mary Schenck spoke to these needs in their first book and showed how a little imagination could go a long way.

Over the years, users have written to us asking for features such as improved resolution, multiple graphics on a page, the ability to place graphics anywhere they wanted, and multicolor printing. As we collected more and more of these ideas from our users, we realized the time had come to enhance The Print Shop, knowing we could make creativity even easier. The original concept of The Print Shop has now been expanded in ways that are consistent with the creativity and simplicity of the original version. The New Print Shop offers more powerful features with the same Print Shop ease of use.

We are proud of the results and look forward to a new generation of loyal users. *The Official New Print Shop Handbook* will help you see many of the features at a glance and show you how to put them to work right away. The original Print Shop software and handbook of ideas proved to be a bestselling pair. I believe, once again, we've delivered another winning combination. I hope your New Print Shop experience proves us right!

Authors' Note

While attending the 1989 New York International Toy Fair, we visited the newly renovated showroom of a major toy manufacturer. An impressive lobby of marble and fresh flowers led to an area of spectacular exhibitry. Upon entering the showroom, we were led down a hallway where a sign directed us to various rooms on the floor — a sign created on The Print Shop!

We continue to document Print Shop sightings in the most unlikely places — from a multimillion dollar showroom in New York to a tiny museum in a French hilltown. In spite of all recent technological advances, The Print Shop appears to be alive and well and as popular as ever. That magic formula combining ease-of-use with the power to create continues to keep The Print Shop in high demand.

Having spent a good deal of time with The New Print Shop, we're keeping our pencils sharpened. Our list of Print Shop sightings is certain to grow. The creators of The New Print Shop have successfully integrated even greater ease-of-use with more Print Shop power than ever before. Our old friend has a new suit of clothes.

When we proposed to write the first *Official Print Shop Handbook*, we believed the sharing of ideas would serve as a valuable resource to fellow Print Shop users. With the success of that book, our belief was confirmed. We began developing ideas for this book much the same way we began the first — by booting up our Print Shop disks and challenging ourselves to once again "think something different." We set out to explore The New Print Shop and exploit the new range of creative opportunities.

We invite you to copy our ideas. Edit them. Embellish them! We hope you'll use this new Handbook to its fullest advantage — let it spark new ideas of your own. As before, the only limit is your imagination!

Acknowledgments

Many thanks to my friends at Broderbund, Bill Rooney, for tirelessly answering the questions, Ruth Friedman, Ann Kronen, Leslie Wilson; to my friends at Bantam, Kenzi Sugihara, for pioneering our first book and so graciously supporting this second effort, Mike Roney, for keeping us on track, John Kilcullen, Terry Nasta, Otto Barz; to my family, for understanding the missed weekends; and finally to my husband, Mark, friend and confidant, for maintaining humor and balance through it all.

Randi Benton

Forest Hills, New York

March, 1990

Grateful appreciation to Gary Schenck for demonstrating no limit to his patience or ideas; to my friend Judi Heiner for living through endless printer noise the summer I stayed with her in San Francisco; to her son, Jess, for his contributions and sense of humor; to Rob Powers for his talents; to Kenzi and Michael at Bantam for sticking with us; and to Broderbund for continuing their excellence in publishing easy-to-use, practical, and fun software for all ages.

Mary Schenck

Santa Fe, New Mexico

March, 1990

Contents

New and Modified Art

Art You Can Create
New Art

Planning Tools

About the Handbook

- WELCOME TO THE NEW PRINT SHOP

- WHY A HANDBOOK OF IDEAS

- WHAT'S IN THIS BOOK

- HOW TO USE THIS BOOK

- LET'S GET STARTED

- A FINAL WORD...

Welcome to The New Print Shop

When the original Print Shop program was introduced, a software phenomenon was born. The extraordinary balance between ease of use and power to create was the secret of Print Shop's appeal. The same program used by third-graders to make school play signs was used by small-business owners to make cash register signs. The Print Shop was truly a program for all ages.

We are delighted to report that the Print Shop has grown up. Thanks to the input of thousands of loyal Print Shop users (young and old), the New Print Shop is loaded with features that provide more flexibility and more creative opportunity. Graphics can be mixed, moved, cloned, flipped, flopped, stretched, shrunk, and more. Fonts can be combined. Margins can be altered. Layouts can be customized. While preserving original Print Shop ease of use, the creators of The New Print Shop have added new dimension to Print Shop power.

Welcome to The Print Shop. It's NEW and improved—and even better than before!

Why a Handbook of Ideas

The pencil and paper are productivity tools. So are the paintbrush and canvas. The New Print Shop is a different kind of productivity tool.

What each of these tools produces depends largely on the user. Of course, there are inherent differences between the tools. The pen and paintbrush allow for a creative environment that is so open-ended and so dependent on the individual user that in most cases it is difficult (if not impossible) for one person to duplicate another's work. Training can certainly hone one's skills, but a person can't be taught to sketch a Picasso or paint a da Vinci—even with a set of instructions from the master himself!

The Print Shop is different. Its creative environment is more structured and more defined. It is quite possible, and in most cases simple, for two people who share ideas to turn out not only similar designs but exact replicas! A set of instructions works wonders with this tool.

This Handbook is a collection of ideas, guides, hints, and facts. The ideas are organized so that you can flip through the pages, find one that suits you, follow step-by-step instructions, and copy or adapt the ideas all in a matter of minutes. It's a book designed to help you get more power in less time whenever you sit down with The New Print Shop.

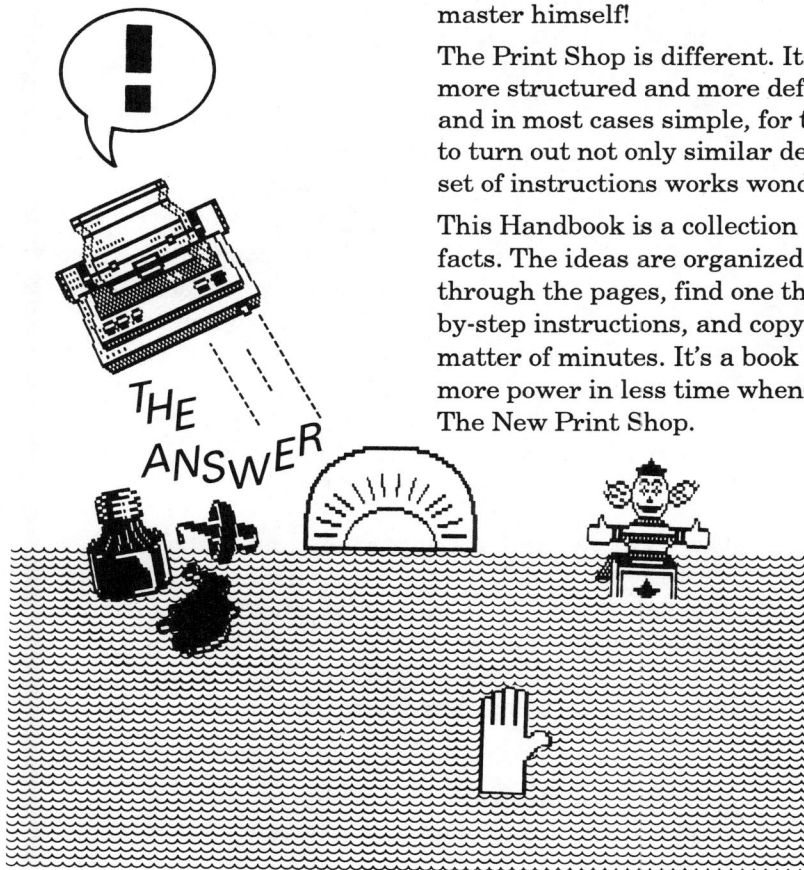

THE
ANSWER

What's in This Book

As New Print Shop users we appreciate the ease with which greeting cards, signs, banners, and letterheads can be created. But most of us only scratch the surface of Print Shop power. In this book are hundreds of ideas to help you get beyond that surface.

Ideas for Home, School, and Professional Use

You need an idea for a party announcement. A school or club announcement. A business announcement. You've come to the right place!

The New Print Shop can be used for so many different reasons. Yet, most applications fall into one of five categories: Home, Party, Learning Materials, School/Organization, or Professional, and that's exactly how the designs in the Handbook are organized. In this way, you can go right to the section that will most appropriately suit your particular need.

New Ideas for Old Applications

You need a sophisticated sign for an office get-together. A playful sign for a child's room. And an attention-getting flyer for a garage sale. Where do you begin? With this book, of course. Included are a large assortment of signs, greeting cards, letterheads and banners with different looks and styles for different purposes. There are ideas to illustrate where, when, and how to make the most of a sign—or a banner. Easy-to-copy techniques used by professional designers will even help give your original designs a more polished look.

New Applications

There's no rule that the sign mode can only be used to create signs. The sign mode can be used to make wrapping paper and flyers or to type memos. The sign and letterhead modes can generate great business cards. In this book are designs for more than 25 different kinds of items you can make using the five basic Print Shop modes.

Design Concepts

Designs often illustrate basic design concepts. For example, a design may show how a certain kind of graphic or font can be used to deliver a message. Fundamental design concepts are illustrated and pointed out for you in many of the Handbook's designs. These concepts can be applied to your original designs and may even open doors to new ideas.

Two Modes Together or One Mode Twice

Here are two ideas that can further broaden the range of what you can do with The New Print Shop.

■ Print a design in one mode, roll back your paper to the starting point, and then add text or art using a different mode.

■ Print a design in one mode, roll back your paper to the starting point, and then add a second graphic using the same mode.

Use the letterhead and sign modes together; or the sign mode twice to mix full panel graphics with other graphics. In the chapter Designs, Designs, Designs you'll find several examples.

Modified Print Shop Art

To make a strong graphic statement you may require a solid silhouetted figure or a simple line drawing. Luckily, with The New Print Shop you may not need to start from scratch! All Print Shop graphics can be easily modified. Included are lots of ideas on how to give Print Shop graphics an entirely new look. There are easy-to-copy techniques to create totally new objects and symbols using existing Print Shop art.

New Art

There are times when even the large assortment of Print Shop graphics just doesn't suit your needs. The New Art section provides easy-to-create alternatives. Each graphic includes suggestions and applications to show you the look or feel each graphic can contribute to a design.

Planning/Time-Saving Devices

A sure way to save time is to plan ahead and know what to expect. Suppose you're about to create a greeting card that calls for a large graphic surrounded by words at the top and bottom. Which graphic layout and which font size and style should you select? On which lines should you type your message? How many lines can you use? The planning section of the Handbook eliminates the guesswork. You'll see every graphic layout and every Print Shop font style and size all in one place.

Hints and Shortcuts

When you set out to use any software program, talking to someone who's spent time with it almost always reveals a personal list of hints and shortcuts. In preparing this book a number of such lists were consolidated. Many hints and shortcuts appear in this book with the items that utilize them. The most widely applicable ones are also in a separate hint section in Designs, Designs, Designs for you to use and apply to your own designs right away!

How to Use This Book

When you're working with The New Print Shop, we hope you'll keep this book nearby. We're certain you'll discover many different ways to use the ideas. Here are our suggestions for getting the most mileage out of each section.

The Designs

COPY A DESIGN

When you find a design idea you like, by all means copy it! All designs come with easy-to-follow, step-by-step instructions precisely for that reason.

ADAPT A DESIGN

You find a design idea that would be just right if only it had a few more lines of text. Or a few less lines of text. Or a different font style. Or a different graphic. Adapt it! Whenever you're looking for an idea, consider adding to the Handbook's ideas. Embellish them. Edit them. Use them as stepping stones to another valuable resource of ideas—you.

SUBSTITUTE A GRAPHIC

It's been said that a picture is worth a thousand words. Then replacing one picture with another very different one should have equally dramatic results. It does! When you're looking at a design idea, think about using that same design with the graphic best suited for your message. For many designs, alternative graphics that work well are suggested. But by no means should you restrict yourself to these suggestions. Only you know what will work best for the message you are trying to convey.

THINK MULTIPURPOSE

For your convenience, the design ideas are organized into five categories: Home, Party, Learning Materials, School/Organization, Professional. However, there may be a letterhead in the professional section that is perfect for your personal use, or a sign in the home section that is perfect for your small business or school. When you're looking for ideas, think multipurpose! Consider ideas from all five sections.

COMBINE TWO IDEAS

Many designs in this book are intended to illustrate a single strong concept. For example, some designs demonstrate how and when to use rules with text. Others focus on the selection and placement of graphics. When you're considering a new design idea, think about combining two ideas from the Handbook. You may find two ideas (or more) that work extremely well together in one of your original creations.

USE A DESIGN FOR A DIFFERENT ITEM

You come across a birthday card design that would be perfect for an invitation. Adapt it and use it. You see a greeting card design that would be perfect for a party sign. Even better! Designs for greeting cards and signs, in fact, are interchangeable. The greeting card and sign modes offer the exact same choices for graphics and text. The only difference is that in the sign mode the design prints larger. Therefore, it's easy to apply a greeting card design to a sign and vice versa. Just make the same choices for graphics and text and you're ready to point!

The Art

DON'T FORGET THE OVERVIEW PAGE

When you need a design idea, you may want to start by selecting a graphic element and building from there. The art overview page is a tool to keep in mind. Here you'll find reduced samples of all the new and modified Handbook art. It's a great place to start thinking about a look for your design. Finding the right graphic on which to focus your design may be exactly what's needed for inspiration.

COPY, ADAPT, EMBELLISH

As with the designs, if you find a piece of art you like, you needn't go further. Copy it! But consider adapting the graphics, too. For example, you may want to add more lines or thicker lines to a graphic. You may want to embellish a graphic with a decorative element or even with your initials. You may want to combine parts of two graphics. Or edit and use just part of one graphic. Remember, let the Handbook's ideas be your springboard.

MODIFY ANY GRAPHIC

Every Print Shop graphic can be modified. Techniques such as turning Print Shop graphics into silhouette drawings or into black line drawings can be applied to many different items. You can start building your own personal library of graphics.

The Planning Tools

GET TO KNOW THE LAYOUTS

When you're working on an original Print Shop design, head straight for the layouts. They show where on a page graphics will appear. So, for example, if you're thinking about creating a greeting card with several small birthday cakes surrounding a larger one, first consult the layouts. Before you even turn on your computer you'll know which layout best suits your idea. And you'll know which layout to call on when you begin your design.

GET TO KNOW THE CUSTOMIZE FEATURES

The key to New Print Shop power lies primarily in the customize features. Layouts can be altered. Graphics can be flipped, stretched, or moved. The customize features add new dimension to Print Shop power.

The Handbook provides a "visual overview" of all Print Shop customize features. For each feature, a sample illustration is shown. You'll see at a glance the results of putting each feature to work. Use the customize features section to spark new design ideas—the possibilities are endless.

GET TO KNOW THE FONTS

You know exactly what words to use in your message, but you're not sure in which font to say them. Turn to the fonts section to review your options. You'll see exactly how each Print Shop font style fits on a page in the small and large sizes. You'll see the maximum number of lines you can use and approximately how many letters will fit on each line. If you have a short, strong message, choose a large bold font. If you have a more detailed message, simply choose one of the smaller fonts.

GET TO KNOW THE GRAPHICS

A picture is worth a thousand words—cliché, but true. Choosing the right picture is critical for any good design. To make the selection process easier for you, the Handbook shows all New Print Shop graphics in one place. Every graphic from The New Print Shop, Sample Edition, School & Business Edition, and Party Edition is included. Simply flip through the pages whenever you need to find just the right picture to express an idea.

GRAPHIC PATTERNS—STUDY THE POSSIBILITIES

When considering design ideas, take a look at the possible patterns formed by the placement of graphics as shown in the graphic layouts. The variety of pattern possibilities may trigger ideas.

THINK CREATIVE LAYOUTS

Try some creative layouts. For example, plan a design with all text on the left and graphics on the right. Try alternating lines of graphics with text, or inserting graphics between words on a line. Think creatively—and then let the planning tools work for you!

Handbook Symbols—At a Glance

Throughout the Handbook design and art pages are easy-to-recognize symbols that tell you at a glance where you are and what you need to create each item. Here are the symbols you'll find:

Home Designs

Party Designs

Learning Materials

School/Organization Designs

Professional Designs

New Art

Modified Print Shop Art

NP The New Print Shop

S Sampler Edition

S/B School & Business Edition

P Party Edition

Let's Get Started

What You Need to Start Creating

You don't need much! If you're a Print Shop owner with an IBM or Apple II compatible computer (and accompanying manual for first time users), you're ready to start creating hundreds of new designs. The ideas are right here! If, in addition, you own the Sampler Edition, School & Business Edition or Party Edition—you'll find lots of ideas for these programs, too.

How the Designs Are Organized

The five design sections (Home, Party, Learning Materials, School/Organization, Professional) each have a variety of categories such as letterheads, business cards, flyers, ads, greeting cards, banners, and wrapping paper. The design categories are listed in alphabetical order.

What You Need for Each Design

To let you know immediately if more than the original Print Shop program itself was used to create a design, every design is marked with symbols for one or more of the following programs shown on the preceding page:

> The New Print Shop
>
> Sampler Edition
>
> School & Business Edition
>
> Party Edition

Consider Every Design—No Matter Which Programs You Own

When you look at a design, one of the first things you'll notice is the symbol(s) indicating which program(s) was used to create that design. If the design calls for The New Print Shop program only or an additional program that you own, you know you'll be able to copy or adapt the design quickly and easily. But keep this in mind: *when you see a design that uses a program you don't have, don't rule it out!* In most cases, alternative graphic choices are suggested in the design notes at the bottom of the page. One of these suggestions may be suitable for your purpose. It may even work better! And for many

Following the Step-by-Step Instructions

designs you're certain to have substitution ideas of your own.

So let's get started! Just pick out a Handbook design and follow the step-by-step instructions. You'll be printing in no time. Instructions are included for every design right on the design page. They lead you through the design, one step at a time, every step of the way. Only one item is left out—the guesswork!

A Final Word

As soon as we began gathering ideas for The New Print Shop, we were met by our single greatest challenge—to think creatively.

In the highly acclaimed film *Dead Poets Society*, Robin Williams, who plays the eccentric Professor John Keating, speaks so effectively of the process of creative thinking when he leaps onto his classroom desk and exclaims, "Why do I stand here? To feel taller than you? I stand on my desk to remind myself that we must constantly look at things differently."

We set out to explore The New Print Shop and to look at things differently. To go beyond the obvious, to use New Print Shop tools in search of new ideas.

We hope you find the ideas in this book useful—and inspiring. Be bold with your own ideas. Unleash your imagination and think big! We'd like nothing better than for you to continue on The New Print Shop discovery road from where we left off.

THINK BIG

Designs, Designs, Designs

- ■ WHAT'S IN THIS SECTION

- ■ USING THIS SECTION

- ■ HINTS, TIPS, AND SHORTCUTS

- ■ THE DESIGN PAGE

- ■ THE PATTERN ABBREVIATIONS

- HOME

- PARTY

- LEARNING MATERIALS

- SCHOOL/ORGANIZATION

- PROFESSIONAL

What's in This Section

Ideas! Ideas! Ideas! The Handbook's design pages contain hundreds and hundreds of ideas. For your convenience, they are organized into five categories: Home, Party, Learning Materials, School/Organization, Professional. Each category is further defined by topics such as letterhead, card, sign, or flyer. Every page is clearly marked so that you can find the design idea you're looking for easily and quickly.

The Handbook's designs show a wide variety of approaches to The New Print Shop. Together, the designs stretch the limits of The New Print Shop and broaden the range of what you can do. Highlighted here is an overview of what you'll find in this section.

New Ideas for Old Applications: A large assortment of signs, greeting cards, letterheads, and banners with different looks and styles for different purposes.

New Applications: Using the five basic Print Shop modes, you'll find designs for more than 25 unique items such as ads, business cards, and wrapping paper.

Designer Techniques: Easy-to-copy techniques used by professional designers that can help give your original designs a more polished look.

Design Concepts: Fundamental design concepts to consider applying to your original designs.

Ideas for Combining Modes: Sample designs created from a single powerful concept — use two different Print Shop modes together.

Hints, Tips, and Shortcuts: Twenty-three hints and shortcuts you can put to work for you right away.

Using This Section

If you were to count the number of designs in this section, you would come up with 109. Not bad. Does that mean there also are 109 ideas? Absolutely not! Many designs combine two, three or more ideas. And there are alternative ideas in the Design Notes on every page.

To get the most out of Designs, Designs, Designs, look beyond the printed designs shown. Think of these designs as examples. They've been included not only for you to copy (which, of course, you're welcome to do!) but also to give you a sense of what can be done — Print Shop possibilities.

Highlighted here are suggestions for using this section.

Suggestion #1: When you find a design idea you like, by all means copy it!

Suggestion #2: When you find a design idea you like, but it isn't quite right for your application, adapt it! Change the design. Make it work for your specific need.

Suggestion #3: Add your own ideas to the Handbook designs. Embellish them! Edit them!

Suggestion #4: When you're looking for a design idea, say a sign for a garage sale, don't restrict yourself only to designs from the most obvious section: Home. There may well be a sign in the School or Professional section that can easily be adapted and better suited for the garage sale sign you want to create. Keep in mind these two words: THINK MULTIPURPOSE! Consider designs from all five sections.

Suggestion #5: When you see a design that uses a Print Shop program you don't have, don't rule it out! In many cases, alternative choices are offered in the Design Notes. And you're likely to have substitution ideas of your own.

Suggestion #6: When you look at a design, think about the graphic best suited for your message. Substituting a graphic is easy and may be the only change needed to make a design work just right for you.

Suggestion #7: Combine ideas from two (or more) Handbook designs.

Suggestion #8: Use one design idea for an entirely different item. Turn a birthday card into a friendship card or a thank you note. Turn the front of the card into a sign.

Suggestion #9: Use the Handbook's ideas as stepping stones to another vast source of original ideas — YOU!

Tricks and Techniques: An Overview

In creating New Print Shop designs, special techniques can be used to achieve even greater variety. Two techniques are worth noting with a brief explanation. Apply them to your original work for added flexibility and more power.

■ **Combining Modes.** New Print Shop designs can be created using two different modes together (e.g. sign and letterhead) or the same mode twice (e.g. sign mode twice to combine full panel graphic with other graphic). With this technique you simply work in one mode and print, then roll back your paper, work in a second mode and print again. It's a terrific way to open doors to new design possibilities. Make sure that all graphics and text fall where you want them to by marking your original print starting point with a light pencil. In this way, you can carefully control where the graphics and/or text from the second printing will appear in relationship to the first. For some designs you will want to start your second printing at the same point as your first. For other designs you may want to start higher or lower.

■ **Cutting and Pasting.** With scissors and glue at hand, The New Print Shop possibilities are limitless. You can use the cut and pasted sample as your original — unless you're planning to send the piece to a printer for reproduction. If so, the printer will photograph your pasted-up design for printing. Or you can copy the piece on a copying machine and duplicate your pasted-up design yourself.

Getting to Know the Symbols

Every Handbook design is clearly marked with easy-to-recognize symbols to let you know immediately if more than just the original Print Shop program was used to create that design. The Handbook's symbols are reviewed for you here.

NP   The New Print Shop

S   Sampler Edition

S/B   School & Business Edition

P   Party Edition

Getting to Know the Design Page

The design page comes complete with the following information:

Category (e.g., Home)

Topic identification (e.g., Flyer)

Printout of the Design

What You Need

What You Do

Hints

Design Notes

Each of these elements is called out and explained on the reduced design page shown on page 31.

Getting to Know the Pattern Abbreviations

Step-by-step instructions that reflect the order of Print Shop screen choices are included for every design right on the page under the heading What You Do. These instructions use easy-to-follow pattern abbreviations. As you move through the Print Shop screens, the pattern abbreviations will become much more obvious. Your design choices can be made quickly and easily.

All pattern abbreviations are outlined on pages 32–35. Refer back to this section whenever you're not sure what a particular abbreviation represents in a pattern.

About the Graphic Positions

In a design, each graphic has a unique position. For the Handbook designs, the position of every graphic is indicated in the step-by-step instructions. The position of a graphic is referenced by 2 numbers: a ROW or COLUMN number and a POSITION number. For example, a graphic in the top left corner of a Handbook design is likely to be in Row 1, Position 1.

For purposes of identifying graphic positions, the Print Shop layouts can be grouped into four categories:

Layouts with ROWS

Layouts with COLUMNS

FRAMED Layouts

Layouts with MIXED GRAPHIC SIZES

An example of each layout category is shown in the illustrations that follow on pages 21 and 22. Each graphic position is labeled. The appropriate Handbook pattern abbreviations are also shown for reference. (For more about the Pattern Abbreviations, see page 32.)

Counting Lines in the Handbook Designs

The step-by-step design instructions indicate the line number on which every line of text is typed. Counting lines is easy. The lines on a page are counted consecutively from top to bottom. Each line of text, regardless of font style or size, counts as one line. Each blank line also counts as one line.

To follow the Handbook's design instructions count each line on screen as one line. Begin entering your message by moving the cursor to the first line indicated in the step-by-step instructions. When the cursor is on the appropriate line, select the font style and size required. Then enter your text. Unless otherwise indicated, all blank lines are in the current font selected in the small

(Continued on page 23)

1. REVERSED DIAMOND (Layout with ROWS)

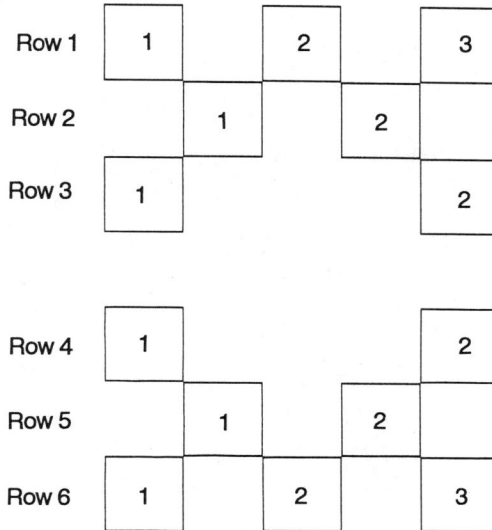

Row 1	1	2	3
Row 2		1	2
Row 3	1		2

Pattern Abbreviations

(ROW 1)1,2,3
(ROW 2)1,2
(ROW 3)1,2
(ROW 4)1,2
(ROW 5)1,2
(ROW 6)1,2,3

Row 4	1		2
Row 5		1	2
Row 6	1	2	3

2. MIXED COLUMNS (Layout with COLUMNS)

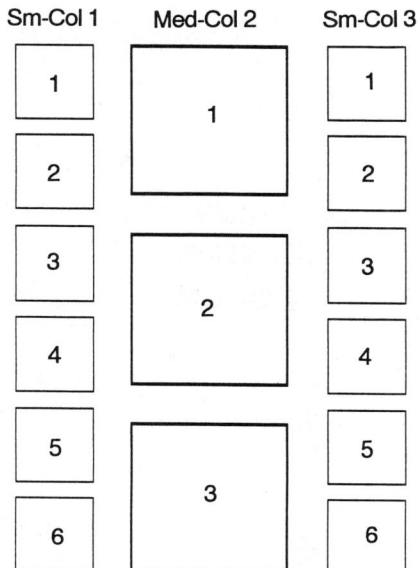

Sm-Col 1   Med-Col 2   Sm-Col 3

Sm-Col 1	Med-Col 2	Sm-Col 3
1	1	1
2		2
3	2	3
4		4
5	3	5
6		6

Pattern Abbreviations

(SM-COL 1)1,2,3,4,5,6
(MED-COL 2)1,2,3
(SM-COL 3)1,2,3,4,5,6

3. SMALL FRAME II (Framed Layout)

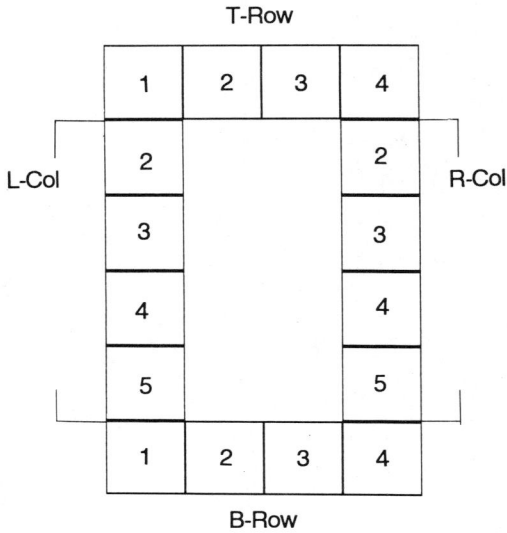

T-Row

1	2	3	4

L-Col

2	2
3	3
4	4
5	5

R-Col

1	2	3	4

B-Row

Pattern Abbreviations

(T-ROW)1,2,3,4

(B-ROW)1,2,3,4

(L-COL)2,3,4,5

(R-COL)2,3,4,5

MIXED ROWS (Layout with Mixed Graphic Sizes)

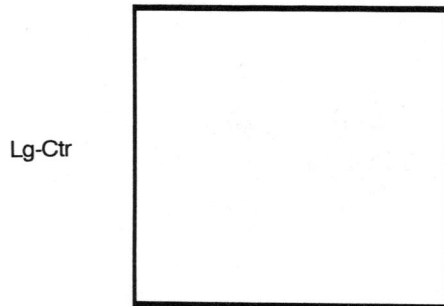

Row-1

| 1 | 2 | 3 | 4 |

Lg-Ctr

Row 2

| 1 | 2 | 3 | 4 |

Pattern Abbreviations

(ROW 1)1,2,3,4

(LG-CENTER)

(ROW 2)1,2,3,4

font size. (Note: The program automatically defaults to the small font size. It is not necessary to select it.)

For a better understanding of line counts, refer to the illustration below. The illustration has a total of 14 lines. Lines 1, 2, 5, 9, 10, 13, and 14 have text. Lines 3, 4, 6, 7, 8, 11, and 12 are blank. (Asterisks are used here to mark the blank lines.) A description for each line is as follows:

> Lines 1 and 2: MADERA font/SMALL size
>
> Lines 3 and 4: blank lines—MADERA font/SMALL size (current font selected)
>
> Line 5: MADERA font/LARGE size

LINE 1	MADERA font / SMALL size
LINE 2	MADERA font / SMALL size
✱	MADERA font / SMALL size
✱	MADERA font / SMALL size
LINE 5	MADERA font / LARGE size
✱	MADERA font / SMALL size
✱	MADERA font / SMALL size
✱	MADERA font / SMALL size
LINE 9	SMALL font / SMALL size
LINE 10	SMALL font / SMALL size
*	SMALL font / SMALL size
*	SMALL font / SMALL size
LINE 13	TINY font / SMALL size
LINE 14	TINY font / SMALL size

Lines 6, 7, and 8: blank lines—MADERA font/SMALL size   (Remember: Program automatically defaults to SMALL size)

Lines 9 and 10: SMALL font/SMALL size

Lines 11 and 12: blank lines — SMALL font/SMALL size (current font selected)

Lines 13 and 14: TINY font/SMALL size

To input the Handbook designs, count lines from top to bottom. Change font styles or sizes only when indicated. It's as simple as that!

Changing Font Size in the Handbook Designs

Whenever a Handbook design calls for a font in the large size, the pattern abbreviation CH SIZE:L appears in the step-by-step instructions in parentheses next to the appropriate line number (see Pattern Abbreviations, page 32). To enter your message, go to the line indicated and select the large font size. Then enter your text. When you press ENTER (or RETURN), the program automatically returns to the small font size.

About the Print Starting Point

Several Handbook designs take advantage of added design power that comes with using two different modes together or the same mode twice.

Inputting designs that combine modes is easy — a full set of instructions is included. As mentioned earlier, simply mark your original print starting point in light pencil. (We recommend placing your mark near the paper holding bar of your printer approximately 1/4 inch above the folding line of your paper.) Always start with a lead-in sheet to mark. If your lead-in sheet is not blank and contains a design or information you want to use, just be certain your pencil mark is very light — for erasing without a trace! Also, for easier measuring, use a clear plastic ruler that is flexible.

The exact position of your print starting mark is not at all critical. But try to be consistent. By always placing your mark in the same spot, you'll be able to find your original print starting point quickly and easily when instructed to roll back your paper.

Some designs require you to roll back your paper to the original print starting point. For these designs, simply roll back your paper to the exact same position as your original printing position. Other designs require that you roll back your paper to a position below your original print starting point. For these designs, roll back your paper to the original print starting point and then roll your paper forward the indicated amount. For designs that require you to roll back your paper to a position above the original print starting point, roll back to your original print starting point and then roll your paper backward the indicated amount.

About Using Color

The use of color can greatly enhance the impact of your New Print Shop designs. The colors available with your four ribbons are the primary yellow, red, and blue, along with black, plus the mix created for green, purple, and orange. Color combinations from even a more limited palette will surprise you with their great variety of visual statements.

Remember, you can print in color with a color printer even if you don't have a color monitor if you are equipped with a 640K machine and a hard disk. Even if you don't have a color printer, you can save your design on disk and check availability for printing at your local computer or copy shop. If you have a color monitor, you can preview your colors on the screen with a color monitor and a EGA or VGA card. Press Alt-F10 at the Project Menu to preview your design in color. The New Print Shop has a fantastic feature for picking colors from the color menu. Any element can be designated an individual color, except the already colorful "multi-colored graphics." You can even go into "Pickcolor" through the customize mode and put color behind all or a single graphic. Watch the sun shine when yellow is printed behind the black outline graphic! Make your own tricks.

The effectiveness of color is determined not only by what colors are chosen for what elements (such as a red for a headline rather than a cool color such as green), but also what colors are used next to one another. Depending on their relative positions on the color wheel, many colors, when placed next to one another, can produce an effect that's different from that produced when they are used by themselves. The more opposite colors are on the color wheel, the greater the contrast. Use this in your designs sparingly in order not to create too much vibration and too many overpowering effects. Brighter colors will create the illusion of a larger size for the chosen element—although position and relative number of brightly colored objects will give unpredictable results. As in all creative endeavors, experiment and enjoy your surprises!

About Hardware Variations

All the Handbook designs can be created on an IBM or Apple II system. (See explanation below of IBM-only designs.) The designs shown in the book were created on an IBM system. Designs created with an Apple II system may look slightly different. Even designs created with a different IBM configuration may look slightly different from the printed samples.

If you're using an Apple II system, use the Preview feature to see your design in progress. Follow the Handbook instructions, but position your words to best suit each layout. Occasionally, you may even want to move a graphic by a few additional key presses. Use the Customize and Preview features of The New Print Shop to fine tune a design before you print.

If your finished design looks slightly different from the Handbook sample, don't be alarmed! There is not one right way for the designs to look. All the designs, except where noted, have been adapted to work for a variety of systems — each with its own unique style.

About the IBM-Only Designs

The IBM and Apple versions of The New Print Shop closely resemble one another. In fact, on the surface the options they offer appear to be identical. However, several unique features are available only to IBM users.

Wide borders are available. Graphics can be enlarged or reduced.

To help IBM users get the most out of this added variety, the Handbook contains several designs that incorporate one or more IBM-unique features. The designs are clearly labeled IBM-only at the top of the design page.

If you're an IBM user, look carefully at the IBM-only designs. You'll see how to put IBM features to work. You'll find ideas for using these features in your own designs.

If you're an Apple user, don't pass the IBM-only designs by! The IBM-unique features are clearly indicated in the step-by-step instructions or discussed in the Design Notes. A simple substitution is often all that's required to adapt the design. And, in most cases, the Handbook suggests alternatives for you.

About the Quick Print Feature for Apple Users

Apple users can customize the positioning, size, and style of text in a design with the Quick Print feature. To position text exactly where you want it in your design, simply save your "design in progress." If you are inputting a Handbook design, be sure to leave a blank line in the same font as the text you will be adding so that the appropriate amount of space is allotted in your design. Go to the Main Menu and select Quick Print. Enter the text you want to add to your design and save it as a graphic.

Only one line of text can be saved at a time. If all of your words don't fit, save your phrase in two parts. If you want to manipulate several lines of text, save each line separately and add to your design one line at a time. Apple users can also add tiny descriptive text to signs by choosing the Tiny font in the Calling Card size.

Once you've saved your text, return to your design and go to the Customize Layout section. Choose the Insert Graphic option to load your text which is saved as a graphic. Position your text exactly where you want it in your design and style it with special effects such as 3-D or Raised. Add as many lines and fonts as you like!

Hints, Tips, and Shortcuts

Hints, tips and shortcuts are all over the New Print Shop Handbook! Turn to any page and you're likely to find at least one of the three. In the design section there are hints for designing. In the art section there are hints for creating new graphics and for giving old graphics a new look. In the planning section there are hints for organizing design ideas.

Some of the Handbook hints are very specific and have limited application. Others are much broader. The 23 hints and tips with the broadest application are highlighted here. Whenever appropriate, put them to work for you!

Hint #1: Customize full panel graphics! Use the Insert Graphic option to combine with other graphics.

Hint #2: Liven up your designs—use brightly colored markers to color in graphics or words in an outline font. Transparent highlight markers also work well.

Hint #3: Photocopy or print your designs on various colors of 8 1/2 X 11 paper and repeat in an interesting repeated design.

Hint #4: Combine borders—print one border, then roll back your paper and add another.

Hint #5: Superimpose one graphic over another graphic that has large open spaces inside.

Hint #6: Cut and paste your graphics and words. Add type and graphics from other sources to your pasted-up design for even greater variety. Then copy on a copying machine or take to a local print shop.

Hint #7: For quick ruled lines—use the dash key repeatedly.

Hint #8: Use any tiled layout with the NOTE LINES graphic on page 182 to create ruled stationery.

Hint #9: Add descriptive information to signs, flyers, and ads in a very tiny size using the address lines of the letterhead mode.

Hint #10: Apple users—use the Quick Print feature to add text exactly where you want it. Use the Tiny font in the Calling Card size to add very small text to signs.

Hint #11: For a short note — use the Tiny font in the sign mode.

Hint #12: Stack several banners on top of one another to create an oversized sign with several lines of copy.

Hint #13: Create customized borders by selecting the Small Tiled layout and erasing all but the outer edge of graphics.

Hint #14: Use the Greeting Card Print Size feature to reduce your designs to make gift enclosure cards, tickets, place cards, name tags, mailing labels and more.

Hint #15: Stop the printing of a Full Panel design near the bottom and use the area to add a separate text message.

Hint #16: Break the rules and print a unique layout by running your paper through the printer more than once.

Hint #17: Wallpaper a bulletin board or part of a wall with several sheets of the same design. Print the design several times or copy your original on a copying machine.

Hint #18: Jazz up your fax forms with a Print Shop design.

Hint #19: Leave extra space between your letters and words for greater interest and readability.

Hint #20: When inputting the Handbook's art, don't be concerned if you don't match every single dot. Even if 90% of your dots match up, your graphic is sure to look like the Handbook's.

Hint #21: The greeting card and sign modes offer the exact same choices for positioning text and graphics. One design idea works for both!

Hint #22: Save time — refer to The Fonts section when planning your message. You'll see approximately how many lines will fit on a page and how many letters will fit on a line.

Hint #23: Sit back, "look at things differently" and have fun!

The Design Page

The design page includes a great deal more than a sample design. The reduced page shown here provides an explanation of the various elements you'll find with every Handbook design.

Topic Identification: Identifies the specific item such as the flyer shown here.

What You Need: Easy-to-recognize symbols (shown on page 11) tell you what Print Shop programs were used to create the design.

What You Do: Step-by-step instructions lead you through the design every step of the way. A complete listing of pattern abbreviations is shown on pages 32–35.

Category Symbol: Symbol at top right tells you if you're in the Home, School/Organization, Party, Learning Materials, or Professional section.

Hints: Includes shortcuts for working on the design.

Design Notes: A variety of information may appear here. For example, there may be alternative design suggestions, alternative graphic choices, a simplified way to create a similar looking design, or an explanation of a design concept or technique.

---

52   THE OFFICIAL NEW PRINT SHOP HANDBOOK

Flyer 2/EVENT

What you need:

NP S

What you do:
SIGN; DYO; TALL; BORDER:RIBBON; LAYOUT:MED MIX; GRAPHIC:SAMP(SCOTTIE); DELETE:(ROW 1)ALL, (ROW 2)ALL, (ROW 3) 1,3, (ROW 5)ALL; CHANGE:(ROW 4) 1 to PROG(PLAYTIME), (ROW 4 2 to PROG(PICNIC), (ROW 4 to PROG(RIBBON); FONT:SMALL; MESSAGE:L1,L2(CENTER,SOLID) text; FONT:SIERRA; MESSAGE:L3(CENTER,SOLID, CH SIZE:L text, L4(1 space between letters)(CENTER, SOLID)text; FONT:TINY; L2(CENTER,SOLID), L13(2 spaces between words) (CENTER,SOLID)text; PRINT

ROYAL OAKS
NEIGHBORHOOD
PET
P A R A D E

SATURDAY, MAY 14th at 10 a.m.
PRIZES! EATS! FUN!

Design Notes:
With so many varied graphics to choose from, this layout is an excellent choice for many needs. Note how changing the font size creates a unique design element. Spacing letters is an easy and attractive enhancement.

Graphic Alternatives:
For SCOTTIE use PARTY(BLACK CAT); for PLAYTIME use PROG(PARTY FAVOR); for PICNIC use PROG(ICE CREAM); for RIBBON use SCH/BUS(TROPHY).

The Design: An actual reduced printout of what you'll get is shown here.

The Pattern Abbreviations

Most of the pattern abbreviations are self-explanatory when working side by side with The New Print Shop program. However, if a pattern abbreviation stumps you, just refer back to this section.

Print Shop features not listed here are written out in full in the design instructions.

DESIGN YOUR OWN BORDERS	**DYO**
Thin Line	THIN
Thick Line	THICK
Blocks	BLOCKS
Deco	DECO
Frilly	FRILLY
Maze	MAZE
Navajo	NAVAJO
Neon	NEON
Ribbon	RIBBON
Rounded	ROUNDED
WIDE BORDERS (IBM only)	
Balloons	WIDE/BALLOONS
Clipboard	WIDE/CLIPBOARD
Columns	WIDE/COLUMNS
Holly	WIDE/HOLLY
Lilies	WIDE/LILIES
DISKS	
New Print Shop program	PROG(GRAPHIC NAME)
Party Edition	PARTY(GRAPHIC NAME)
Sampler Edition	SAMP(GRAPHIC NAME)
School & Business Edition	SCH/BUS(GRAPHIC NAME)
New Art (from Handbook)	NEW(GRAPHIC NAME, PAGE 000)

Modified Art (from Handbook)	MOD(GRAPHIC NAME,PAGE 000)

SIZE/DIMENSION

Small	SM
Medium	MED
Large	LG
Vertical	VERT
Horizontal	HORIZ

STYLE (for Graphics and Text)

Outline	OUTLINE
3-D	3-D
Raised	RAISED
Shadow	SHADOW

LAYOUT POSITIONS (for explanation, see page 20)

Staggered Layouts

Row 1—Positions 1,2,3	(ROW 1)1,2,3
Row 2—Positions 1,2	(ROW 2)1,2
Row 3—All Positions	(ROW 3)ALL

Framed Layouts

Top Row—Positions 1,2,3	(T-ROW)1,2,3
Left Column—Positions 2,3,4	(L-COL)2,3,4
Right Column—Positions 2,3,4	(R-COL)2,3,4
Bottom Row—Positions 1,2,3	(B-ROW)1,2,3

Mixed Layouts

Small Column 1—Positions 1,2,3	(SM-COL 1)1,2,3
Medium Column 2—Positions 1,2,3	(MED-COL 2)1,2,3
Small Column 3—Positions 1,2,3	(SM-COL 3)1,2,3
Large Center Graphic	LG-CTR

MESSAGE

LINE 1	L1(text)
LINE 2	L2(text)
LINE 3	L3(text)
etc.	etc.

ALIGNMENT OF TEXT

Center	CENTER
Left	LEFT
Right	RIGHT

FONT SIZE

Change Size of Font to Large	CH SIZE:L

POSITION OF TEXT

Center Top to Bottom	CENTER TOP TO BOTTOM

CUSTOMIZE FEATURES

Change Graphic in Row 1, Position 1 to Disk Name (Graphic Name)	CHANGE:(ROW 1)1 to DISK(GRAPHIC NAME)
Move Graphic in Row 1, Position 1 up 1 key press for IBM up 4 key presses for Apple	MOVE:(ROW 1)1 up 1(IBM)/4(APP) key presses
Delete Graphic in Row 1, Position 1	DELETE:(ROW 1)1
Flip Vertical Graphic in Row 1, Position 1	FLIP VERT:(ROW 1)1
Flip Horizontal Graphic in Row 1, Position 1	FLIP HORIZ:(ROW 1)1
Insert Graphic to Layout	INSERT:SIZE/ DISK(GRAPHIC NAME) to (position on page)

Graphic Style Row 1, Position 1	STYLE:(ROW 1)1 (STYLE NAME)
Stretch Graphic in Row 1, Position 1 approximately 3 Key Presses Down	STRETCH:(ROW 1)1 down 3 key presses
Shrink Graphic in Row 1, Position 1 approximately 3 Key Presses Up	SHRINK:(ROW 1)1 up 3 key presses

IBM only

Enlarge Graphic in Row 1, Position 1 approximately 3 Key Presses	ENLARGE:(ROW 1)1 (+) 3 key presses
Reduce Graphic in Row 1, Position 1 approximately 3 Key Presses	REDUCE:(ROW 1)1 (-) 3 key presses

Calendar/YEARLY

What you need:

What you do:

CALENDAR TOP; DYO; YEARLY;
LAYOUT:FULL PANEL;
GRAPHIC:PROG(HOUSES);
FONT:SUTTER;
MESSAGE:L1(CENTER,SOLID)
text; RULED LINE:DOUBLE

CALENDAR BOTTOM; LAYOUT:
SM TILED; GRAPHIC:PARTY
(PARTY HAT); DELETE:(ROW 1)
3,4,7,8, (ROW 2) 3,4,7,8; CHANGE:
(ROW 1) 2 to PROG(CAKE
SLICE), (ROW 1) 6 to
PROG(MUSIC), (ROW 2) 2 to
PROG(MUSIC), (ROW 1) 5 to
PARTY(ST. PATRICK'S), (ROW 1)
9 to PARTY(GRADUATION),
(ROW 1) 10 to PARTY(RINGS),
(ROW 2) 1 to PARTY(PICNIC
TIME), (ROW 2) 6 to
PARTY(BLACK CAT), (ROW 2) 9
to PARTY(PENGUIN), (ROW 2) 10
to PARTY(ORNAMENT), (ROW 2)
5 to SCH/BUS(SCHOOL; RULED
LINE:THIN; PRINT

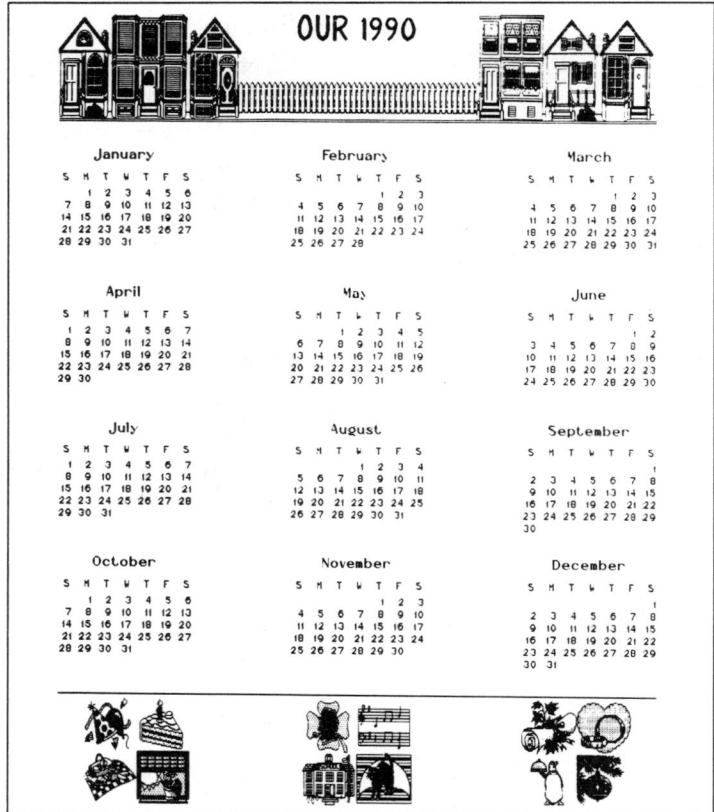

Design Notes:

Liven up a yearly calendar by using 12 unique graphics to
represent each month of the year.

Graphic Alternatives:

Choose graphics for the 12 months that reflect your areas of
emphasis such as: SCH/BUS(BAND) for football season,
(DOLLARS) for tax time, (GEOGRAPHY) for a trip and any
sports symbol for the athletes in the family!

Calendar/MONTHLY

What you need:

What you do:

CALENDAR; DYO; MONTHLY; MONTH; YEAR

CALENDAR TOP; LAYOUT:MED STAGGERED; GRAPHIC:MOD (SUN CREST,PAGE 200); DELETE: (ROW 1) 2,3,4; FONT:SMALL; MESSAGE:L1(CENTER,OUTLINE, CH SIZE:L)text; L3(CENTER, SOLID)text; FONT:TINY; MESSAGE:L5,L6(CENTER,SOLID) text; RULED LINE:DOUBLE

CALENDAR MIDDLE; MAY 4/GRAPHIC:MOD(CAT,PAGE 205); TEXT; MAY 6/GRAPHIC: MOD(AIRPLANE,PAGE 202); TEXT; MAY 10/TEXT; MAY 12/GRAPHIC:PROG(CASH BOX); MAY 15/GRAPHIC: PROG(COMPUTER); TEXT; MAY 18/PROG(BOOKS); TEXT; MAY 24/GRAPHIC:PARTY(RINGS); TEXT; MAY 26/PARTY(PARTY HAT); TEXT; MAY 27/GRAPHIC:PARTY (GRADUATION); TEXT; MAY 31/GRAPHIC:NEW(FINGER, PAGE 184); TEXT

CALENDAR BOTTOM; LAYOUT: SM STAGGERED; GRAPHIC:NEW (HANDS,PAGE 178); FONT: SMALL; MESSAGE:L1(CENTER, SOLID,CH SIZE:L)text; L5 (CENTER,SOLID)text; PRINT

Design Notes:

Scattered graphics liven up your calendar...too many create confusion. It's fun to personalize the calendar top, also. The "joke of the month," a reminder or main event at the bottom helps focus your thoughts.

Graphic Alternatives:

Select simple graphics that work well in the small size such as: PROG(PENS) for study, (PIANO) for lessons and recitals and (POINSETTIA) for Christmas parties. The many sports and seasonal graphics positioned at the bottom can be used to highlight a special month.

Card 1/INVITATION

What you need:

What you do:

CARD FRONT; DYO; SIDE FOLD;
LAYOUT:SM TILED;GRAPHIC:
NEW(ROW HOUSES,PAGE 185);
DELETE:(ROW 1) 2,3,4, (ROW 2)
ALL, (ROW 3)ALL;CHANGE:
(ROW 1) 1,5 to NEW(FINGER,
PAGE 184); FLIP VERT:(ROW 1)
1; FLIP VERT and HORIZ:(ROW 1)
5; FONT: MADERA; MESSAGE:
L1-L3(CENTER,RAISED,CH
SIZE:L)text

CARD INSIDE; LAYOUT:FULL
PANEL; GRAPHIC:PARTY(NEW
YEAR); FONT:SMALL;
MESSAGE:L1-L4(LEFT,SOLID)
text; FONT:TINY; MESSAGE:L5
(blank); L6-L8,L11(CENTER,
SOLID)text,PRINT

Card Front

Card Inside

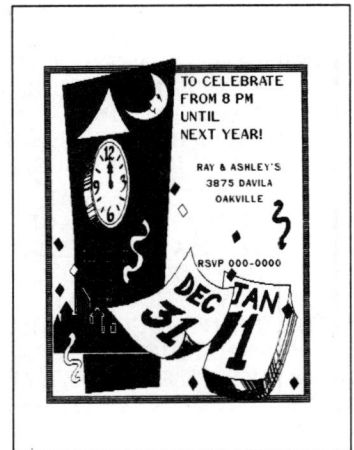

Design Notes:

Full panels create an instant impact. Contrast with a very
different layout for the card front. A repeat graphic, as used here,
is a contrasting pattern but appears uncluttered due to the
repetition.

Graphic Alternatives:

Try varying panels according to your event. Several New and
Modified Art samples make nice repeat graphics such as:
(SPORTS SYMBOL, PAGE 187), (CAKE, PAGE 162),
(SUNSHINE, PAGE 189), (PUMPKIN, PAGE 218), and
(CHRISTMAS TREE, PAGE 194).

Card 2/BABY ANNOUNCEMENT

What you need:

Card Front

Card Inside

What you do:

CARD FRONT; DYO; TOP FOLD;
BORDER:RIBBON; LAYOUT:MED
CENTERED; GRAPHIC:NEW
(TEDDY BEAR,PAGE 190);
INSERT:PROG(PARTY FAVOR)
8(IBM)/32(APP) key presses down,
1(IBM)/4(APP) key press right,
PROG(PARTY FAVOR)
8(IBM)/32(APP) key presses down,
16(IBM)/64(APP) key presses right;
FLIP HORIZ:PROG(PARTY
FAVOR) at bottom right corner;
FONT:SONOMA; MESSAGE:L1(1
space between letters, 2 spaces
between words)(CENTER,
RAISED)text

CARD INSIDE; BORDER:THIN;
LAYOUT:SM STAGGERED;
GRAPHIC:SAMP(BABY BOTTLE);
DELETE:(ROW 2) 1,2, (ROW 3) 2;
FONT:SONOMA; MESSAGE:L3
(CENTER,RAISED)text; FONT:
SMALL; MESSAGE:L4-L6
(CENTER,SOLID)text; PRINT

Design Notes:

Bolder graphics used prominently work well with more illustrative
images. Try to avoid using busy art with more busy art. Balanced
use of white space works well in this card front. Borders "clip"
graphics and create a nice finished look.

Graphic Alternatives:
For TEDDY BEAR use PROG(TEDDY BEAR),(BALLOONS);
NEW(JACK-IN-THE-BOX)

For BABY RATTLE use PROG(PARTY FAVOR);
PARTY(RATTLE).

Card 3/BIRTHDAY

What you need:

What you do:

CARD FRONT; DYO; TOP FOLD;
BORDER:THIN LINE;
LAYOUT:MED CENTERED;
GRAPHIC:SAMPLER(TIME
FLIES); MOVE:MED-CTR to left
5(IBM)/20(APP) key presses, down
2(IBM)/8(APP) key presses;
FONT:SIERRA;
MESSAGE:L1(LEFT,SOLID)text;
L2(indent 3 spaces)(LEFT,SOLID)
text; FONT:SMALL; MESSAGE:L3
(indent 16-IBM/19-APP spaces)
(1 space between W and I, 2 spaces
between I and N, 3 spaces between
N and G, 4 spaces between G and S)
(LEFT,SOLID)text; FONT:TINY;
MESSAGE:L5-L7(RIGHT,SOLID)

CARD INSIDE; LAYOUT:SM
TILED; BORDER:THIN LINE;
GRAPHIC:PROG(BALLOONS;
FONT:SIERRA; MESSAGE:L2-L4
(CENTER,SOLID)text; FONT:
SMALL; MESSAGE:L5(blank),
L6(CENTER,SOLID)text; PRINT

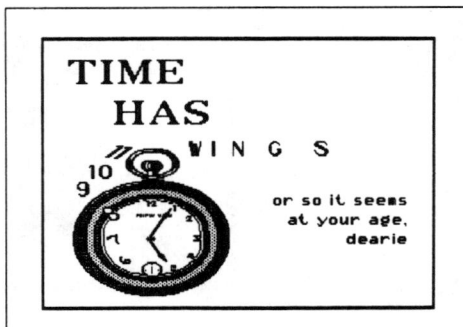

Card Front

Card Inside

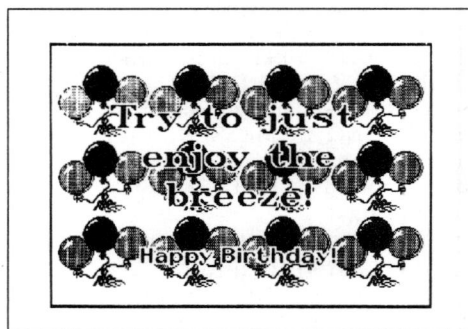

Design Notes:

Switching fonts and spacing out your letters can create a
statement unto itself. This particular design shows this technique
nicely. The inside of the card illustrates an example of dropping
text over graphics. The font in this size still allows for readability.

Graphic Alternatives:
Try PROG(BUBBLY) to offer solace or (TOP SECRET) for
whimsy.

Card 4/BIRTHDAY—CHILD (IBM ONLY)

What you need:

NP S/B P

Card Front

Card Inside

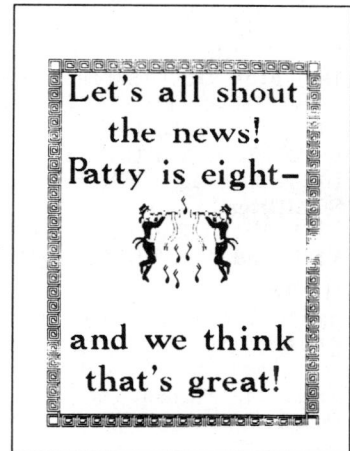

What you do:

CARD FRONT; DYO; SIDE FOLD;
LAYOUT:SM TILED;
GRAPHIC:SCH/BUS(BAND);
DELETE:(ROW 1) 1,2,4,5, (ROW
2)ALL, (ROW 3) 1,2,4,5, (ROW 4)
1,4,5, (ROW 5) 1,5, (ROW 7)ALL;
MOVE:(ROW 4) 3 to right 4(IBM)
/16(APP) key presses, (ROW 2) 2 to
right 3(IBM)/12(APP) key presses;
REDUCE (IBM only):
(ROW 1) 1 3 key presses; FONT:
SMALL; MESSAGE:L1-L3(blank);
FONT:IMPERIAL; MESSAGE:L4
(CENTER,SOLID)text; FONT:
SMALL; MESSAGE:L5-L16(blank);
FONT:IMPERIAL; MESSAGE:
L17(CENTER,SOLID)text;
CUSTOMIZE/CHANGE TEXT TO
GRAPHIC (IBM only)—MOVE:
L17 down 1 key press

CARD INSIDE; BORDER:MAZE;
LAYOUT:MED CENTER;
GRAPHIC:PARTY(TRUMPETS);
FONT:IMPERIAL; MESSAGE:
L1-L3,L7-L8(SOLID,CENTER)
text; PRINT

Design Notes:

Apple Users: This same design can be created without reducing the
graphic at top or moving the line of text at bottom. Simply
eliminate those two steps.

An interesting layout is achieved by positioning the leading
graphics and then moving them to create a staggered look. This
pyramid format makes a strong design element. Also, try a
diamond or cross shape.

Graphic Alternatives:
For BAND use PROG(BUBBLY) or PARTY(GINGERBREAD,
PENGUIN).

Card 5/CHRISTMAS

What you need:

What you do:

SIGN; DYO; TALL;
LAYOUT:MIXED COLUMNS;
GRAPHIC:PROG(POINSETTIA);
DELETE:(SM-COL 1) 1,3,4,5,6,
(MED-COL)ALL, (SM-COL 2)
1,2,3; CHANGE:(SM-COL 1) 2 to
MOD(CHRISTMAS TREE,PAGE
194); FLIP VERT:(SM-COL 1) 2;
FONT:SMALL; MESSAGE:
L1(LEFT SOLID)"HOLIDAYS!",
L2(LEFT,SOLID)"HAPPY",
L12-L13,L15-L16(CENTER,
SOLID)text, L19-L20
(CENTER,OUTLINE)text; FLIP
VERT and HORIZ:L1,L2; PRINT

HINTS: To fold card, first fold in
half from top to bottom as a normal
side fold card. Then fold over front
of card so that front right edge of
card aligns with left edge of
Poinsettias as shown in illustration.
Poinsettias should remain visible
when card is folded.

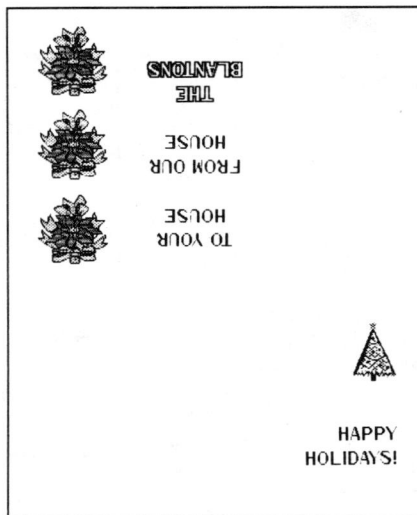

(Before Folding)

(After Folding)

Design Notes:

A different approach to creating a card is to use the sign mode,
printing the Card Front upside down at the top left quarter section
of the design. A fold over card in which the inside is wider makes
an interesting and fun statement. Many different graphics and
text styles can be used with this technique...just be sure you're
within the space boundaries as shown in this example.

Graphic Alternatives:
For POINSETTIA use PARTY(ORNAMENT); for CHRISTMAS
TREE use SAMP(PRESENT).

Card 6/FRIENDSHIP

What you need:

What you do:

CARD FRONT; DYO; SIDE FOLD; LAYOUT:MED FRAMED; GRAPHIC:NEW(FLOWER,PAGE 169); DELETE:MED-CTR; FONT:MERCED; MESSAGE:L3-L6 (CENTER,OUTLINE)text

CARD INSIDE; LAYOUT:MED FRAMED; GRAPHIC:NEW (HAND,PAGE 178); CHANGE:MED-CTR to NEW (SUNSHINE,PAGE 189); FONT: SMALL; MESSAGE:L4(CENTER, OUTLINE,CH SIZE:L)text, L6,L14 (CENTER,SOLID)text; PRINT

HINTS: Create customized borders with your choice of graphics by selecting the Medium Framed layout and deleting the Medium Center graphic.

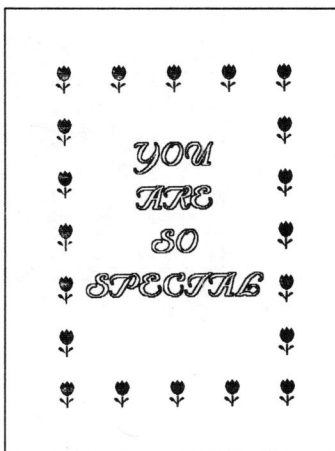

Card Front

Card Inside

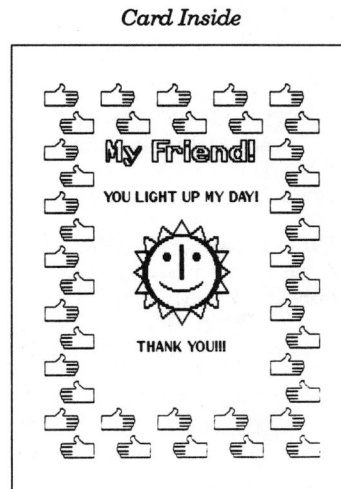

Design Notes:

Cards using simple text work well with The New Print Shop. Try selecting graphics that personalize your message. Personalization is the real advantage to creating Print Shop greeting cards! Felt tip fine- line pens can be used to fill in outline type for highlights.

Graphic Alternatives:
For text, use "you mean the world to me," changing SUNSHINE graphic to SCH/BUS(GLOBE). Also, for SUNSHINE use PARTY(TRUMPETERS), for FLOWERS use PROG(ROSEBUD).

Card 7/FATHER'S DAY (IBM ONLY)

What you need:

NP S/B

What you do:

CARD FRONT; DYO; SIDE FOLD;
LAYOUT:SM TILED II;
GRAPHIC:NEW(GRAPHIC TILE
PATTERN 1,PAGE 173);
DELETE:(ROW 1) 3,4, (ROW 2)
3,4, (ROW 5)ALL, (ROW 6) 2,3,4;
CHANGE:(ROW 6) 1 to PROG(INK
BOTTLE); MOVE:(ROW 6) 1 up 1
key press, right 1 key press;
INSERT:MED/PROG(LETTER)
down 2 key presses, flush right and
then left 2 key presses;
INSERT:MED/SCH-BUS(QUOTE)
down 15 key presses, right 14 key
presses; ENLARGE(IBM only):
SCH/BUS(QUOTE) by 5 key
presses; FONT:SMALL; MESSAGE:
L16(CENTER,SOLID)text;
CUSTOMIZE/CHANGE TEXT TO
GRAPHIC (IBM only)—MOVE:L16
to right 6 key presses

CARD INSIDE; BORDER:THIN
LINE; LAYOUT:MED STAGGERED
II; GRAPHIC:SCH/BUS(TROPHY);
DELETE:(ROW 2)ALL, (ROW 3)
ALL; FONT:SMALL; MESSAGE:
L7,L8(CENTER,SOLID)text;
FONT:SONOMA;
MESSAGE:L10-L12
(CENTER,SOLID)text; FONT:
SMALL; MESSAGE:L14,L15
(CENTER,SOLID)text; PRINT

Card Front

Card Inside

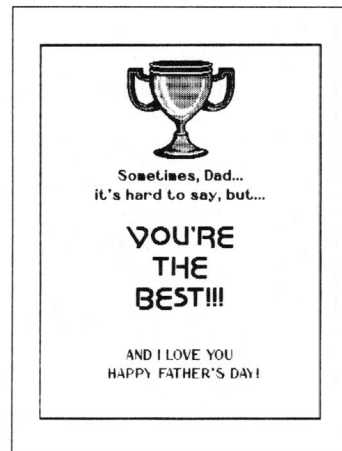

Design Notes:

The Tile Pattern graphics make interesting design devices even
when not used in an overall tiled pattern. The use of text inside
the Quote or Emblem graphics is a simple, yet strong, concept that
creates a sense of whimsy in a design.

Graphic Alternatives:

For INK use SCH/BUS(CONFIDENTIAL); for TROPHY use
PROG(RIBBON); for QUOTE use text alone without graphic.

Card 8/GET WELL

What you need:

NP S S/B

What you do:

CARD FRONT; DYO; SIDE FOLD;
LAYOUT:MED STAGGERED II;
DELETE:(ROW 2)ALL, (ROW 3)
ALL; FONT:IMPERIAL;
MESSAGE:L4(CENTER,
OUTLINE,CH SIZE:L)text, L5
(CENTER,RAISED,CH SIZE:L)
text, L6(CENTER,SOLID)text;
FONT:SMALL; MESSAGE:L7
(CENTER,SOLID)text

CARD INSIDE; LAYOUT:MED
FRAMED; GRAPHIC:
SCH/BUS(BAND); DELETE:
(T-ROW)ALL, (L-COL) 2,3,4,5,6,
(R-COL) 2,3,4,5,6, (MED-CTR);
FONT:SMALL; MESSAGE:L3
(CENTER,SOLID)text; FONT:
IMPERIAL; MESSAGE:L4-L6
(CENTER,SOLID,CH SIZE:L)text;
FONT:SMALL; MESSAGE:L7
(CENTER,SOLID)text; PRINT

Card Front

Card Inside

Design Notes:

Try altering typeface styles and sizes for interesting looks. Adding
one row of graphics makes a statement especially when the
graphic is one that links well through its full-box design or
symmetry.

Graphic Alternatives:
For TIME FLIES use PROG(BALLOONS). For BEAR use
PROG(PENS) or PARTY(GINGERBREAD).

Card 9/GRADUATION

What you need:

What you do:

CARD FRONT; DYO; SIDE FOLD; LAYOUT:SM FRAME II; GRAPHIC:NEW(GRAPHIC TILE PATTERN 1,PAGE 173); INSERT: MED/MOD(BOOKS,PAGE 192) to right 8(IBM)/32(APP) key presses, down 8(IBM)/32(APP) key presses; FONT:TINY; MESSAGE:L17,L18 (IBM)/L20,L21(APP)(CENTER, SOLID)text

CARD INSIDE; BORDER:SCH/BUS (BOOKS); FONT:IMPERIAL; MESSAGE:L3,L4(CENTER, RAISED)text; PRINT

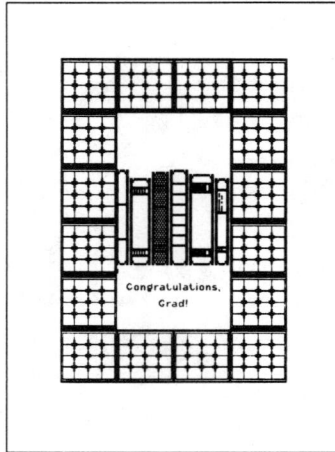

Card Front

Card Inside

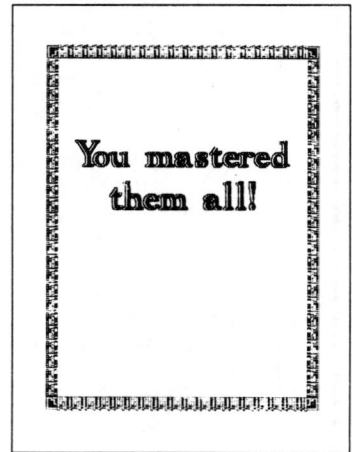

Design Notes:

For a formal and bold look, use a geometric graphic as a border with two or four sides. The use of the MOD(BOOKS) gives a more generic application. Straight-edged graphics work particularly well butting up to borders.

Graphic Alternatives:
For MOD(BOOKS) use PROG(BOOKS); for BOOKS border use PROG(DECO) border.

Card 10/HALLOWEEN

What you need:

What you do:

CARD FRONT; BORDER:THIN LINE; LAYOUT:MED MIX; GRAPHIC:PARTY(BATS); DELETE:(COL 1) 2,3,4, (COL 2) ALL, (COL 3) 2,3,4; CHANGE: MED-CTR to PARTY(BLACK CAT); FONT:SUTTER; MESSAGE: L1-L3,L6-L7(SOLID,CENTER)text

CARD INSIDE; BORDER:RIBBON; LAYOUT:MIXED ROWS; GRAPHIC:PARTY(PENGUIN); DELETE:(SM-ROW 1) 1,2,3, (SM-ROW 2)ALL; CHANGE: (SM-ROW 1) 4 to PARTY (MASQUERADE); MOVE:(ROW 1) 4 left 9(IBM)/36(APP) key presses, down 4(IBM)/16(APP) key presses (NOTE:Mask is positioned over face of penguin); FONT:TINY; MESSAGE:L1(blank); FONT: SUTTER; MESSAGE:L2-L8 (SOLID,CENTER)text; PRINT

Card Front

Card Inside

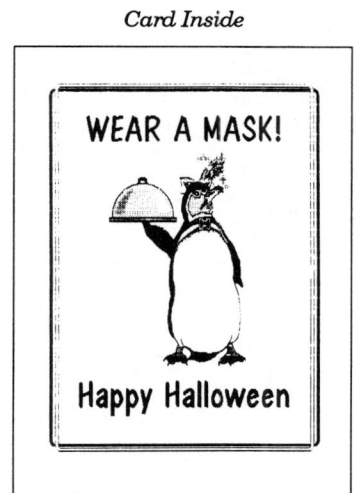

Design Notes:

Moving a smaller graphic over a larger graphic creates an interesting and often humorous new image. The four-corner layout of the card inside is a good layout useful for many applications. Try coloring the interior of the images for a bright look.

Graphic Alternatives:
Try MOD(PUMPKIN, PAGE 218) on the inside of the card.

Card 11/MOTHER'S DAY

What you need:

NP

Card Front

What you do:

CARD FRONT; DYO; SIDE FOLD;
BORDER:FRILLY; LAYOUT:SM
TILED II; PATTERN:PROG
(LACE); DELETE:(ROW 3) 2,3,
(ROW 4) 2,3; FONT:MERCED;
MESSAGE:L4,L5(CENTER,
SOLID)text

CARD INSIDE; LAYOUT:MED
STAGGERED II; GRAPHIC:
PROG(ROSEBUD);
DELETE:(ROW 1) 1, (ROW 2) 1,2;
FONT:MERCED;
MESSAGE:L1,L2,L4-L6(CENTER,
SOLID)text; PRINT

Card Inside

Design Notes:

The technique of using a tiled pattern and deleting a clear shape
makes an interesting look. Text or another graphic can then be
inserted into the open space.

Graphic Alternatives:

The most modern of Moms still loves sweet images at Mother's
Day. Try a breakfast in bed I.O.U. with SCH/BUS(LUNCHTIME)
or SAMPLER(VALLEY LILY).

Diary 1/ADULT

What you need:

NP

What you do:

SIGN; DYO; TALL; LAYOUT:SM
TILED II; GRAPHIC:NEW ART
(NOTE LINES, PAGE 182);
DELETE:(ROW 1) 1,2,3,4, (ROW 6)
1,2,3,4; FONT:MERCED;
MESSAGE:L8(1 space between all
letters)(CENTER,SOLID)text;
PRINT

To add graphics and text at top, roll
back paper to original print starting
point.

LETTERHEAD TOP; DYO;
LAYOUT:SM STAGGERED;
GRAPHIC:PROG(PENS); DELETE:
(ROW 1) 2,3,4,5; RULED LINE:
THIN; FONT:MERCED;
MESSAGE:L1,L2(CENTER,
SOLID)text; PRINT

Sarah's Thoughts
Today's Date: _____

journal

Design Notes:

This design in multiples is well suited for a notebook of memoirs.
Try creating pages identified by goal for a personalized
self-improvement handbook.

Graphic Alternatives:
For PENS use SCH/BUS(CONFIDENTIAL).

Diary 2/YOUTH

What you need:

What you do:
SIGN; DYO; TALL; BORDER:THIN;
LAYOUT:SM FRAME;
GRAPHIC:MOD(PENCIL,PAGE
196); DELETE:(ROW 1)ALL,
(L-COL) 3,4,5,6, (R-COL) 3,4,5,6;
FONT:LASSEN; MESSAGE:L1
(CENTER,SOLID)text, L3(LEFT,
SOLID)text; FONT:SMALL;
MESSAGE:L4,L6,L8,L10,L12
(CENTER,SOLID)text; PRINT

Design Notes:
This design is easy to create and shows how the "dash" key on the keyboard can be used to create notepaper lines. Substituting graphics can quickly alter the look and age appropriateness of the design.

Graphic Alternatives:
For PENCIL use PROG(PENS, LETTER, INK BOTTLE), SAMPLER(TIME FLIES) or SCH/BUS(KEY).

Flyer 1/SALE

What you need:

NP **S** **S/B**

What you do:

SIGN; DYO; TALL; LAYOUT:MED
MIX; GRAPHIC:SAMP(TIME
FLIES); DELETE:(COL 1)
3,4,(COL 2) 1,2,3,4,(COL 3)
3,4,MED-CTR; CHANGE:(COL 1) 2
to SCH/BUS(POINTER), (COL 3) 2
to SCH/BUS(KEY), (COL 1) 5 to
PROG(TELEPHONE), (COL 3) 5
to SCH/BUS(MOVING VAN);
FONT:SUTTER; MESSAGE:L1
(CENTER,3-D)text; FONT:SMALL;
MESSAGE:L2-L4,L11-L14
(CENTER,SOLID)text;
FONT:TINY;
MESSAGE:L16,L17(CENTER,
SOLID)text; PRINT

LOOK!
The time is now
for this home
to be yours!

**314 S. El Monte Avenue
Phillipsburg Manor!
3 Bedrooms/3 Baths/Cottage!
Only $375,500**

Call the Halston's
000-0000

MOVING

Design Notes:

This layout works well for a poster sign and also as a fold-over
mailer. Seal with a colored, circular label to add a bright touch to
your mailing. Varied graphics add interest and visually
communicate your message.

Graphic Alternatives:

For TIME FLIES use SCH/BUS(CLOCK); for TELEPHONE use
SCH/BUS(QUOTE) with an exclamation mark inside; for
POINTER use NEW(HOME); for MOVING VAN use
SCH/BUS(SWITCH); for KEY use SAMP(FIREPLACE).

Flyer 2/EVENT

What you need:

NP **S**

What you do:

SIGN; DYO; TALL;
BORDER:RIBBON; LAYOUT:MED
MIX; GRAPHIC:SAMP(SCOTTIE);
DELETE:(ROW 1)ALL, (ROW
2)ALL, (ROW 3) 1,3, (ROW 5)ALL;
CHANGE:(ROW 4) 1 to
PROG(PLAYTIME), (ROW 4) 2 to
PROG(PICNIC), (ROW 4) 3 to
PROG(RIBBON); FONT:SMALL;
MESSAGE:L1,L2(CENTER,SOLID)
text; FONT:SIERRA;
MESSAGE:L3(CENTER,SOLID,
CH SIZE:L)text, L4(1 space
between letters)(CENTER,
SOLID)text; FONT:TINY;
L12(CENTER,SOLID), L13(2
spaces between words)
(CENTER,SOLID)text; PRINT

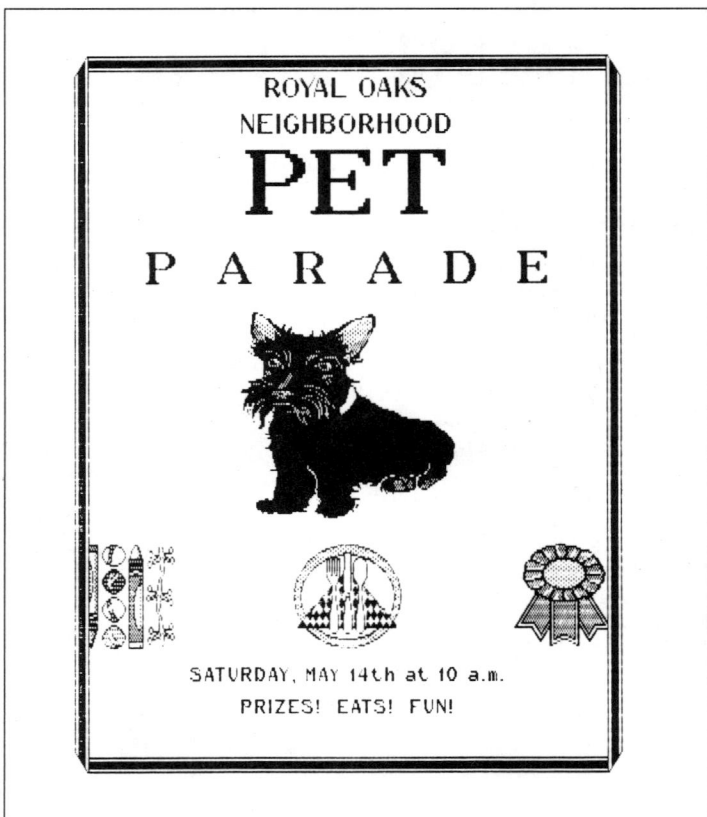

ROYAL OAKS
NEIGHBORHOOD
PET
P A R A D E

SATURDAY, MAY 14th at 10 a.m.

PRIZES! EATS! FUN!

Design Notes:

With so many varied graphics to choose from, this layout is an
excellent choice for many needs. Note how changing the font size
creates a unique design element. Spacing letters is an easy and
attractive enhancement.

Graphic Alternatives:
For SCOTTIE use PARTY(BLACK CAT); for PLAYTIME use
PROG(PARTY FAVOR); for PICNIC use PROG(ICE CREAM); for
RIBBON use SCH/BUS(TROPHY).

Flyer 3/GARAGE SALE

What you need:

What you do:

SIGN; DYO; TALL;
LAYOUT:MIXED COLUMNS;
GRAPHIC:SAMP(BICYCLE);
DELETE:(SM-COL 1) 3,4,
(MED-COL) 2, (SM-COL 2) 3,4;
CHANGE:SM-COL 1) 2 to
SAMP(HIGHTOP), (SM-COL 1) 5
to PROG(PRINTER), (SM-COL 1)
6 to PROG(COMPUTER),
(MED-COL) 1 to
NEW(HOUSE,PAGE 180),
(MED-COL) 3 to SAMP(PIGGY
BANK), (SM-COL 2) 1 to
SAMP(TOOLS), (SM-COL 2) 2 to
SAMP(GARDENING), (SM-COL 2)
5 to PROG(SOCCER), (SM-COL 2)
6 to PROG(TEDDY BEAR);
FONT:TINY; MESSAGE:L1-L7
(IBM)/L1-L9(APP)(blank);
FONT:SONOMA; MESSAGE:L8,L9
(IBM)/L10,L11(APP)(CENTER,
RAISED,CH SIZE:L)text;
FONT:SMALL; MESSAGE:L10
(IBM)/L12(APP)(CENTER,SOLID),
 L11(IBM)/L13(APP)(1 space
between letters, 3 spaces
between words)(CENTER,
SOLID)text; PRINT

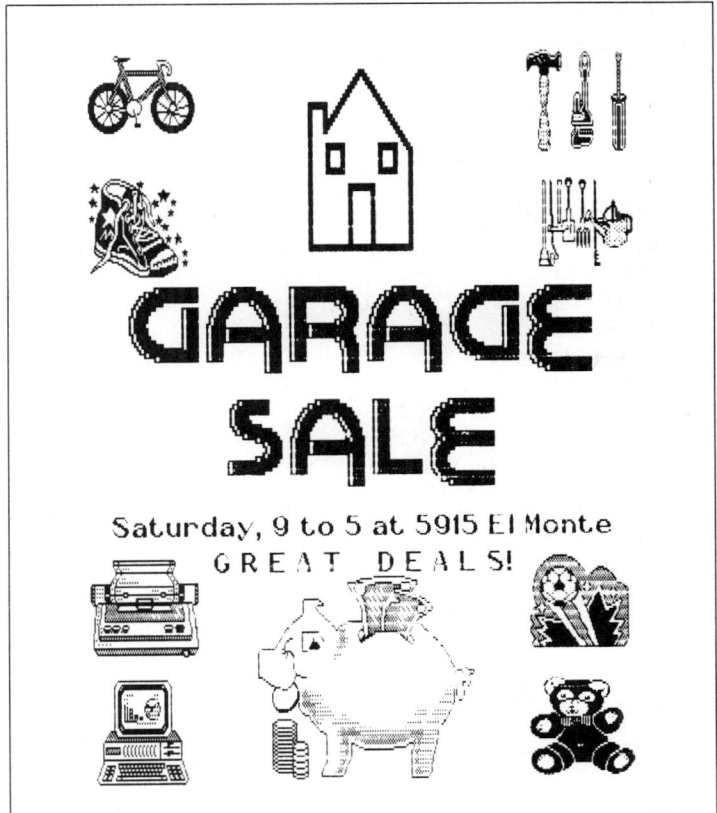

Design Notes:

Contrasting multiple graphics work well in a layout when
medium-sized graphics balance the design and thus avoid a busy
look. The "raised" style works well in this font. Use felt tip
markers to highlight your text and graphics.

Graphic Alternatives:

For HOUSE use NEW(ROW HOUSES, PAGE 185); for PIGGY
BANK use SCH/BUS(DOLLARS). For smaller art spots try
PROG(BASEBALL, BASKETBALL, CASH, PLAYTIME).

Letterhead 1/ADULT FORMAL

What you need:

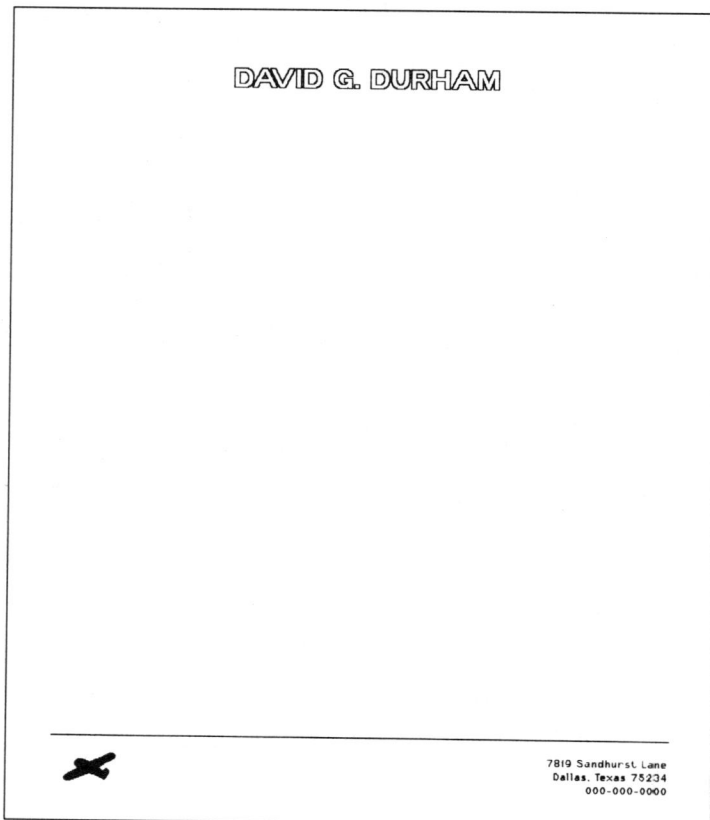

What you do:
LETTERHEAD TOP; DYO;
FONT:MADERA;
MESSAGE:L2(CENTER,OUTLINE)
text

LETTERHEAD BOTTOM;
LAYOUT:SM ENDS II;
GRAPHIC:MOD(AIRPLANE
SOLID, PAGE 202); DELETE:
(ROW 1) 2; MOVE:(ROW 1) 1 to
right 1(IBM)/4(APP) key press;
FONT:TINY; MESSAGE:L2-L4
(RIGHT,SOLID)text; RULED
LINE:THIN; PRINT

Design Notes:
Try several different fonts in outline for this formal, more
sophisticated look. Also, many different graphics will work. Choose
one that best suits your personality or purpose.

Graphic Alternatives:
Create a professional look for this layout by selecting a very bold
and simple graphic. Many examples can be found in the New and
Modified Art section.

Letterhead 2/ADULT FORMAL

What you need:

NP **S/B**

Michael Charles
NATHAN

3402 Windy Ridge
Breckenridge, Texas 65391
000-000-0000

What you do:

LETTERHEAD TOP; DYO;
LAYOUT:SM ENDS II;
GRAPHIC:SCH/BUS(BUILDINGS);
FONT:SMALL;
MESSAGE:L1(blank);
FONT:VENTURA;
MESSAGE:L2(CENTER,SOLID)
text, L3(CENTER,SOLID,CH
SIZE:L)text; RULED LINE:THICK

LETTERHEAD BOTTOM;
FONT:SMALL;
MESSAGE:L2-L4(CENTER,SOLID)
text; PRINT

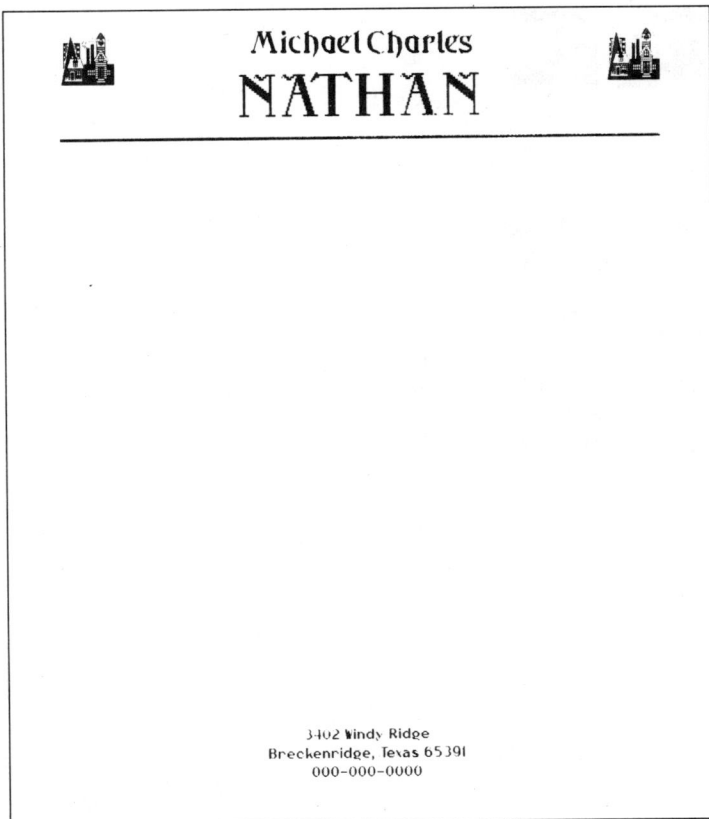

Design Notes:

This easy-to-create letterhead works well for all purposes. If you prefer a letterhead without graphics, simply delete the graphics at top.

Graphic Alternatives:
Choose a slightly illustrative graphic for a formal but decorative layout such as: PROG(SUNSHINE, LETTER) or SCH/BUS(PAINT TUBE) for an artist, (SAILBOAT) for a sportsman.

Letterhead 3/ADULT PERSONAL

What you need:

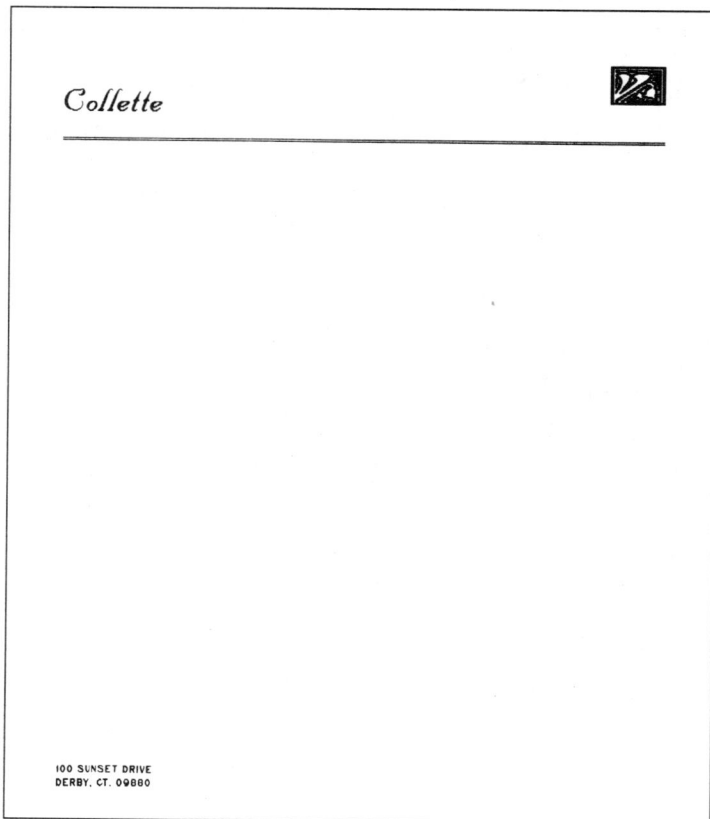

What you do:
LETTERHEAD TOP;DYO;
LAYOUT:SM ENDS
III;GRAPHIC:SAMP(VALLEY
LILY);DELETE:(ROW 1) 1;
FONT:MERCED;
MESSAGE:L3(LEFT,RAISED)text;
RULED LINE:DOUBLE

LETTERHEAD BOTTOM;
FONT:TINY;MESSAGE:L5,L6
(LEFT,SOLID);PRINT

Design Notes:
This clean and simple design works well for personal stationery for adults or children.

Graphic Alternatives:
ADULT: PROG(DAISIES);SCH/BUS(LEAVES) CHILD:
PROG(PLAYTIME, TEDDY BEAR).

Letterhead 4/HOME BUSINESS

What you need:

NP  **S/B**

What you do:

LETTERHEAD TOP; DYO;
LAYOUT:SM TILED;
GRAPHIC:NEW ART(NOTE
LINES, PAGE 182);
DELETE:(ROW 1)ALL;
FONT:LASSEN;
MESSAGE:L1(LEFT,OUTLINE)
text; MARGIN:MOVE to left
3(IBM)/12(APP) key presses

LETTERHEAD BOTTOM;
LAYOUT:SM ENDS;
GRAPHIC:SCH/BUS(ART);
DELETE:(COL 1) 1,(COL 2) 1;
FONT:LASSEN;
MESSAGE:L1(CENTER,SOLID)
text; FONT:TINY;
MESSAGE:L4(CENTER,SOLID)
text; PRINT

Framers Unlimited

4342 Crowley Drive   Ft. Worth, Texas 98053

000/000-0000

Design Notes:

Select a graphic that best reflects your business image. A repeat
graphic (Note Lines) at top is balanced by large text and small
graphics at bottom. Avoid using busy graphics in all locations with
this type of layout.

Graphic Alternatives:
For generic use SCH/BUS(POINTER)—select HORIZ FLIP for
position at right. For food related business use PROG(PICNIC).
For music-related business use PROG(MUSIC). For design-related
business use SCH/BUS(DRAFTING).

Letterhead 5/CHILD

What you need:

NP

What you do:

LETTERHEAD TOP; DYO;
FONT:SONOMA; MESSAGE:L1(3
spaces between letters)(CENTER,
RAISED,CH SIZE:L)text;
FONT:TINY;
MESSAGE:L2(4 spaces between
words)(CENTER,SOLID)text;
RULED LINE:THICK

LETTERHEAD BOTTOM;
LAYOUT:FULL PANEL;
GRAPHIC:PROG(SWEETS);
FONT:SONOMA;
MESSAGE:L2(CENTER,SOLID)
text; FONT:TINY; MESSAGE:L3
(CENTER,SOLID)text; Mark
original print starting point and
then PRINT.

To add ICE CREAM graphics, roll
back paper to approximately 1 3/8
inches below original print starting
point.

LETTERHEAD TOP; DYO;
LAYOUT:SM STAGGERED;
GRAPHIC:PROG(ICE CREAM);
PRINT

Design Notes:

Full Panels are a new addition to The Print Shop. They make a
bold statement whether used at the top or bottom of a letterhead.
The panel shown here works particularly well at bottom because it
surrounds and contains text so nicely.

By rolling back your paper and adding more graphics, you can
make a more decorative design. This idea works especially well for
children's stationery. Raised text is easy to color with fine-point,
colored felt tip pens. Try using multi-colors!

Graphic Alternatives:
For ICE CREAM use PROG(TEDDY BEAR, PLAYTIME) or
PARTY(GINGERBREAD).

Letterhead 6/CHILD

What you need:

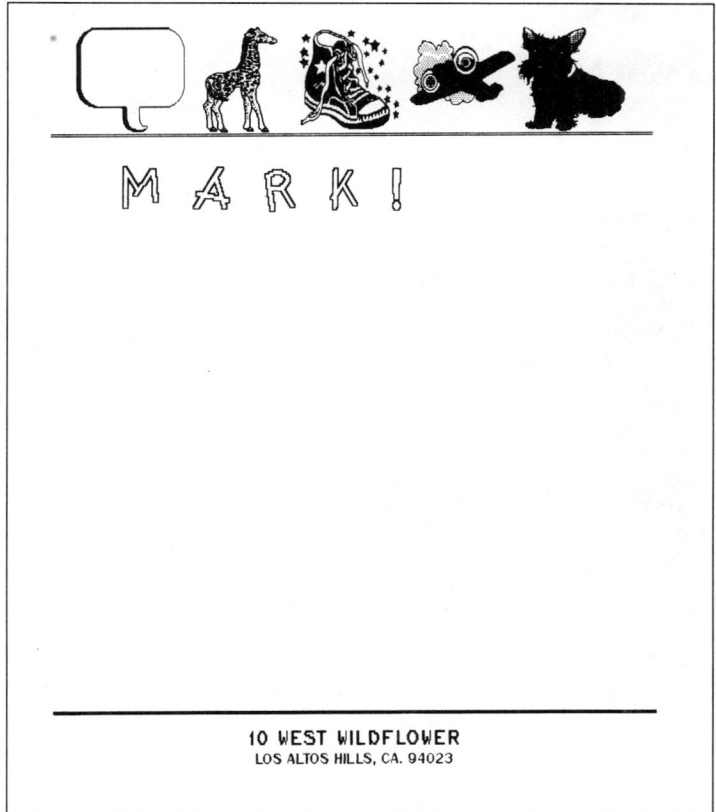

What you do:

LETTERHEAD TOP;
DYO;LAYOUT:MED TILED;
GRAPHIC:SCH/BUS
(QUOTE); POSITION:(ROW1) 1;
GRAPHIC:SAMP(GIRAFFE);
POSITION(ROW1) 2;
GRAPHIC:SAMP(HIGH TOP);
POSITION(ROW1) 3;
GRAPHIC:SAMP(AIRPLANE);
POSITION(ROW1) 4;
GRAPHIC:SAMP(SCOTTIE);
POSITION(ROW1) 5; RULED
LINE:DOUBLE

LETTERHEAD BOTTOM;
FONT:SMALL;
MESSAGE:L2(CENTER,SOLID,
CH SIZE:L)text; L3(CENTER,
SOLID)text; RULED LINE:THICK;
PRINT

To add CHILD'S NAME, roll back
paper to approximately 2 inches
below original print starting point.

LETTERHEAD TOP; DYO;
FONT:SCH/BUS(CHILDREN);
MESSAGE:L1(LEFT,OUTLINE,
CH SIZE:L)text; MARGIN:MOVE
to left 5(IBM)/20(APP) key presses;
PRINT

Design Notes:

Help a small child personalize his or her stationery with
appropriate graphic choices. There are many New Print Shop
graphics well suited to children's stationery. Below are some
suggestions.

Graphic Alternatives:
For sports theme use PROG(BASEBALL, BASKETBALL,
FOOTBALL, SOCCER),SAMP(BOWLING). For generic use
PROG(ICE CREAM, TEDDY BEAR, PLAYTIME),
SCH/BUS(CHEERLEADER), SAMP(RABBIT).

Letterhead 7/CHILD (IBM ONLY)

What you need:

What you do:

SIGN; DYO; TALL;
BORDER:PARTY(WIDE/BEACH—
IBM only); LAYOUT:SM PAIR;
GRAPHIC:MOD(EMBLEM,PAGE
195); DELETE:ROW 2) 1;
MOVE:(ROW 1) 1 up 3(IBM)/12
(APP) key presses; FONT:SMALL;
MESSAGE:L1-L4(blank);
FONT:PARTY(BRUSH);
MESSAGE:L5(CENTER,OUTLINE)
text; FONT:SMALL; MESSAGE:
L6-L12(blank); L13-L14(CENTER,
SOLID)text; PRINT

Design Notes:

Apple Users: Replace wide border with a thin border and a big, fun graphic such as the JACK-IN-THE-BOX, page 181.

Kids love to write short notes. Reproduce on a copying machine for a supply of sheets. Any graphic that is open and simple is good for coloring and will work well.

Graphic Alternatives:
For EMBLEM use PROG(BALLOONS, ICE CREAM), SCH/BUS(QUOTE, CHALKBOARD) with personalization or MOD(CREST, PAGE 216).

List 1/GROCERY

What you need:

What you do:

SIGN; DYO; TALL; BORDER:THIN
LINE; LAYOUT:SM TILED;
GRAPHIC:NEW(NOTE
LINES,PAGE 182);
DELETE:(ROW 1)ALL; (ROW 2)
2,3,4,5; CHANGE:(ROW 2) 1 to
PARTY(PICNIC TIME);
MOVE:(ROW 2) 1 right
1(IBM)/4(APP) key press;
FONT:SUTTER;
MESSAGE:L1(RIGHT,
SHADOW)text,
L2(RIGHT,SOLID)text; PRINT

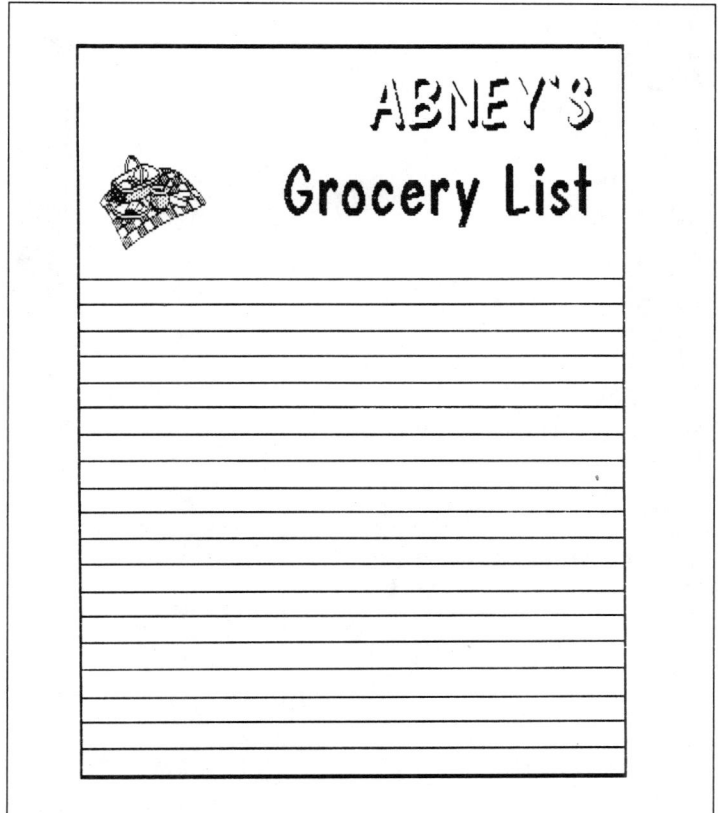

Design Notes:

The NOTE LINES pattern is simple to create and can be used for
many kinds of designs. You may want more lines for your list.
Simply keep the NOTE LINES graphic in Row 2 of the Small Tiled
layout and choose a smaller font for your heading.

Graphic Alternatives:
For PICNIC TIME use PROG(PICNIC) or
SCH/BUS(LUNCHTIME).

List 2/DAILY TO DO

What you need:

What you do:

SIGN; DYO; TALL;
BORDER:PROG(NAVAJO);
LAYOUT:SM TILED II;
GRAPHIC:NEW(NOTE
LINES,PAGE 182);
DELETE:(ROW 6) 2,3;
CHANGE:(ROW 6) 1 to
PROG(SUNSHINE), (ROW 6) 4 to
PROG(TELEPHONE);
FONT:SMALL;
MESSAGE:L1(blank);
FONT:SUTTER;
MESSAGE:L2(CENTER,SOLID)
text, L3(CENTER,SOLID,CH
SIZE:L)text; PRINT

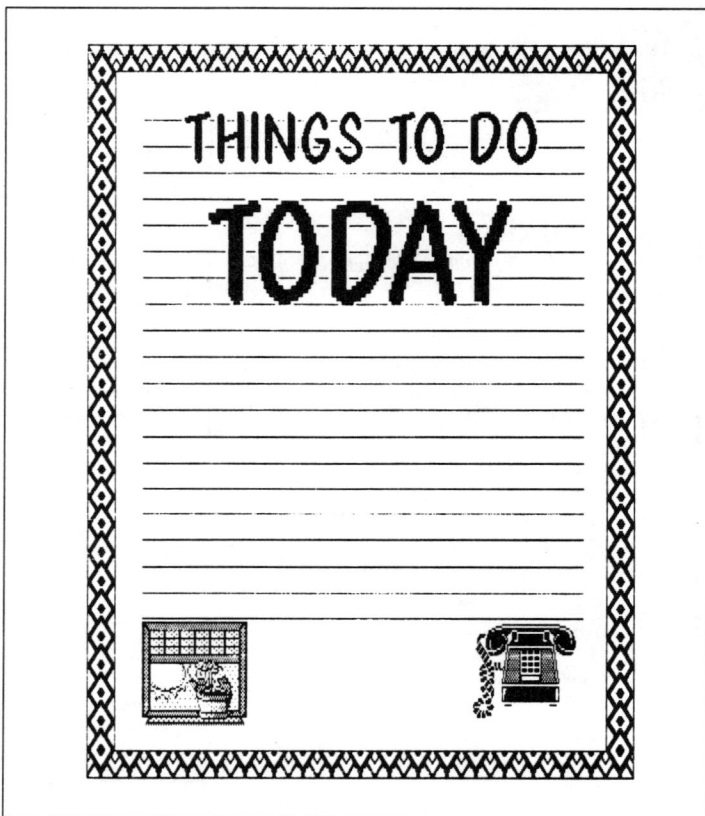

Design Notes:

This design is generic and can be used with almost any
combination of graphics. For a simpler design, delete the border.
The line pattern can also be drawn so that the lines are closer
together or further apart.

Graphic Alternatives:
For TELEPHONE use PROG(PENS) or SCH/BUS(POINTER); for
SUNSHINE use PARTY(COLLEGE) or NEW(SUNSHINE, PAGE
189).

Sign 1/ FAMILY INFORMATION

What you need:

What you do:

SIGN; DYO; WIDE;
BORDER:NAVAJO; LAYOUT:SM
CENTERED; GRAPHIC:MOD
(LARGE HOUSE,PAGE 211);
MOVE:(ROW 1) 1 up 3(IBM)/12
(APP) key presses; FONT:
IMPERIAL; MESSAGE:L1(LEFT,
SOLID)text; FONT:SMALL;
MESSAGE:L2(RIGHT,SOLID)text;
FONT:TINY; MESSAGE:L3
(CENTER,SOLID)dashes with shift
key, L4-L9(LEFT,SOLID)text;
CUSTOMIZE/CHANGE TEXT TO
GRAPHIC(IBM only): MOVE L1
down 1 key press; PRINT

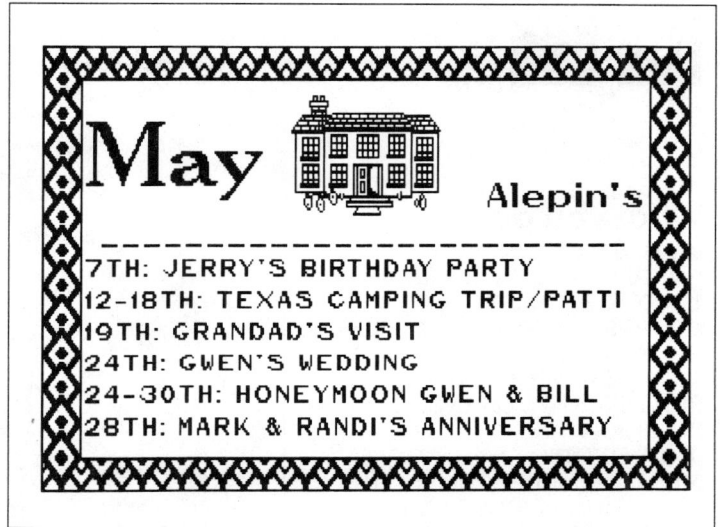

Design Notes:

Graphic Alternatives:

NEW(HOUSE, PAGE 180) can be used to create a strong image
for signs. A main event can be highlighted as well with New Print
Shop sports or holiday symbols.

Sign 2/CHILD'S ROOM

What you need:

What you do:

SIGN; DYO; TALL;
BORDER:SAMP(PLACARD);
LAYOUT:REVERSED DIAMOND;
GRAPHIC:SAMP(JOLLY ROGER);
DELETE:(ROW 1) 1,2,3,(ROW 6)
1,2,3; CHANGE(ROW 5) 1 to
SCH/BUS(KEY); CHANGE(ROW
5) 2 to SCH/BUS
(CONFIDENTIAL); FONT:SMALL;
MESSAGE:L2(CENTER,SOLID)
text; FONT:SAMP(WILDE);
MESSAGE:L4,L5(CENTER,
SHADOW)text;PRINT

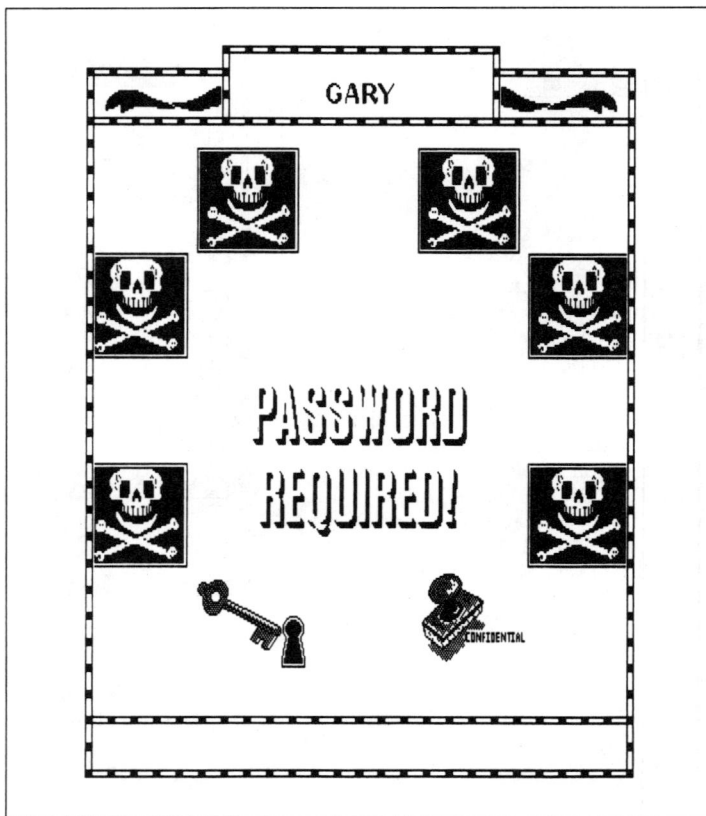

Design Notes:

Children of any age will enjoy creating their own room signs to
keep out parents and siblings. There are many appropriately
repelling graphics that will appeal to varying ages.

Graphic Alternatives:
Substitute JOLLY ROGER with an age-appropriate graphic: for ages
5-7 use PARTY(MAGIC); for ages 8-11 use PARTY(JAM
SESSION) or PROG(CAUTION); for ages 11 and up use SCH/BUS
(CONFIDENTIAL).

Sign 3/LEMONADE STAND

What you need:

What you do:

SIGN; DYO; TALL;
LAYOUT:MIXED ROWS;
GRAPHIC:PARTY(COOL DRINK);
DELETE:(SM-ROW 1)ALL;
CHANGE:(SM-ROW 2)ALL to
NEW(SUNSHINE,PAGE 189);
FONT:SUTTER;
MESSAGE:L1(CENTER,OUTLINE,
CH SIZE:L)text,
L5(CENTER,SOLID)text,
L6(CENTER,OUTLINE)text;
CUSTOMIZE/CHANGE TEXT TO
GRAPHIC (IBM only) —
MOVE:L1,L5,L6 down 1 key press
(Apple Users: Use Quick Print
feature to add text, see page 27);
PRINT

HINTS: To create the cents ("¢")
symbol, type a small "c" and add a
vertical rule with a fine-tip black
pen after printing.

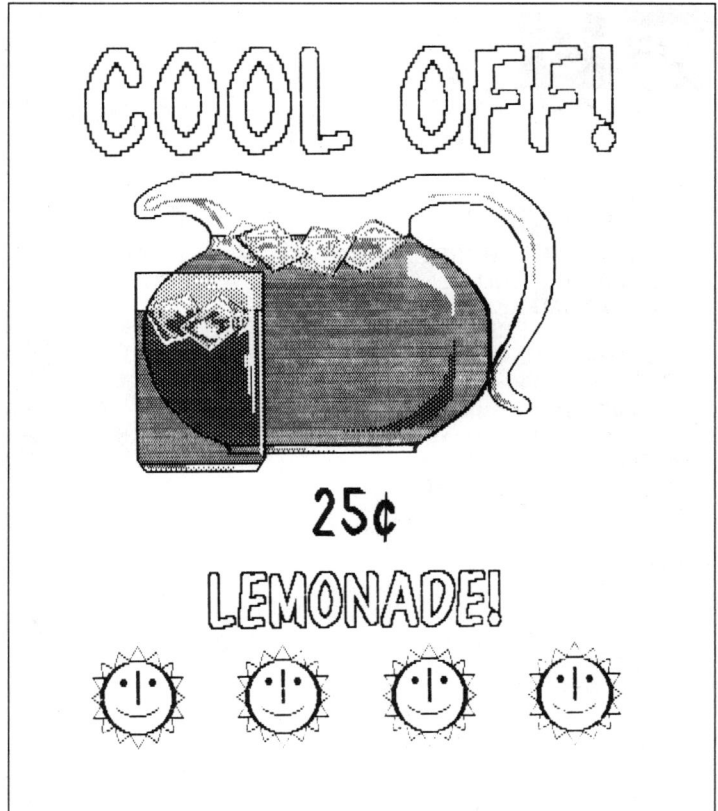

Design Notes:

Apple Users: An alternative to adding text with the Quick Print
feature is to use text lines 1 and 6 only placing "LEMONADE 25¢"
all on Line 6.

Try using felt tip markers to fill in outline text for greater impact.
Graphics such as the bold SUNSHINE can benefit from color as
well.

Graphic Alternatives:
For SUNSHINE use PROG(PICNIC, BALLOONS).

Sign 4/REFRIGERATOR

What you need:

What you do:

SIGN; DYO; TALL; BORDER:THIN LINE; LAYOUT:MED CENTERED; GRAPHIC:SAMPLER(BURGER and SHAKE); INSERT:MED/MOD (NO SYMBOL,PAGE 213) to right 8(IBM)/32(APP) key presses, down 8(IBM)/32(APP) key presses; INSERT:SM/SAMP(WOMAN) to right 11(IBM)/44(APP) key presses, down 17(IBM)/68(APP) key presses; FONT:AMADOR; MESSAGE:L1(CENTER,SOLID) text, L2(1 space between letters)(CENTER,SOLID, CH SIZE:L)text, L6(5 spaces between words)(CENTER,SOLID) text; PRINT

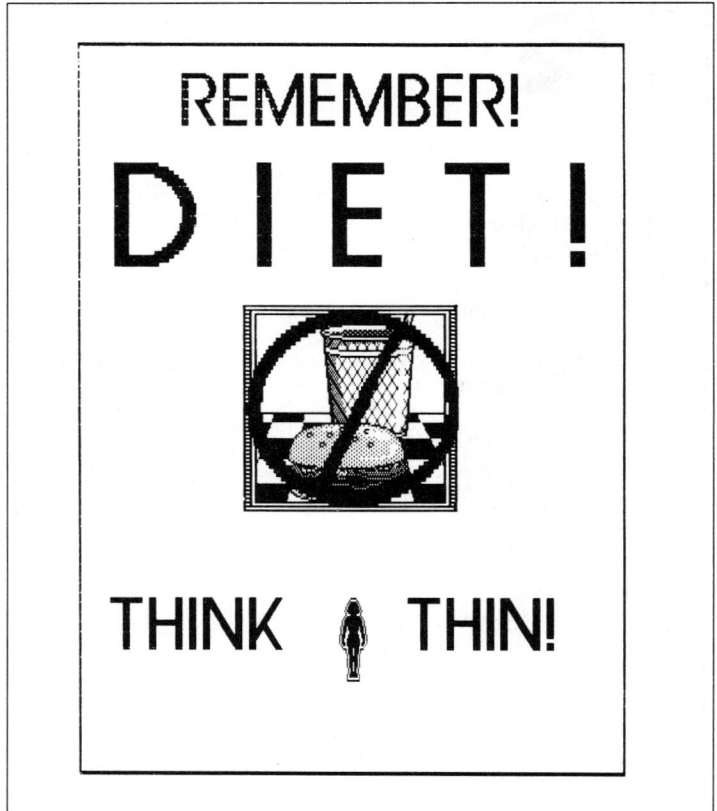

Design Notes:

For a quicker sign, use the thin woman as the primary graphic. The NO SYMBOL works well over ICE CREAM, BUBBLY, COFFEE or any other established habit.

Graphic Alternatives:
For WOMAN use SAMPLER(MAN) or MOD(MAN OF STRENGTH SYMBOL, PAGE 207).

Stencil

What you need:

NP

What you do:

BANNER; LAYOUT:TWO EQUAL
LINES; FONT:SIERRA;
MESSAGE:L1,L2(CENTER,SOLID)
text; PRINT

> B O A T   F O R   S A L E !
> P E R F E C T !   O O O – O O O O

Design Notes:

Print Shop banners make great stencils! For a more durable
stencil, attach your printed banner to lightweight cardboard with
rubber cement or spray mount and then cut out your letters. To
make sure your letter placement is accurate, first trace your
message on the surface to be stenciled. Check your layout and
then, leaving your stencil in place, transfer your message. Spray
paint works best with large stencils.

Banner 1/BIRTHDAY

What you need:

NP

What you do:

BANNER; DYO; HORIZONTAL; LAYOUT:LG GRAPHIC BOTH ENDS; GRAPHIC:NEW(CAKE,PAGE 162); CHANGE:(ROW 1) 2 to NEW(JACK-IN-THE-BOX,PAGE 181); TEXT:ONE LINE TEXT; FONT:LASSEN; MESSAGE:(RAISED)text; TRIM:PROG(BLOCKS); PRINT

Design Notes:

Customize your banner with art you have either modified or created from scratch for a more personal look. The simpler and bolder the graphic, the more readable it will be when printed in the large banner size.

Graphic Alternatives:
Try using NEW(CLOWN, PAGE 163)

Banner 2/BIRTHDAY

What you need:

NP

What you do:
BANNER; DYO; VERTICAL; LAYOUT:LG GRAPHIC BOTH ENDS; GRAPHIC:MOD(MAN PROFILE, PAGE 212); CHANGE:(POS 2) to MOD(FESTIVE GRAPHIC, PAGE 217); FONT:SIERRA; MESSAGE:(SOLID)text; PRINT

Design Notes:
Vertical banners make a bold and whimsical statement. Hang from the ceiling, out on a porch or out a window. There are many graphics appropriate for birthdays. Tailor your text to complement a graphic in your design.

Graphic Alternatives:
Try using PROG(ROSEBUD, BALLOONS, ICE CREAM, PARTY FAVOR) or PARTY(SIXTEEN, TWENTY-ONE, TWENTY-FIVE).

S H H H ! Michael is FORTY !

Card 1/INVITATION

What you need:

Card Front

Card Inside

What you do:

CARD FRONT; DYO; TOP FOLD;
BORDER:PARTY(BALLOONS);
LAYOUT:FULL PANEL;
GRAPHIC:PARTY(CAKES);
FONT:SMALL;
MESSAGE:L1,L2(CENTER,
RAISED,CH SIZE:L)text

CARD INSIDE;
BORDER:PARTY(CAKES);
LAYOUT:SM CORNERS;
GRAPHIC:PARTY(PARTY HAT);
INSERT:SM/PARTY(PARTY HAT)
to right 2(IBM)/8(APP) key
presses, down 1(IBM)/4(APP) key
presses; to right 2(IBM)/8(APP)
key presses, down 7(IBM)/28(APP)
key presses; FONT:SMALL,
MESSAGE:L4-L6(indent
12-IBM/14-APP
spaces)(RIGHT,SOLID) text,
L7,L8(indent 16-IBM/19-APP
spaces)(RIGHT,SOLID)text; PRINT

Design Notes:

By combining words with a Full Panel graphic containing text, you can create a very decorative card. Try customizing your graphic layouts by inserting graphics. Print a second copy of a graphic over its original image for a more interesting, asymmetrical design. Notice that borders overprint graphics, so choose a graphic that looks good when trimmed.

Graphic Alternatives:
Other partylike graphics include PROG(BALLOONS), PARTY(PARTY FAVOR) and NEW(CAKE, PAGE 162).

Card 2/THANK YOU (IBM ONLY)

What you need:

Card Front

Card Inside

What you do:

CARD FRONT; DYO; SIDE FOLD; BORDER:PROG(WIDE/ CLIPBOARD); LAYOUT:MED TILED; GRAPHIC:NEW(NOTE LINES,PAGE 182); CHANGE:(ROW 1) 1 to NEW(CLOWN,PAGE 163); DELETE:(ROW 1) 2; FONT:TINY; MESSAGE:L1(blank); FONT:SUTTER; MESSAGE:L2(indent 2 spaces, 1 space between letters) (RIGHT,OUTLINE)text; FONT:TINY; MESSAGE:L3-L7(blank); FONT:SMALL; MESSAGE:L8,L11,L14(CENTER, SOLID)text

CARD INSIDE; BORDER:PROG(DOUBLE LINE); LAYOUT:LARGE TOP; GRAPHIC:SCH/BUS(QUOTE); INSERT:MED/NEW(CLOWN,PAGE 163) to right 15(IBM)/60(APP) key presses, down 15(IBM)/60(APP) key presses); FONT:SUTTER; MESSAGE:L2-L4(CENTER, SOLID)text; PRINT

Design Notes:

Apple Users: Combine a decorative border such as DECO on Program Disk with a second fun graphic and substitute for the clipboard image. Insert text on Card Front ruled lines with Quick Print feature, see page 27.

The NOTE LINES art can be used to create a "list" look. Personalize your card with the recipient's name or initials. A second printing is quick and easy and allows you to combine the speech balloon in the larger size with a smaller character image.

Graphic Alternatives:
For CLOWN use NEW(JACK-IN-THE-BOX, PAGE 181).

Favor/COLORING SOUVENIR

What you need:

What you do:
SIGN; DYO; WIDE;
BORDER:PROG(THIN);
LAYOUT:SM TILED II;
GRAPHIC:NEW(SUNSHINE,PAGE
189); CHANGE:(ROW 1) 2,4,
(ROW 2) 2,4, (ROW 3) 2,4 to
NEW(JACK-IN-THE-BOX,PAGE
181); FONT:MADERA;
MESSAGE:L2,L4(1 space between
letters)(CENTER,OUTLINE)text;
PRINT

HINTS: Turn a coloring souvenir
into a fan.

Design Notes:
Personalize an activity at a party for 4-, 5- or 6-year-olds by
printing a coloring page for each little guest with his or her own
name—or the name of the host or hostess. After the sheets have
been colored, show the youngsters how to turn their colorful
creations into fans! Fold between the columns for best results.

Graphic Alternatives:
Try using open graphics such as NEW(CAKE, PAGE 162),
NEW(HOUSE, PAGE 180), NEW(CACTUS, PAGE 161) or
PARTY(PARTY FAVOR).

Game/PIN-THE-TAIL

What you need:

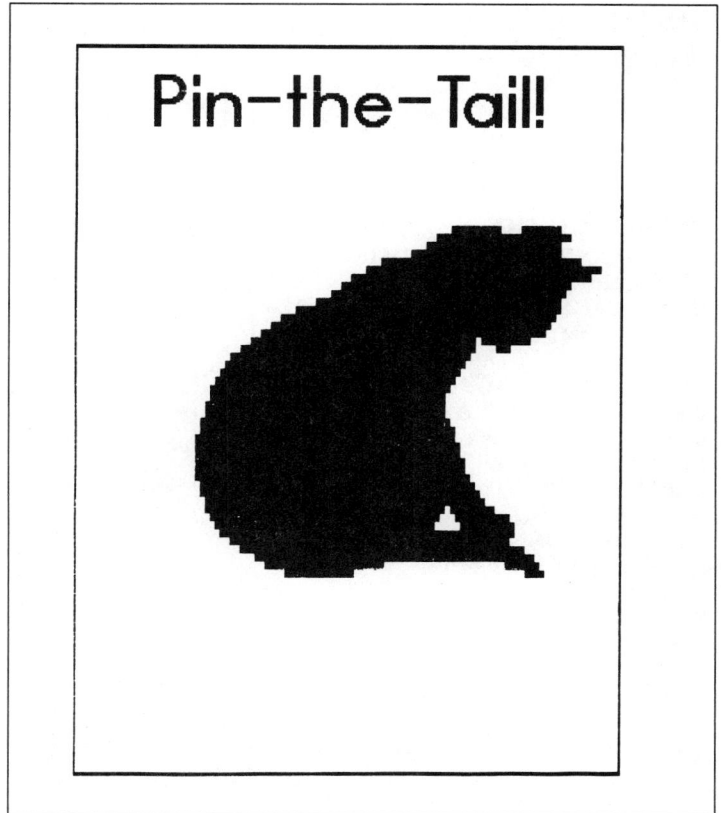

What you do:

SIGN; DYO; TALL;
BORDER:THIN; LAYOUT:LG
CENTERED;
GRAPHIC:MOD(KITTY CAT,
PAGE 205); MOVE:MOD(KITTY
CAT) to right 3(IBM)/12(APP) key
presses; FONT:AMADOR;
MESSAGE:L1(CENTER,SOLID)
text; PRINT

Design Notes:

Use the banner mode to print oversized graphics for party games
or decorations or use the sign mode as shown. For this game
simply use the modified Kitty Cat or the version on the Sampler
disk and cut colored construction paper tails or make a long curly
tail of yarn or ribbon. Run the ribbon over a blunt edge of a scissor
to make a curl.

Graphic Alternatives:
Try using PARTY(PENGUIN) or SAMP(GIRAFFE, SCOTTIE,
RABBIT).

Nametags

What you need:

What you do:
SIGN; DYO; TALL; LAYOUT:MED
TILED; GRAPHIC:MOD(SUN
CREST,PAGE 200); MOVE:(ROW
1) 1 up 1(IBM)/4(APP) key press,
left 2(IBM)/8(APP) key presses;
(ROW 1) 2 up 1(IBM)/4(APP) key
press, right 2(IBM)/8(APP) key
presses; (ROW 2) 1 left 2(IBM)/8
(APP) key presses; (ROW 2) 2 right
2(IBM)/8(APP) key presses; (ROW
3) 1 down 2(IBM)/8(APP) key
presses, left 2(IBM)/8(APP) key
presses; (ROW 3) 2 down
2(IBM)/8(APP) key presses, right
2(IBM)/8(APP) key presses;
FONT:MADERA;
MESSAGE:L4,L8,L12(CENTER,
OUTLINE)text (Note: Type first
name and then leave appropriate
number of blank spaces before
typing second name. For example,
for 2 names with 5 letters each,
leave 6 or 7 blank spaces between
names.); PRINT

Design Notes:
Use an outline font and try filling in with felt tip markers for
accent. Choosing graphics with a symmetrical design works well.
However, any graphic can be used with the name printed
underneath.

Graphic Alternatives:
Try using MOD(CREST FRAME, PAGE 216) or
MOD(CHALKBOARD, PAGE 214).

Sign/PIN-UP

What you need:

What you do:

For Part 1(top left):

SIGN; DYO; WIDE; LAYOUT:MED
CENTERED; GRAPHIC:NEW
(ARROW1,PAGE 157); MOVE:NEW
(ARROW1) to left 5(IBM)/20(APP)
key presses, up 1(IBM)/4(APP) key
press; FONT:MARIN;
MESSAGE:L1(RIGHT,SOLID,CH
SIZE:L)text; FONT:SONOMA;
MESSAGE:L3
(RIGHT,SOLID,CH SIZE:L)text;
PRINT

For Part 2(top right):

SIGN; DYO; WIDE; LAYOUT:MED
CENTERED; GRAPHIC:NEW
(ARROW1,PAGE 157); MOVE:NEW
(ARROW1) to right
5(IBM)/20(APP) key presses, up
1(IBM)/4(APP) key press; HORIZ
FLIP:NEW
(ARROW1); FONT:MARIN;
MESSAGE:L1(LEFT,SOLID,
CH SIZE:L)text; FONT:SONOMA;
MESSAGE:L3(LEFT,SOLID,
CH SIZE:L)text; PRINT

For Part 3(bottom left):

SIGN; DYO; WIDE; LAYOUT:SM
STAGGERED; GRAPHIC:SCH/BUS
(CONFIDENTIAL); DELETE:
(ROW 1) 2, (ROW 2)ALL, (ROW
3)ALL; FONT:SMALL; MESSAGE:
L2(CENTER,SOLID,CH SIZE:L)
text;, L3-L4,L6-L8,L10-L13
(CENTER,SOLID)text; PRINT

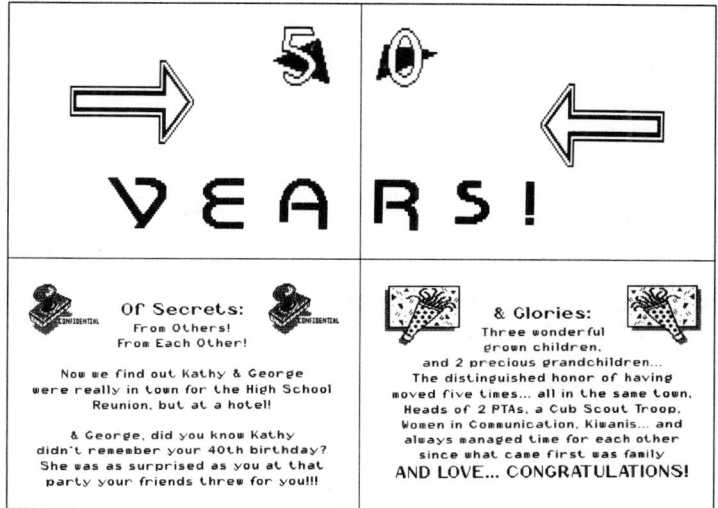

For Part 4(bottom right):

SIGN; DYO; WIDE; LAYOUT:SM STAGGERED;
GRAPHIC:PROG(PARTY FAVOR); DELETE:
(ROW 1) 2, (ROW 2)ALL, (ROW 3)ALL; HORIZ FLIP:(ROW 1) 3;
FONT:SMALL; MESSAGE:L2(CENTER,SOLID,CH SIZE:L)text,
L3-L11(CENTER,SOLID)text,L12(CENTER,SOLID,CH
SIZE:L)text; PRINT

Design Notes:

This example of multiple pages forming an overall large design has
many applications. Try a second row of two pages that are banner
designs, or use large text in the sign mode for this row.

Graphic Alternatives:

For ARROW use SCH/BUS(POINTER); for CONFIDENTIAL use
PROG(BALLOONS) or NEW(FLOWER, PAGE 169); for PARTY
FAVOR use SCH/BUS(TROPHY).

Wrapping Paper 1

What you need:

NP

What you do:

SIGN; DYO; TALL; LAYOUT:SM
STAGGERED II;
GRAPHIC:PROG(PARTY FAVOR);
DELETE:(ROW 2)ALL, (ROW
4)ALL; CHANGE:(ROW 1) 2,4,
(ROW 3) 1,3, (ROW 5) 2,4 to
PROG(BUBBLES); FONT:MARIN;
MESSAGE:L3,L6(CENTER,
OUTLINE)text; PRINT

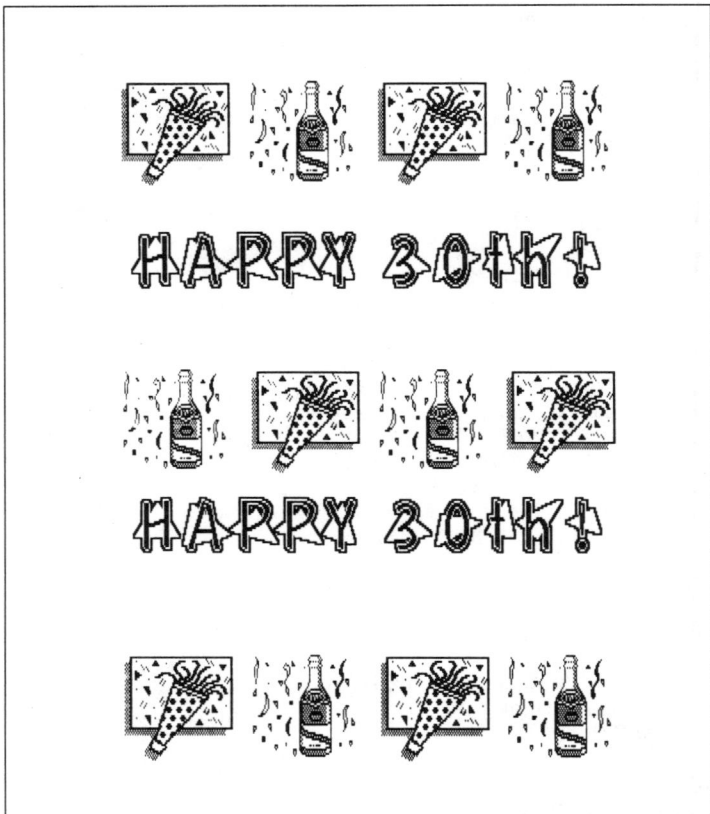

Design Notes:

Try using graphics that have a good amount of white space and
color in with colored markers. Select your font in outline and color
in your text, too. It's easy to change the look of your wrapping
paper by selecting different graphics.

Graphic Alternatives:
Other graphics with white space include
NEW(JACK-IN-THE-BOX, PAGE 181), NEW(CAKE, PAGE 162),
NEW(SUNSHINE, PAGE 189). Also try using
PROG(BALLOONS) with this design.

Wrapping Paper 2

What you need:

NP

What you do:

SIGN; DYO; TALL; LAYOUT:SM
STAGGERED;
GRAPHIC:PROG(BALLOONS);
CHANGE:(ROW 1) 2, (ROW 3) 2,
(ROW 5) 2 to PROG(CAKE
SLICE); (ROW 3) 1,3, to
PROG(ICE CREAM); PRINT

Design Notes:

Many graphics will complement one another in this staggered
pattern. Contrasting graphics will work best (e.g.bold/detailed,
animate/inanimate). Try graphics with large areas of white space
and color in with markers.

Graphic Alternatives:
Several graphics in the New Art section have good amounts of
white space such as NEW(CAKE, PAGE 162), NEW(CROWN,
PAGE 164), NEW(PLANT, PAGE 183) and NEW(STAR, PAGE
188).

Coloring 1/ASSORTED

What you need:

NP **S** ✍

What you do:

For CAT coloring sheet:

SIGN; DYO; TALL
BORDER:DOUBLE LINE;
LAYOUT:LG CENTER;
GRAPHIC:SAMP(KITTY CAT);
FONT:AMADOR;
MESSAGE:L7(CENTER,OUTLINE)
text; PRINT

For SUNSHINE coloring sheet:

SIGN; DYO; TALL;
BORDER:FRILLY; LAYOUT:LG
CENTER;
GRAPHIC:NEW(SUNSHINE,PAGE
189); FONT:MADERA;
MESSAGE:L8(CENTER,OUTLINE)
text; PRINT

Design Notes:

Print Shop animals and objects make terrific coloring sheets!
Select animals or objects with a good amount of white space for
better coloring opportunities. For an additional challenge, omit one
letter from label at bottom for child to complete or use dashes and
let child fill in all letters. For group use, copy on a copying machine.

Graphic Alternatives:

Try using SAMP(RABBIT, GIRAFFE) or MOD(PUMPKIN, PAGE
218).

Coloring 2/PERSONALIZED

What you need:

What you do:

SIGN; DYO; TALL;
BORDER:DECO; LAYOUT:LG
CENTER; GRAPHIC:NEW
(JACK-IN-THE-BOX, PAGE 181);
FONT:MADERA;
MESSAGE:L1,L9(CENTER,
OUTLINE)text; PRINT

Design Notes

Children love to see their names in print. Any open graphic makes an attractive coloring candidate. Select an open and simple font. Try other sight words such as "Smile," "I love," etc.

Graphic Alternatives:

Try using SAMP(RABBIT, KITTY CAT, GIRAFFE) or NEW(SUNSHINE, PAGE 189).

Coloring 3/PICTURE FRAME (IBM ONLY)

What you need:

What you do:

SIGN; DYO; TALL;
BORDER:PROG(WIDE/LILIES—
IBM only); LAYOUT:SM PAIR;
GRAPHIC:NEW(FLOWER,PAGE
169); MOVE:TOP FLOWER left
6(IBM)/24(APP) key presses, down
10(IBM)/40(APP) key presses;
BOTTOM FLOWER right
6(IBM)/24(APP) key presses, down
5(IBM)/20(APP) key presses;
FONT:LASSEN;
MESSAGE:L2(CENTER,SOLID)
text; PRINT

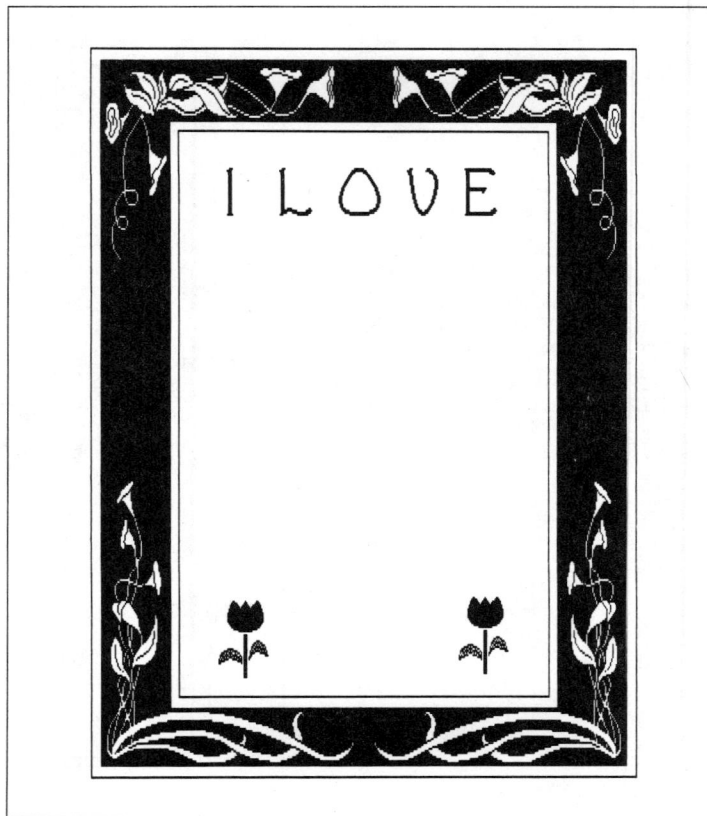

Design Notes

Apple Users: Substitute DECO border on Program Disk for
LILIES border shown.

Copy on a copier or print multiple copies of this design for many
"lovely" favorites.

Graphic Alternatives:
For FLOWER use PROG(ROSEBUD).

Coloring 4/SAFETY

What you need:

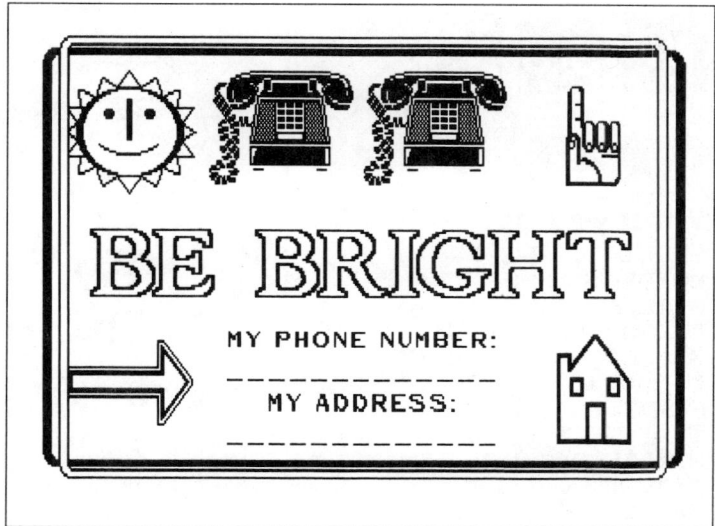

What you do:

SIGN; DYO; WIDE;
BORDER:NEON;
LAYOUT:SM TILED;
GRAPHIC:PROG(TELEPHONE);
DELETE:(ROW 2)ALL, (ROW 3)
2,3; CHANGE:(ROW 1) to
NEW(SUNSHINE,PAGE 189),
(ROW 1) 4 to NEW(POINTING
FINGER,PAGE 184), (ROW 3) 1 to
NEW(ARROW 1,PAGE 157),
(ROW 3) 4 to NEW(HOUSE,PAGE
180); FONT:TINY;
MESSAGE:L1-L5(IBM)/L1-L4(APP)
(blank); FONT:IMPERIAL;
MESSAGE:L6(IBM)/L5(APP)
(CENTER,OUTLINE)text;
FONT:TINY;
MESSAGE:L7-L10(IBM)/L6-L9
(APP)(CENTER,SOLID)text;
PRINT

Design Notes

Choose graphics that are clean and open for coloring. Copy on a copying machine for group use.

Graphic Alternatives:
For SUNSHINE use SCH/BUS(KEY); for TELEPHONES use SCH/BUS(LIGHT SWITCH) and SCH/BUS(LIGHT BULB); for POINTING FINGER use PROG(RIBBON); for ARROW 1 use SCH/BUS(POINTER); for HOUSE use SCH/BUS(KEY) or SAMP(FIREPLACE).

Coloring 5/ALL ABOUT ME (IBM ONLY)

What you need:

What you do:

SIGN; DYO; TALL;
BORDER:SCH/BUS
(WIDE/SCROLL—IBM only);
LAYOUT:MIXED COLUMNS;
GRAPHIC:NEW(SUNSHINE,PAGE
189); DELETE:(SM-COL 1) 2,3,4,5,
(MED-COL 2) 2,3, (SM-COL 3)
2,3,4,5; CHANGE:(SM-COL 1) 6 to
NEW(ARROW1,PAGE 157),
(SM-COL 3) 6 to
NEW(CLOWN,PAGE 163);
FONT:SONOMA;
MESSAGE:L4,L5(indent 1
space)(LEFT,SOLID)text,
L6,L7(indent 1 space,
12-IBM/14-APP spaces between
numbers)(LEFT,SOLID)text;
FONT:LASSEN;
MESSAGE:L8(CENTER,SOLID)
text; PRINT

Design Notes

Apple Users and IBM Users without School & Business Edition:
Substitute DOUBLE LINE border on Program Disk for SCROLL
border shown.

Children love activities involving fill-ins, especially about
themselves. Copy this design on a copying machine for classroom,
group, or repeated use. Choose graphics that are easy to color.

Graphic Alternatives:
For SUNSHINE use SAMP(KITTY CAT); for ARROW use
NEW(POINTING FINGER, PAGE 184) or SCH/BUS(POINTER);
for CLOWN use SAMP(RABBIT).

Creature Maker

What you need:

What you do:
SIGN; DYO; TALL;
LAYOUT:LG CENTER;
GRAPHIC:MOD(CREATURE
MAKER/RABBIT,PAGE 204);
PRINT

Design Notes
Print out and copy for hours of silly drawings. Erase the head, legs
or tail of any Print Shop animal. Just be sure to leave enough room
for a child to fill in his or her own creation. Print in Medium
Staggered for an entire cast of characters. Try printing various
animals on a long banner, tape up, offer crayons and start a party
off right...instant activity and laughs!

Graphic Alternatives:
Try using SAMP(GIRAFFE, KITTY CAT, SCOTTIE) or
NEW(JACK-IN-THE-BOX, PAGE 181).

Memory Game

What you need:

NP S

What you do:

SIGN; DYO; TALL; LAYOUT:SM
TILED; GRAPHIC:PROG(TEDDY
BEAR); DELETE:(ROW 2)ALL,
(ROW 4)ALL, (ROW 6)ALL;
CHANGE:(ROW 1) 2,4, (ROW 3)
2,5, (ROW 5) 3,4, (ROW 7) 1,3 to
SAMP(RABBIT); CHANGE:(ROW
3) 3, (ROW 5) 5, (ROW 7) 2 to
SAMP(AIRPLANE); FONT:
SMALL;
MESSAGE:L5,L11,L17(LEFT,
SOLID)(dashes); PRINT 3 copies

Game Rules:

Create a fun memory building activity for you and your child. Design 4 rows with 5 graphics each. Repeat the same graphics in each row in a unique order with increasing complexity as shown.

Print 2 copies of the Memory Game sheet. Cut one sheet on the dotted lines into 4 memory card strips. Cut the second sheet into individual memory cards and give 3 cards of each graphic to your child.

Hold up one memory card strip for your child to see for about 5 seconds. Let your child lay down the matching memory cards in the same order.

Graphic Alternatives:

Try using other childlike arrangements such as PROG(BALLOONS, ICE CREAM) and NEW(SUNSHINE, PAGE 189) or SAMP(KITTY CAT, BICYCLE) and NEW(CLOWN, PAGE 163).

Number Signs

What you need:

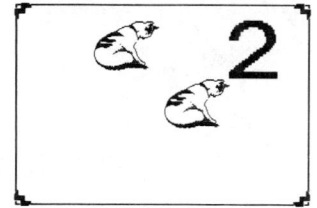

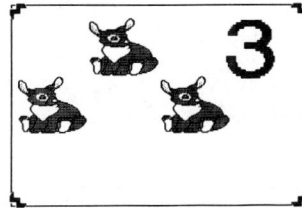

What you do:

For Number 1 Sign:

SIGN; DYO; WIDE; BORDER:
SAMP(CORNER); LAYOUT:SM
TILED; GRAPHIC:NEW
(SUNSHINE,PAGE 189); DELETE:
(ROW 1)ALL, (ROW 2) 1,3,4,
(ROW 3)ALL; FONT:AMADOR;
MESSAGE:L1(indent 6 spaces)
(CENTER,SOLID,CH SIZE:L)
text; PRINT

For Number 2 Sign:

SIGN; DYO; WIDE; BORDER:
SAMP(CORNER); LAYOUT:SM
TILED; GRAPHIC:SAMP(KITTY
CAT); DELETE:(ROW 1) 1,3,4,
(ROW 2) 1,2,4, (ROW 3)ALL;
FONT:AMADOR;
MESSAGE:L1(indent 6
spaces)(CENTER,SOLID,CH
SIZE:L)text; PRINT

For Number 3 Sign:

SIGN; DYO; WIDE; BORDER:
SAMP(CORNER); LAYOUT:SM
TILED; GRAPHIC:SAMP
(RABBIT); DELETE:(ROW 1)
1,3,4, (ROW 2) 2,4, (ROW 3)ALL;
FONT:AMADOR; MESSAGE:L1
(indent 6 spaces)(CENTER,
SOLID,CH SIZE:L)text; PRINT

For Number 4 Sign:

SIGN; DYO; WIDE; BORDER:
SAMP(CORNER); LAYOUT:SM
TILED; GRAPHIC:SAMP
(AIRPLANE); DELETE:(ROW 1)
1,3,4; (ROW 2) 2,4, (ROW 3) 1,3,4;
FONT:AMADOR; MESSAGE:L1

(indent 6 spaces)(CENTER,SOLID,CH SIZE:L)text; PRINT

For Number 5 Sign:

SIGN; DYO; WIDE; BORDER:SAMP(CORNER); LAYOUT:SM
TILED; GRAPHIC:PROG(TEDDY BEAR); DELETE:(ROW 1)
1,3,4, (ROW 2) 4, (ROW 3) 1,3,4; FONT:AMADOR;
MESSAGE:L1(indent 6 spaces)(CENTER,SOLID,CH SIZE:L)text;
PRINT

Design Notes:

Adding color with markers will make your number signs more
eye-catching. Try copying the number signs on a copying machine
and letting children color them in. It's a great group activity. For
coloring, choose graphics with clean areas in which to color.

Graphic Alternatives:
For SUNSHINE use SAMP(SCOTTIE); for KITTY CAT use
SAMP(GIRAFFE); for RABBIT use PROG(RIBBON) or
SCH/BUS(TROPHY); for AIRPLANE use NEW(HOUSE, PAGE
180); for TEDDY BEAR use NEW(FLOWER, PAGE 169).

Puzzle Game

What you need:

NP

What you do:
SIGN; DYO; TALL; LAYOUT:
LG CENTERED;
GRAPHIC:PROG(BALLOONS);
INSERT:LG/NEW(GAME BOX,
PAGE 170) to right
3(IBM)/12(APP) key presses, down
5(IBM)/20(APP) key presses;
PRINT

Cut into four pieces.

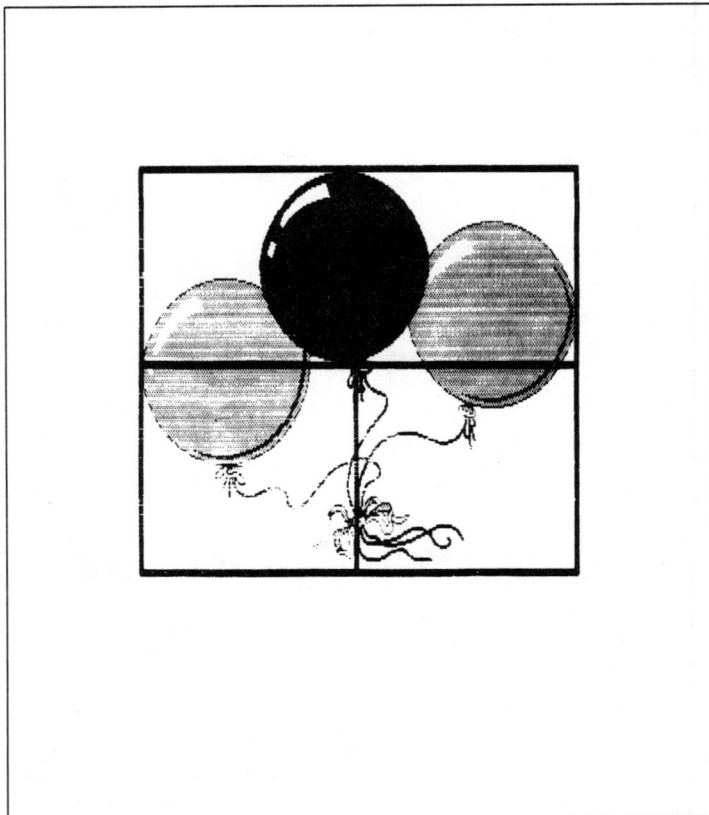

Design Notes:
This jigsaw-like puzzle game can be created using any New Print Shop graphic. For a very young child select an item that is easy to identify such as an animal or car. For a more advanced preschooler try a graphic like Balloons for a greater challenge at problem solving.

Graphic Alternatives:
Try using SCH/BUS(CLOCK); PARTY(BLACK CAT); SAMP(VALLEY LILY).

Tic-Tac-Toe

What you need:

What you do:

SIGN; DYO; TALL; LAYOUT:SM
STAGGERED;
GRAPHIC:NEW(TIC-TAC-TOE,
PAGE 191); DELETE:(ROW 1) 1,
(ROW 3) 2, (ROW 4) 2, (ROW 5) 3;
FONT:SONOMA;
MESSAGE:L1,L2(LEFT,SOLID)
text, L8(LEFT,SOLID)(dashes),
L6(CENTER,SOLID)text,
L8(CENTER,SOLID)(dashes),
L10,L11(RIGHT,SOLID)text,
L12(RIGHT,SOLID)(dashes);
CHANGE TEXT TO
GRAPHIC(IBM only)/MOVE:L8 up
1 key press (Apple Users: Use
Quick Print feature to insert L8
into position, see PAGE 27); PRINT

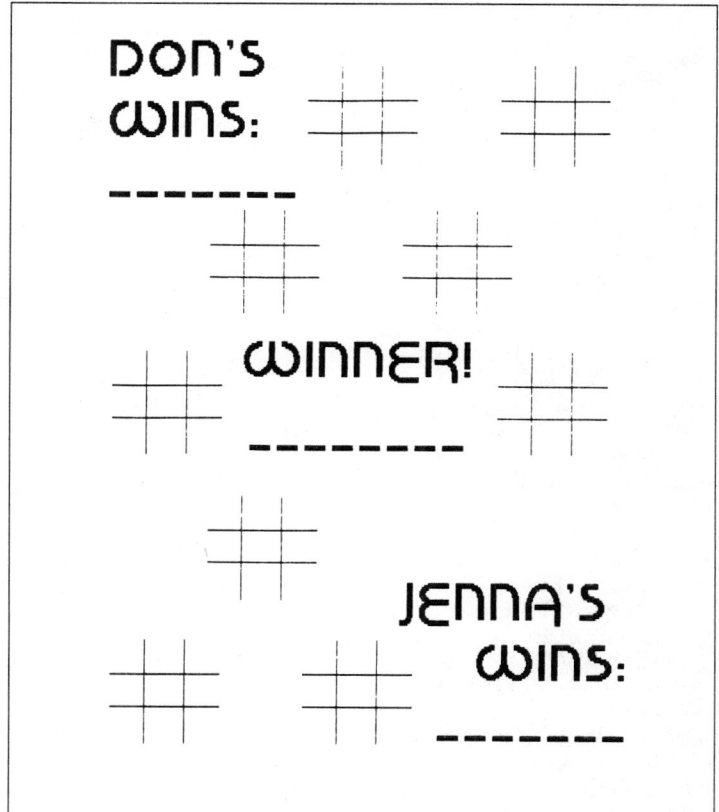

Design Notes:

Print personalized game sheets for new enthusiasm to an old
game. In addition to creating a Tic-Tac-Toe game, the graphic
shown here can be used as an interesting symbol or decorative
graphic. Try using it in a tiled pattern on a letterhead.

"Top Secret" Game/GAMEMAT

What you need:

What you do:

GRAPHIC EDITOR; draw NEW(GAMEBOX, PAGE 170) without inside horizontal and vertical lines; SAVE as BOX SIGN; DYO; TALL; BORDER:THIN LINE; LAYOUT:MATRIX; GRAPHIC:NEW(BOX); DELETE:(ROW 2) 1,2; MOVE:(ROW 1)ALL up 1(IBM)/4(APP) key press, (ROW 2) 3 down 2(IBM)/8(APP) key presses, (ROW 3)ALL down 1(IBM)/4(APP) key press; INSERT: MED/NEW(BOX) to right 4(IBM)/16(APP) key presses, down 6(IBM)/24(APP) key presses; INSERT:SM/PROG(FOLDERS) to right 8(IBM)/32(APP) key presses, down 7(IBM)/28(APP) key presses; FONT:SIERRA; MESSAGE:L2(LEFT SOLID) indent approx. 5 spaces and type "1," leave approx. 6 spaces and type "2," leave approx. 6 spaces and type "3," L7(LEFT,SOLID) indent 20-IBM/24-APP spaces and type "4," L9(LEFT SOLID) indent approx. 5 spaces and type "5," leave approx. 6 spaces and type "6," leave approx. 6 spaces and type "7," L11(LEFT, SOLID) indent approx. 5 spaces and type "8," leave approx. 6 spaces and type "9," leave approx. 6 spaces and type "10," PRINT 4 copies

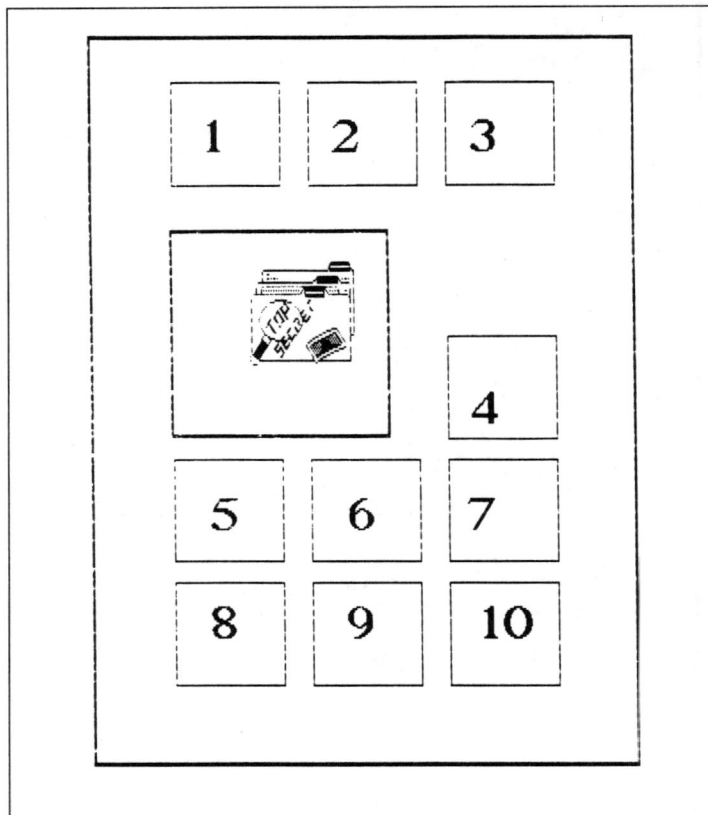

Game Rules:

Ages 7 & up

Two Players

OBJECT OF THE GAME:

Guess who stole the "Top Secret" file. To win, guess the correct "Suspect File Number" card and "Evidence" card that is face down on the gamemat.

HOW TO PLAY:

Print 3 "Evidence" card sheets and 4 gamemats. Give each player one of each sheet for "checking off" eliminated and guessed items during the game.Cut up one sheet of "Evidence" cards and one gamemat. Discard the large card with the Top Secret File graphic.

(Continued on next page.)

"Top Secret Game"/EVIDENCE CARDS

What you need:

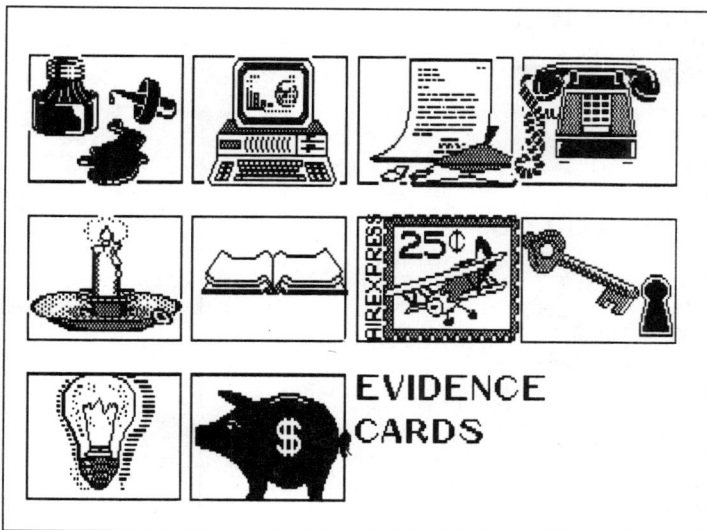

EVIDENCE
CARDS

What you do:

SIGN; DYO; WIDE; LAYOUT:SM
TILED II; GRAPHIC:NEW(BOX);
DELETE:(ROW 3) 3,4; INSERT:
SM/PROG(INK BOTTLE) to top left
corner; SM/PROG(COMPUTER)
to right 6(IBM)/24(APP) key presses;
SM/PROG(LETTER) to right
12(IBM)/48(APP) key presses;
SM/PROG(TELEPHONE) to right
18(IBM)/72(APP) key presses;
SM/SAMP(CANDLESTICK) down
4(IBM)/16(APP) key presses;
SM/NEW(BOOK, PAGE 159) to right 6(IBM)/24(APP) key presses, down 4(IBM)/16(APP) key presses;
SM/SCH/BUS(STAMP) to right 12(IBM)/48(APP) key presses, down 4(IBM)/16(APP) key presses;
SM/SCH/BUS(KEY) to right 18(IBM)/72(APP) key presses, down 4(IBM)/16(APP) key presses;
SM/SAMP(LIGHT BULB) down 8(IBM)/32(APP) key presses; SM/MOD(PIGGY BANK, PAGE 208) to right
6(IBM)/24(APP) key presses, down 8(IBM)/32(APP) key presses; FONT:SMALL;
MESSAGE:L8,L9(LEFT,SOLID)(indent 15-IBM/18-APP spaces)text; PRINT 3 copies

Turn the remaining cards face down in two separate piles and without looking draw one card from each pile. Place the selected cards face down in the Top Secret File box on the gamemat.

Deal the remaining cards. Each player secretly checks off on his or her reference sheets the cards he or she is holding. Players move around the gamemat with tokens or pennies, taking turns at guessing the face down "Suspect File Number" card and "Evidence" card. A "Suspect File Number" can be guessed only when the player has actually landed on that file number. If a guess is incorrect, it's up to the player's opponent to prove the player wrong by showing that card from his or her own hand. The first player to guess correctly wins!

HOW TO MOVE:

Players put hands behind backs and on the count of 3 reveal a number pattern from 1 to 10 with fingers. The lower number gets to move. The goal is to get a number you want to move ahead without getting a number bigger than your opponent. If two "ones" are presented—the winner is the first out there!

Keep score and see who can win the most games out of ten!

Travel Game

What you need:

NP **S/B**

What you do:

SIGN; DYO; TALL; BORDER:THIN
LINE; LAYOUT:SM CORNERS;
GRAPHIC:SCH/BUS(MOVING
VAN); DELETE:(ROW 2)ALL;
CHANGE:(ROW 1) 2 to
SCH/BUS(POINTER);
FONT:SMALL; MESSAGE:
L1,L2(CENTER,SOLID,
CH SIZE:L)text, L3(1 space
between letters)(CENTER,SOLID)
text; FONT:TINY; MESSAGE:
L5-L7, L9-L14(3 spaces between
states)(CENTER,SOLID,CH
SIZE:L)text, L8(4 spaces between
states)(CENTER,SOLID,CH
SIZE:L)text; PRINT

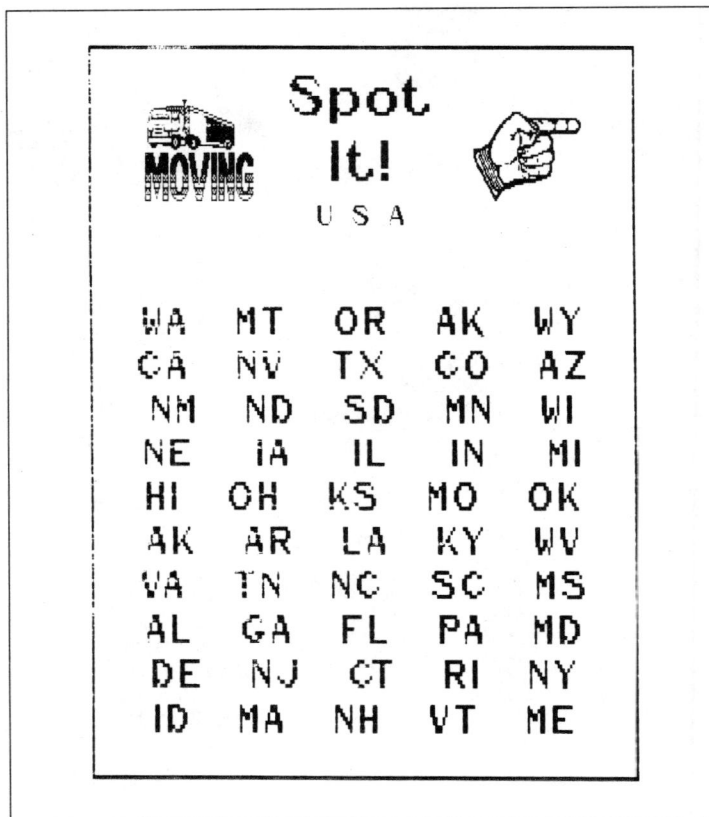

Spot
It!
U S A

WA	MT	OR	AK	WY
CA	NV	TX	CO	AZ
NM	ND	SD	MN	WI
NE	IA	IL	IN	MI
HI	OH	KS	MO	OK
AK	AR	LA	KY	WV
VA	TN	NC	SC	MS
AL	GA	FL	PA	MD
DE	NJ	CT	RI	NY
ID	MA	NH	VT	ME

Design Notes

Copy sheets of this game for hours of travel fun. Match state
license plates on the road to your game sheet. Be the first player to
spot a state on your sheet and you've "captured" that state. Only
one player can "capture" each state. So work fast! Use different
colored crayons or pencils for each player to circle a "captured"
state (or mark the "captured" state with and "X" or "O"). Mix up
the abbreviations for a brand new game.

Graphic Alternatives:
Try using PROG(FOLDERS), SCH/BUS(MAGNIFIER, GLOBE)
or NEW(POINTING FINGER, PAGE 184).

Tri-Dot Game

What you need:

What you do:
SIGN; DYO; TALL; LAYOUT:
SM TILED;
GRAPHIC:NEW(DOTS,PAGE
168); PRINT

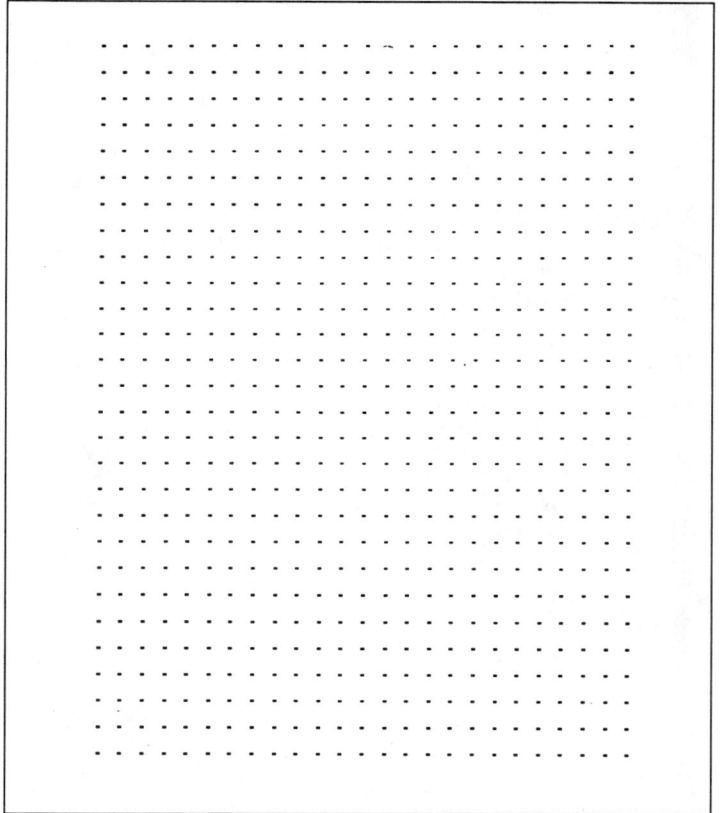

Design Notes
Create hours of travel fun with this classic connect-the-dots game.
Each player takes a turn connecting two dots either horizontally or
vertically. Each time a player draws a line that completes a box,
the player "wins" the box by filling in his or her initials and gets
another turn. The player who completes the most boxes wins the
game!

Ad/EVENT

What you need:

NP

What you do:

SIGN; DYO; TALL; BORDER:THIN
LINE; LAYOUT:MED TILED II;
GRAPHIC:MOD(MAN OF
STRENGTH SYMBOL, PAGE 207);
MOVE:(ROW 2) 1,2 down 2(IBM)/8
(APP) key presses; FONT:
MERCED; MESSAGE:L3(CENTER,
SOLID)text; FONT:TINY;
MESSAGE:L4-L6(CENTER,SOLID)
text; FONT:SMALL; MESSAGE:L8,
L9,L11-L15(CENTER,SOLID)text;
CHANGE TEXT TO GRAPHIC
(IBM only)/MOVE:L3 down 1 key
press (*Apple Users:* Use Quick Print
feature to insert Line 3, see page
27); PRINT

Design Notes:

Combine horizontal and vertical text for an interesting design
effect. Use the customize feature to move graphics to exactly
where you want them to allow space for your words.

Graphic Alternatives:
Try using PROG(DAISIES).

Badge

What you need:

What you do:

GRAPHIC EDITOR; draw
NEW(GAME BOX,PAGE 170)
eliminating the inside horizontal
and vertical lines; SAVE as BOX.

SIGN; DYO; TALL; LAYOUT:MED
CENTER; GRAPHIC:NEW(BOX);
INSERT:SM/PROG(PICNIC) to
right 11(IBM)/44(APP) key
presses, down 9(IBM)/36(APP) key
presses; FONT:SMALL;
MESSAGE:L3(CENTER,SOLID)(12
dashes); FONT:IMPERIAL;
MESSAGE:L4(CENTER,
SOLID)text; FONT:SMALL;
MESSAGE:L5(CENTER,SOLID)(12
dashes with shift key),
L10,L11(CENTER,SOLID)text;
PRINT

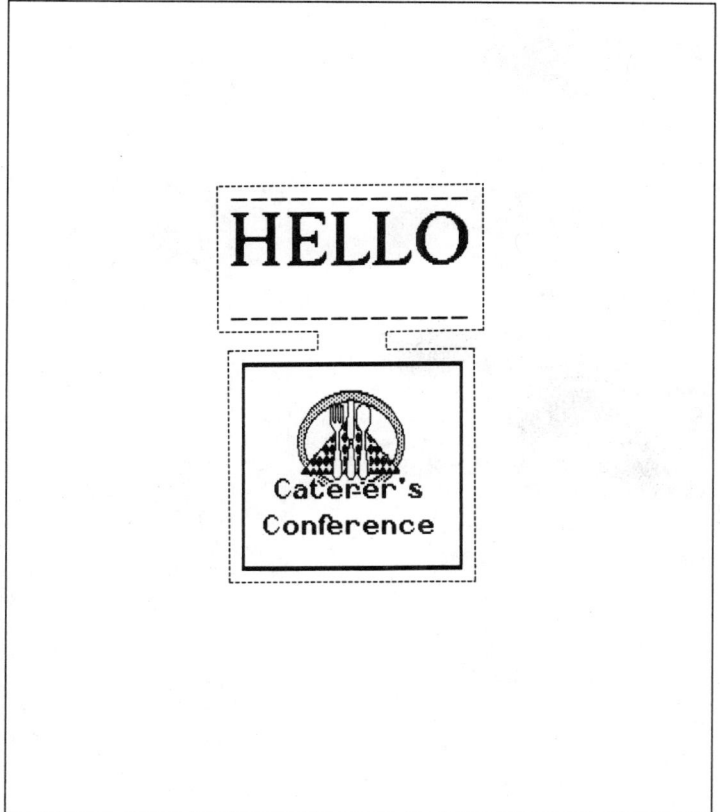

Design Notes:

A small graphic can easily be superimposed on top of a
medium-size graphic as shown here. Print and cut and you're
ready to pin this badge on the recipient. For multiple badges, copy
the badge on a copying machine and then add names or text by
hand. If individual printing is desired, personalize with names.
IBM users can use the name file feature to personalize badges.

Graphic Alternatives:

Select a graphic that represents your event. For generic message
use NEW(STAR, PAGE 188) or NEW(SUNSHINE, PAGE 189).

Banner/ (IBM ONLY)

What you need:

NP

What you do:

To create top banner:

BANNER; HORIZONTAL; TEXT:SM LINE OVER LG; FONT:SUTTER; MESSAGE:L1(1 space between letters, 4 spaces between words)(CENTER, SOLID)text; FONT:MADERA; MESSAGE:L2(2 spaces between letters)(CENTER,SOLID)text; PRINT

To create middle banner:

BANNER; HORIZONTAL; LAYOUT:LG GRAPHIC BOTH ENDS; GRAPHIC:PROG (FOOTBALL); TEXT:ONE LINE TEXT; FONT:MARIN; MESSAGE:(CENTER,OUTLINE) (3 dashes/1 space to word, 3 spaces between letters, 1 space to dashes/3 dashes); PRINT

To create bottom banner:

BANNER; HORIZONTAL; TEXT:LG LINE OVER SM; FONT:MADERA; MESSAGE:(2 spaces between letters)(CENTER, SOLID)text; FONT:SUTTER; MESSAGE:(1 space between letters, 4 spaces between words)(CENTER,SOLID)text; PRINT

Design Notes:

Apple Users: Print one line of text at a time for the top and bottom banners and then cut and paste the smaller line of text to sit on top of the larger line as shown.

Stacked banners can be used to create oversized sale signs or cheerleading signs as shown here. The middle section can hold any message desired. Simply add dashes to create the length desired to match the length of the top and bottom banners. If you make a mistake it's easy to correct even after printing by cutting out unwanted dash sections and retaping! Trim off excess paper at the ends.

Graphic Alternatives:

Try using SAMP(HIGH TOP, SKIER, BICYCLE), SCH/BUS(TROPHY) or PROG(RIBBON).

Chart/SEATING

What you need:

NP

What you do:

SIGN; DYO; TALL; LAYOUT:SM
TILED II; GRAPHIC:MOD(CREST
FRAME, PAGE 216);
FONT:SMALL;
MESSAGE:L1(CENTER,SOLID)
text; PRINT

CLASSROOM SEATING CHART

Design Notes:

For larger classes or for seating arrangements with additional
rows across, choose a different tiled pattern or attach additional
sheets with tape. This chart also works horizontally without the
text. Use at the beginning of school or as a quick reference for a
substitute or visiting teacher.

Flyer 1/BANQUET

What you need:

NP

What you do:

SIGN; DYO; TALL;
BORDER:DECO; LAYOUT:MED
CENTER; GRAPHIC:PROG
(PICNIC); FONT:AMADOR;
MESSAGE:L1(CENTER,SOLID)
text, L2(2 spaces between letters)
(CENTER,SOLID)text, L3(1 space
between letters)(CENTER,SOLID)
text; FONT:SMALL; MESSAGE:
L4(indent 4 spaces, leave
35-IBM/42-APP spaces between
words)(LEFT,SOLID)text; FONT:
MARIN; MESSAGE:L9(CENTER,
SOLID)text; FONT:AMADOR;
MESSAGE:L10(CENTER,SOLID)
text; CHANGE TEXT TO
GRAPHIC(IBM only)/MOVE:L3 up
1 key press (Apple Users: Use
Quick Print feature to insert L3
into position, see page 27); PRINT

Moss Farm
P T A
A N N U A L

6:30   Feb.15

BANQUET
FEAST

Design Notes:

Varying fonts hold together when there are few graphics or a
symmetrical layout. This design satisfies both requirements. Move
2 lines of a simple, sans serif font close together to form a linked
logo in your design.

Graphic Alternatives:
Try using PROG(COFFEE).

Flyer 2/MEETING

What you need:

What you do:

SIGN; DYO; TALL;
BORDER:NEON; LAYOUT:SM
PAIR; GRAPHIC:SCH/BUS(KEY);
CHANGE:(COL 1) 2 to
NEW(DOLLAR,PAGE 167);
MOVE:(COL 1) 1 up
1(IBM)/4(APP) key press;
FONT:MADERA;
MESSAGE:L1(CENTER,SOLID,
CH SIZE:L)text, L2,L5,L8,L9
(CENTER,SOLID)text;
FONT:SMALL(IBM)/TINY(APP);
MESSAGE:L10,L11(CENTER,
SOLID)text; CHANGE TEXT TO
GRAPHIC (IBM only)/MOVE:L5 up
1 key press (*Apple Users:* Use Quick
Print feature to insert Line 5, see
page 27); PRINT

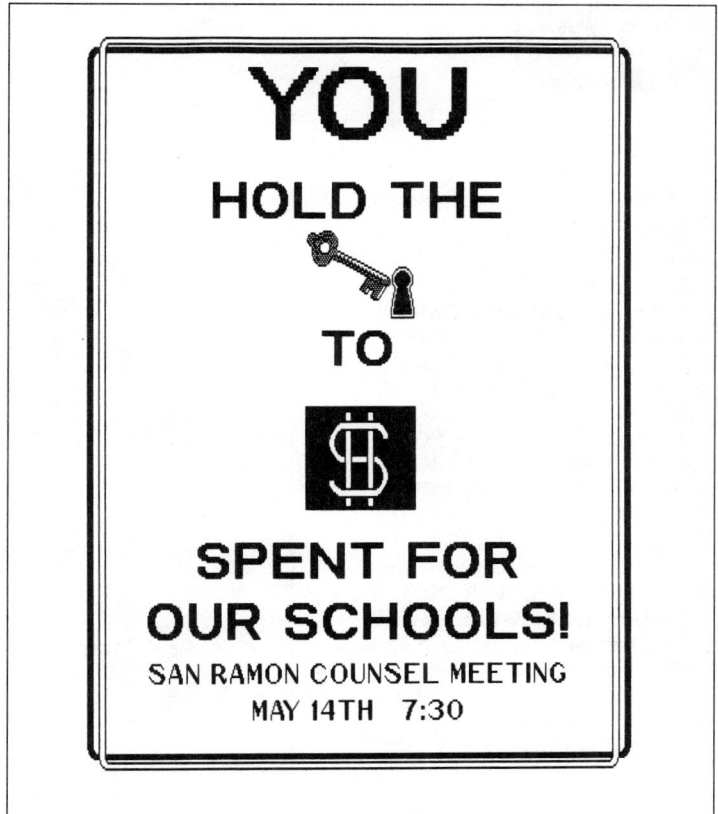

Design Notes:

By centering all elements in the design, you can quickly create a
powerful flyer. Print on colored paper for an even greater impact.

Graphic Alternatives:
For DOLLAR use SCH/BUS(DOLLARS).

Flyer 3/EVENT

What you need:

NP **S/B**

What you do:

SIGN; DYO; TALL; LAYOUT:SM
STAGGERED;
GRAPHIC:SCH/BUS(DRAMA);
DELETE:(ROW 1) 1,3, (ROW
2)ALL, (ROW 3) 1,3, (ROW 4)ALL,
(ROW 5) 2; CHANGE:(ROW 3) 2 to
PROG(NIGHT SKY), (ROW 5) 1,3
to SCH/BUS(SCHOOL); FONT:
SMALL; MESSAGE:L1-L4(blank);
FONT:MERCED; MESSAGE:
L5-L6(CENTER,RAISED)text;
FONT:SMALL; MESSAGE:L7
(8-IBM/10-APP spaces between
words)(CENTER,OUTLINE,CH
SIZE:L)text, L8(10-IBM/12-APP
spaces between words)(CENTER,
OUTLINE,CH SIZE:L)text,
L10-L12(CENTER,SOLID)text;
FONT:TINY; MESSAGE:L14-L16
(CENTER,SOLID)text; PRINT

Design Notes:

Symmetrical layouts can have great diversity. Many different
graphics and fonts can hold together with a centered design. Print
on colored paper for more impact.

Graphic Alternatives:
For DRAMA use PROG(ROSEBUD); for NIGHT SKY use
PROG(DAISIES) or SAMP(CANDLESTICK); for SCHOOL use
SCH/BUS(BUILDINGS) or SCH/BUS(QUOTE) and type ! inside.

Letterhead 1/SCHOOL

What you need:

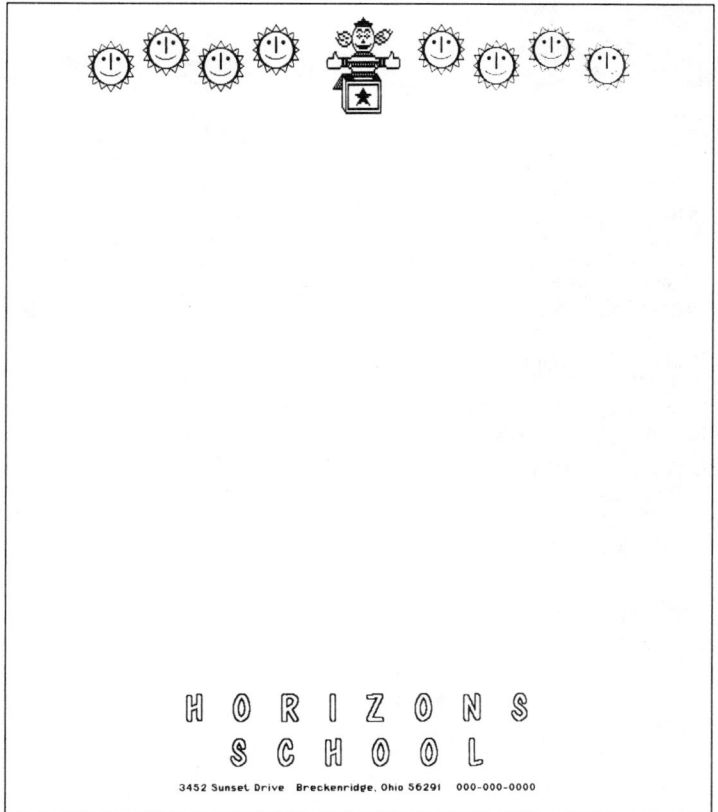

What you do:

LETTERHEAD TOP; DYO;
LAYOUT:SM CENTER ROW;
GRAPHIC:NEW(SUNSHINE,PAGE
189); DELETE:(ROW 1) 5,6;
INSERT:MED/NEW(JACK-IN-
THE-BOX,PAGE 181) to right
25(IBM)/100(APP) key presses;
MOVE:(ROW 1) 2,4,7,9 up
1(IBM)/4(APP) key press

LETTERHEAD BOTTOM;
FONT:SUTTER;
MESSAGE:L1,L2(3 spaces between
letters)(CENTER,SOLID)text;
FONT:TINY; MESSAGE:L3
(3 spaces between phrases)
(CENTER,SOLID)text; PRINT

Design Notes:

A simple technique can be used with the customize feature. Simply
move every other picture for a whimsical, yet graphic effect.

Graphic Alternatives:

For SUNSHINE use SAMP(GIRAFFE, KITTY CAT) or
PARTY(GINGERBREAD); for JACK-IN-THE-BOX use
PROG(SUNSHINE).

Letterhead 2/CLUB

What you need:

What you do:

LETTERHEAD TOP; DYO;
LAYOUT:SM ENDS;
GRAPHIC:SCH/BUS(STAMPS);
FONT:VENTURA;
MESSAGE:L1(CENTER,RAISED)
text; FONT:TINY;
MESSAGE:L5(CENTER,SOLID);
RULED LINE:THIN

LETTERHEAD BOTTOM;
FONT:SMALL;
MESSAGE:L2,L3(indent 3
spaces)(LEFT,SOLID,CH SIZE:L)
text; RULED LINE:THICK

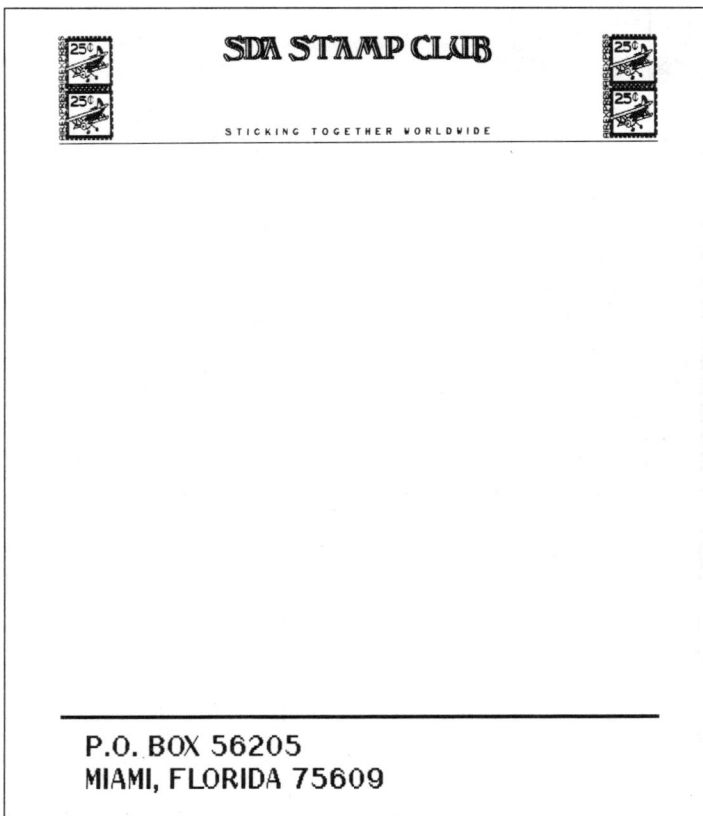

Design Notes:

An unusual look is created with 2 stacked graphics on each side of
a letterhead. By using the same graphic in all 4 positions a more
solid feel is given to the layout. This design needs the balance of a
text line under the name.

Graphic Alternatives:
For Art Club use SCH/BUS(ART); for Chemistry Club use
SCH/BUS(BEAKER); for Real Estate or City Charity group use
SCH/BUS(BUILDINGS); for Investment Club use
SCH/BUS(DOLLARS); for Computer Users group use
PROG(COMPUTER); for Piano or Music group use
PROG(MUSIC).

Letterhead 3/CLUB

What you need:

NP

What you do:

LETTERHEAD TOP; DYO;
LAYOUT:SM TILED;
GRAPHIC:NEW(STAR,PAGE 188);
DELETE:(ROW 2) 2,3,4,5,6,7,8,9;
CHANGE:(ROW 2) 1,10 to
PROG(BASEBALL);
FONT:SMALL;
MESSAGE:L1-L4(blank);
FONT:MARIN;
MESSAGE:L5(CENTER,SOLID)
text; RULED LINE:DOUBLE

LETTERHEAD BOTTOM;
FONT:TINY;
MESSAGE:L2-L4(CENTER,SOLID)
text; PRINT

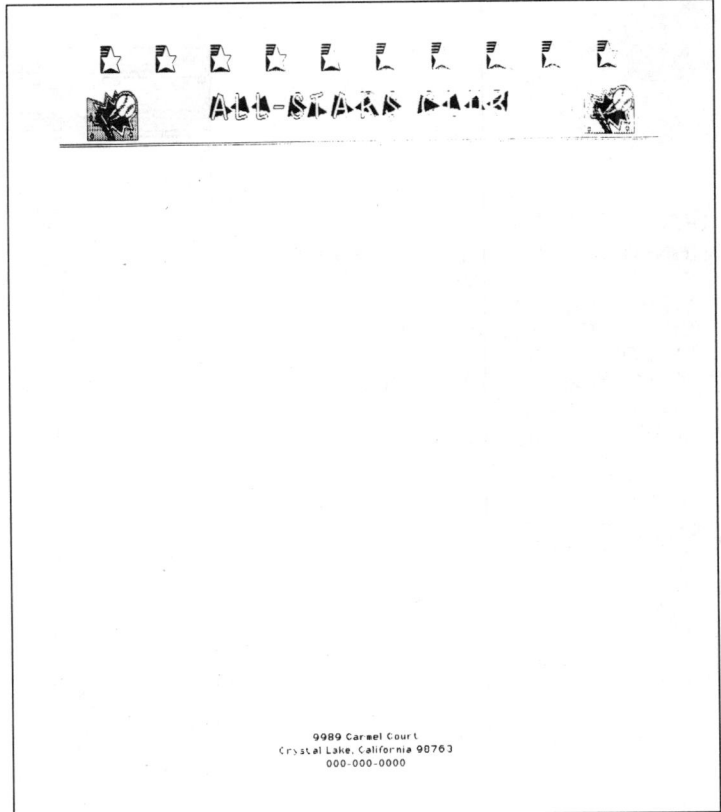

ALL-STARS

9989 Carmel Court
Crystal Lake, California 98763
000-000-0000

Design Notes:

A decorative band at the top creates a unifying element. An alternating graphic pattern satisfies this need as well.

Graphic Alternatives:
Try using other sports symbols to represent other activities.

Masthead/NEWSPAPER

What you need:

NP

What you do:

SIGN; DYO; TALL; BORDER:THIN
LINE; LAYOUT:MIXED ROWS;
GRAPHIC:PROG(MUSIC);
DELETE:LG-CTR, (SM-ROW 2)
ALL; FONT:SIERRA;
MESSAGE:L3(CENTER,SOLID)
text;L4(CENTER,SOLID)dashes;
PRINT

Design Notes:

A simple pattern of repeated graphics creates a bold design. For a
masthead the dashed line works well to divide the heading from
the body copy. Use The New Print Shop to create your newsletter
with the Small or Tiny font, or type normally. Children can place
graphics within their body copy for greater impact and whimsy.

Graphic Alternatives:
Try using SCH/BUS(TROPHY), PROG(RIBBON) or graphics that
relate to your specific club theme.

Program Cover/RECITAL

What you need:

NP

What you do:

SIGN; DYO; TALL; LAYOUT:SM
TILED; GRAPHIC:PROG(MUSIC);
DELETE:(ROW 2) 2,3,4, (ROW
3)ALL, (ROW 4)ALL, (ROW
5)ALL, (ROW 6)ALL; CHANGE
(ROW 1) 3 to PROG(NIGHT SKY);
CHANGE (ROW 2) 1,5 to
PROG(PARTY FAVOR); CHANGE
(ROW 7) 1,5 to PROG(PIANO);
FONT:MARIN;
MESSAGE:L4(CENTER,SOLID)
text; FONT:AMADOR;
MESSAGE:L5(CENTER,OUTLINE);
FONT:SMALL;
MESSAGE:L6-L8(CENTER,SOLID)
text,L10(1 space between all
letters, 2 spaces between
words)(CENTER,
SOLID)text; PRINT

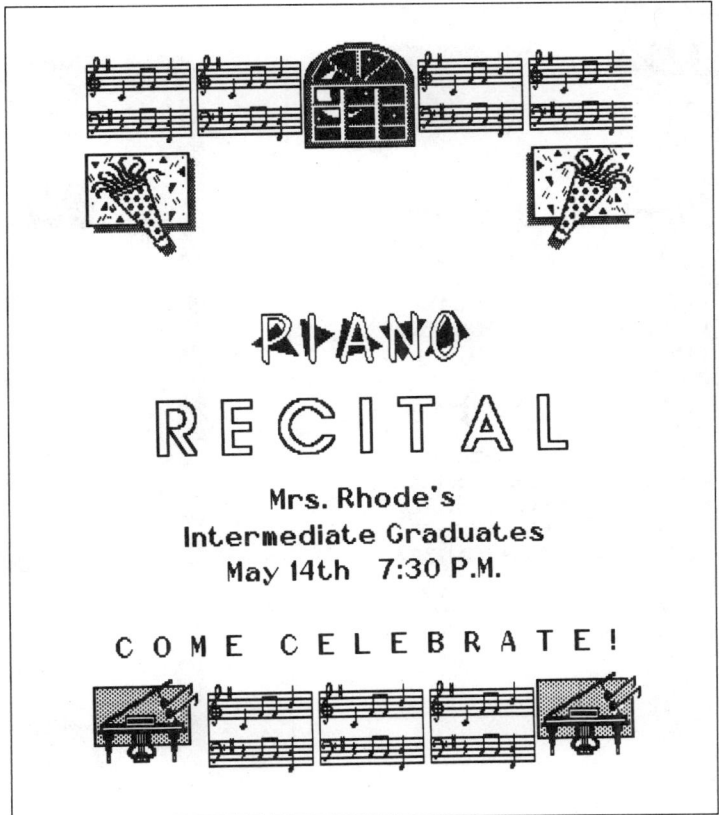

Design Notes:

Piano, ballet, voice... any recital program cover can be produced
easily with The New Print Shop. Mixing graphics adds interest to
your design. Mixing fonts allows you to place emphasis where you
need it.

Graphic Alternatives:
For PIANO use SCH/BUS(BAND, CHEERLEADER).

Sign/DIRECTION (IBM ONLY)

What you need:

NP

What you do:

SIGN; DYO; TALL;
BORDER:PROG(WIDE/CLIPBOARD
—IBM only); LAYOUT:MED
CENTERED; GRAPHIC:NEW
(ARROW 1,PAGE 157);
MOVE:(ROW 1) 1 up
1(IBM)/4(APP) key press;
FONT:MADERA;
MESSAGE:L1(CENTER,SOLID)
text (Note: This text will be moved
to bottom.); FONT:MERCED;
MESSAGE:L2,L5-L6(CENTER,
RAISED) text; CUSTOMIZE/
CHANGE TEXT TO GRAPHIC
(IBM only): MOVE:L1 down 16 key
presses; PRINT

Ms. Brown's

**MATH
CLASS**

ROOM 514

Design Notes:

Apple Users: For CLIPBOARD use DECO border; type classroom
number on Line 7 or use Quick Print to insert text, see page 27.

A single arrow is effective for any kind of directional sign. Color in
outline of arrow with brightly colored markers for added emphasis.

Sign/INVITATION

What you need:

NP **S/B**

What you do:

SIGN; DYO; TALL; LAYOUT:FULL
PANEL; GRAPHIC:PROG
(ROBOT); INSERT:MED/SCH/BUS
(QUOTE) to right 1(IBM)/4(APP)
key press, down 1(IBM)/4(APP)
key press; FONT:SMALL;
MESSAGE:L2(indent approx. 4
spaces)(LEFT,SOLID,CH SIZE:L)
text, L3(indent approx. 3 spaces)
(LEFT,SOLID,CH SIZE:L)text;
FONT:TINY:L7-L10(indent 1 space)
(LEFT,SOLID)text; PRINT

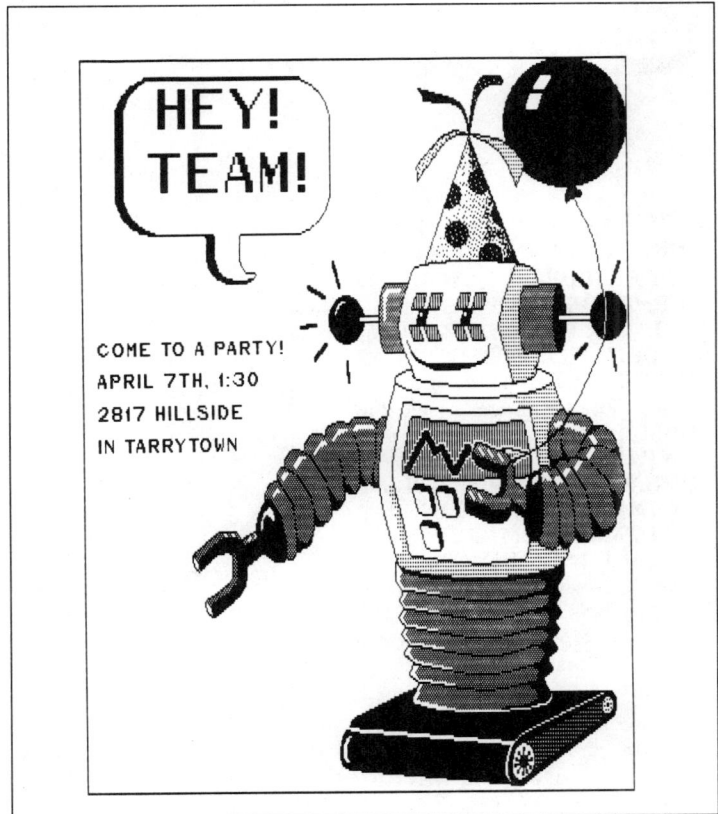

Design Notes:

Combine full panel graphics with other graphics by using the
Insert feature.

Tickets

What you need:

NP

What you do:

CARD FRONT; DYO; TOP FOLD;
BORDER:RIBBON; LAYOUT:SM
PAIR; GRAPHIC:NEW(STAR,
PAGE 188); FLIP HORIZ:(ROW 1)
2; INSERT:SM/NEW(POINTING
FINGER,PAGE 184) to right
9(IBM)/36(APP) key presses, down
7(IBM)/28(APP) key presses;
FONT:MADERA;
MESSAGE:L1(CENTER,SOLID)
text, L3(CENTER,OUTLINE)text;
FONT:SMALL(IBM)/TINY(APP);
MESSAGE:L5(15-IBM/25-APP
spaces between "day" and
"time")(CENTER,SOLID)text,
L6(17-IBM/27-APP spaces between
"date" and "casual")(CENTER,
SOLID)text

For a second copy on same sheet,
make the same choices for CARD
INSIDE and then go to PRINT.

SELECT SIZE:SMALL(67%);
PRINT

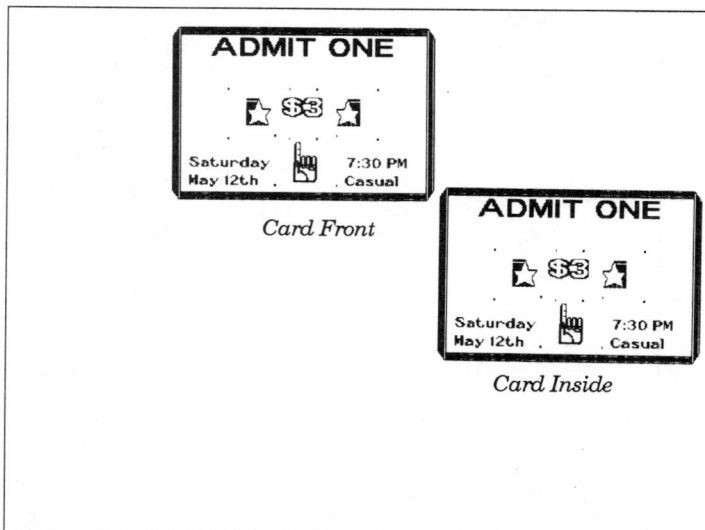

Card Front

Card Inside

Design Notes:

The greeting card mode has an interesting feature which allows for
the reduction of your design. A 67% reduction works well for
tickets. Choose contrasting size fonts to replicate a classic ticket
look. By flipping the graphic on the right side of your price, a more
professional look is achieved.

Print in multiples, paste as many as you can fit on an 8 1/2 X 11
colored sheet and trim for tickets.

Ad 1/HELP WANTED

What you need:

NP **S/B**

What you do:

LETTERHEAD TOP; DYO;
LAYOUT:MED ENDS;
GRAPHIC:PROG(FILE DRAWER);
FLIP HORIZ:(ROW 1) 2;
FONT:SCH/BUS(CLASSIC);
MESSAGE:L1(2 spaces between
letters, 4 spaces between words)
(CENTER,RAISED);
FONT:AMADOR;
MESSAGE:L2(3 spaces between
letters)(CENTER,SOLID);
FONT:TINY;
MESSAGE:L3(CENTER,SOLID);
RULED LINE:THIN; PRINT

Design Notes:

Print Shop art and type can be used quite successfully for
reproduction. This ad was created in the letterhead mode. You can
be even more elaborate (e.g. add borders) by cutting and pasting.

Graphic Alternatives
For other jobs use PROG(CASH BOX, COFFEE, COMPUTER,
TELEPHONE); SCH/BUS(POINTER, BRIEFCASE, DOLLARS)

Ad 2/PROMOTION (IBM ONLY)

What you need:

NP **P** **S/B**
S

What you do:

SIGN; DYO; TALL; BORDER:SCH/
BUS(WIDE/FILM—IBM only);
LAYOUT: SM FRAME II;
GRAPHIC:PARTY(POPCORN);
DELETE:(T-ROW) 1,2,3,4,
(B-ROW) 1,4;
FONT:SAMP(SULLIVAN);
MESSAGE:L1(1 space between
letters)(CENTER,SOLID),
L2(CENTER,SOLID);
FONT:SCH/BUS(CHILDREN);
MESSAGE:L3-L5(CENTER,SOLID);
FONT:TINY;
MESSAGE:L6-L8(CENTER,SOLID);
PRINT

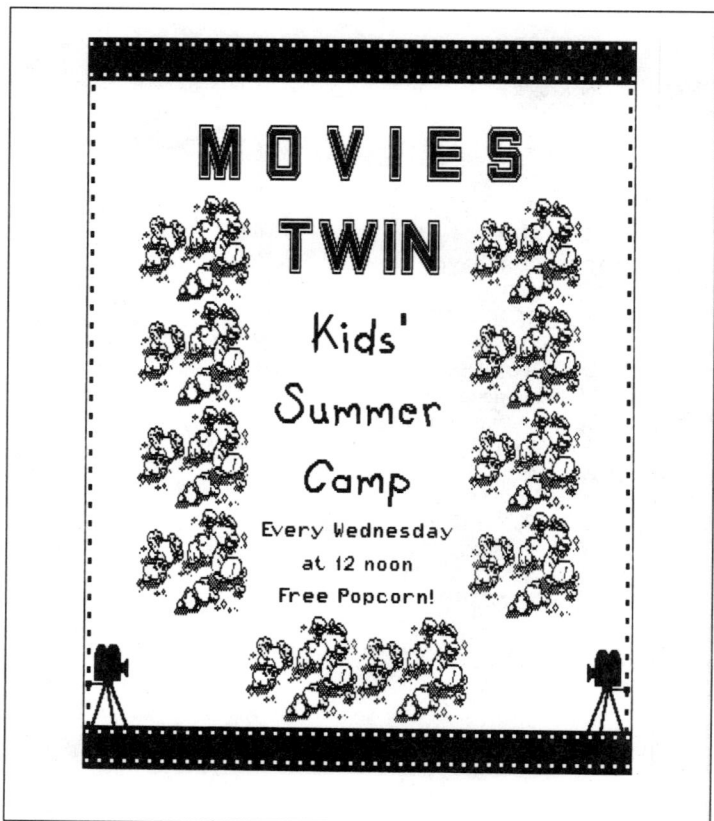

Design Notes:

Apple Users: For FILM border use DECO border.

Graphics which are more irregular or free form work well in this
unusual layout. A fun font mimics the more dynamic design and
irregular graphic placement.

Graphic Alternatives:
For POPCORN use PROG(BALLOONS) or PARTY(COOL
DRINK), for CAMERA use PROG(PARTY FAVOR) or
SAMP(PRESENT).

Ad 3/OPENING—RETAIL (IBM ONLY)

What you need:

NP

What you do:

GRAPHIC EDITOR;
GRAPHIC:PROG(DESERT);
HORIZ FLIP; NEGATIVE; SAVE
as NEGDES

SIGN; DYO; WIDE;
BORDER:NAVAJO; LAYOUT:SM
TILED; GRAPHIC:PROG
(DESERT); DELETE:(ROW 1) 1,4,
(ROW 2)ALL, (ROW 3)ALL;
CHANGE:(ROW 1) 2 to
NEW(NEGDES); FONT:SMALL;
MESSAGE:L4(CENTER,SOLID);
FONT:SIERRA;
MESSAGE:L5(CENTER,SHADOW),
L6(CENTER,SOLID); FONT:TINY;
MESSAGE:L7,L8(CENTER,SOLID);
PRINT

Don't miss our opening
DAY & NIGHT
PLANT SALE
at THE OASIS, 212 Aztec Ave.
Open Saturday 7 a.m. til 11 p.m.

Design Notes:

Apple Users: You can create this same design without Line 8 of the
message.

Reverse graphics are interesting whether used to literally connote
a message or just for effect. How you achieve this look is simple.
Just go to the Graphic Editor, select Negative and save your
graphic to use in a design. Change font styles for an interesting
effect.

Graphic Alternatives:
Other graphics suitable for reverse printing include:
SCH/BUS(DOLLARS, LIGHT SWITCH), PARTY(PARTY HAT,
TWENTY-ONE), and SAMP(VALLEY LILY).

Ad 4/PROMOTION (IBM ONLY)

What you need:

What you do:

GRAPHIC EDITOR; draw
horizontal line at Y=44 across
entire box; SAVE as LINE

SIGN; DYO; TALL;
BORDER:PARTY(WIDE/SHIRT—
IBM only); LAYOUT:MED PAIR;
GRAPHIC:MOD(RIBBON, PAGE
199); CHANGE:(COL 1) 2 to
NEW(LINE); FONT:SMALL;
MESSAGE:L8(CENTER,SOLID);
FONT:TINY;
MESSAGE:L10,L11,L15,L16
(CENTER,SOLID); PRINT

Design Notes:

A playful border created with multiple graphics or IBM wide
borders complements a clever, to-the-point message. A rule created
in the Graphic Editor can be used to separate text and add
emphasis to a message. Leave plenty of white space for this layout
to be effective.

Graphic Alternatives:
For RIBBON use SCH/BUS(TROPHY).

Ad 5/COUPON

What you need:

NP **S/B**

What you do:

SIGN; DYO; TALL;
BORDER:SCH/BUS(BOOKS);
LAYOUT:SM TILED II;
GRAPHIC:SCH/BUS(BOOKS);
DELETE:(ROW 1) 2,3, (ROW
2)ALL; (ROW 3)ALL, (ROW
4)ALL, (ROW 5)ALL,
CHANGE:(ROW 1) 1,4 to
SCH/BUS(SCHOOL);
FONT:MADERA; MESSAGE:L3,L4
(CENTER,RAISED)text;
L5(CENTER,RAISED)dashes;
FONT:SUTTER; MESSAGE:L6
(CENTER,3-D)text; FONT:
MADERA; MESSAGE:L7(CENTER,
RAISED)dashes; FONT:TINY;
MESSAGE:L8-L10(CENTER,
SOLID)text; PRINT

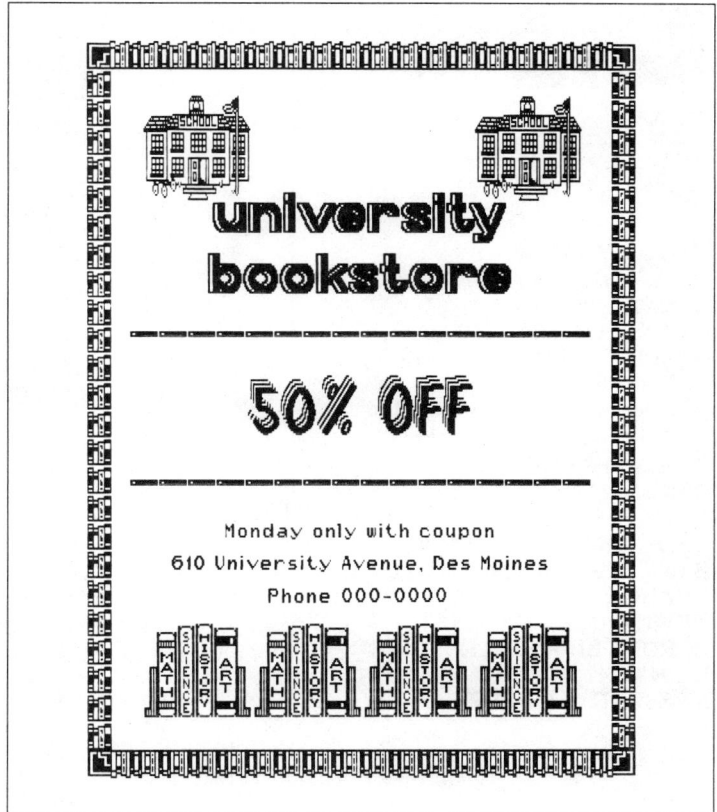

Design Notes:

A raised font dash creates an interesting design element dividing a
layout into the needed areas. Use for coupons, tickets and place
cards, or for cut lines.

Graphic Alternatives:
For art of office supplies: PROG(PENS) or
SCH/BUS(DRAFTING). For computer store or supplies:
PROG(COMPUTER) For savings: PROG(CASH BOX).

Banner/SALE (STACKED)

What you need:

What you do:

To create top and bottom banners:
BANNER; HORIZONTAL;
LAYOUT:LG GRAPHIC LEFT;
GRAPHIC:SCH/BUS(MOVING);
PRINT; PRINT again 3 times or
however many times you need to
equal the length of your message.

To create middle banner:
BANNER; HORIZONTAL;
LAYOUT:LG GRAPHIC BOTH
ENDS; GRAPHIC:MOD(PIGGY
BANK GRAPHIC, PAGE 208);
CHANGE:POS 2 to
NEW(DOLLAR, PAGE 167);
BORDER:BLOCKS; TEXT:ONE
LINE TEXT; FONT:AMADOR;
MESSAGE:text; PRINT

Design Notes:

By choosing Large Graphic Left and printing over and over, a
dramatic stacked sale border can be produced. Simply print your
middle banner first and count the number of pages you will need to
match the length. Then print that same number of pages of
graphics for your top and bottom banners.

Graphic Alternatives:
Pick a graphic appropriate for your message. Some examples are:
SCH/BUS(SWITCH) for "Lights Out Sale,"
SCH/BUS(BUILDINGS) for "Losing Our Lease," NEW(BOOKS,
PAGE 192) for "Book Sale."

Business Card 1

What you need:

NP **S**

What you do:

SIGN; DYO; TALL;
LAYOUT:SM TILED II;
GRAPHIC:SAMP(COCKATIEL);
DELETE:(ROW 1)ALL, (ROW 2)
1,4, (ROW 3)ALL, (ROW 4)ALL,
(ROW 5)ALL, (ROW 6)ALL; FLIP
HORIZ:(ROW 2) 2;
FONT:LASSEN;
MESSAGE:L1(CENTER,SOLID)
text; FONT:TINY; MESSAGE:L2
(1 space between letters, 3 spaces
between words)(CENTER,SOLID);
FONT:SMALL; MESSAGE:L3
(CENTER,SOLID); FONT:TINY;
MESSAGE:L7,L8(CENTER,SOLID)
text

Mark your original print starting
point and then PRINT.

To add bottom card to page, roll
back paper approximately 5 1/2
inches below original print starting
point. Make identical graphic and
text choices as above and then
PRINT.

Fold paper in half and then cut with
scissors.

"Birds of a Feather"

EXOTIC BIRDS & PETS
Roger Lindsay, Manager

212 Lakehurst, Great Falls, MN 67001
Telephone (000) 000-0000

"Birds of a Feather"

EXOTIC BIRDS & PETS
Roger Lindsay, Manager

212 Lakehurst, Great Falls, MN 67001
Telephone (000) 000-0000

Design Notes:

Business cards don't have to be small! Make a statement with an
oversized card that is personalized and easy to update. You may
want to print on colored paper or photostat to a smaller size and
have a local print shop reproduce on colored stock.

Graphic Alternatives:
Flipped graphics placed side-by-side create a bold and decorative
design element. Several graphics will work well with this
technique: PROG(ICE CREAM, BALLOONS), PARTY(RATTLE),
SCH/BUS(KEY) or SAMP(BICYCLE, AIRPLANE).)

Business Card 2

What you need:

What you do:

SIGN; DYO; TALL; BORDER:THIN
LINE; LAYOUT:SM TILED;
PATTERN:PARTY(LACE);
CHANGE:(ROW 3) 3 to PROG
(ROSEBUD); FONT:MERCED;
MESSAGE:L1(CENTER,SOLID)
text; FONT:MADERA; MESSAGE:
L2(CENTER,SOLID)text;
FONT:TINY MESSAGE:L3
(CENTER,SOLID)text; PRINT

Cut in half and use top portion only.

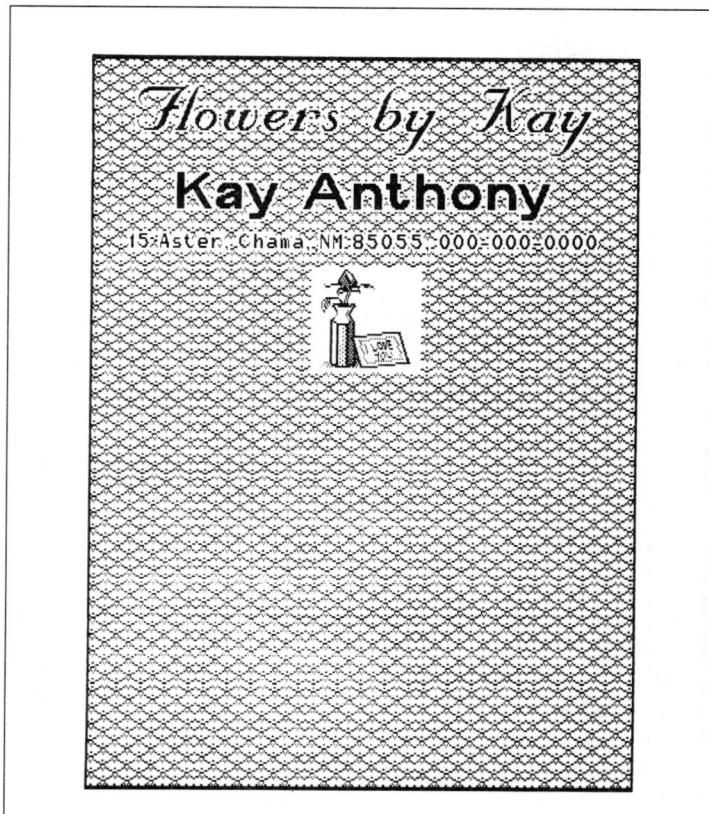

Design Notes:

Print an overall pattern for an interesting textual feel to an
oversized business card. Trim in half to eliminate bottom. To save
printing, erase your graphics from Line 7 down.

Graphic Alternatives:
For flower services: PROG(DAISIES), for delivery:
PROG(POINSETTIA), for bakery: PARTY(GINGERBREAD), for
childcare: PARTY(RATTLE) or SAMP(BABY BOTTLE), for pet
services: SAMP(COCKATIEL), for nursing care: SCH/BUS
(LUNCHTIME).

Business Card 3

What you need:

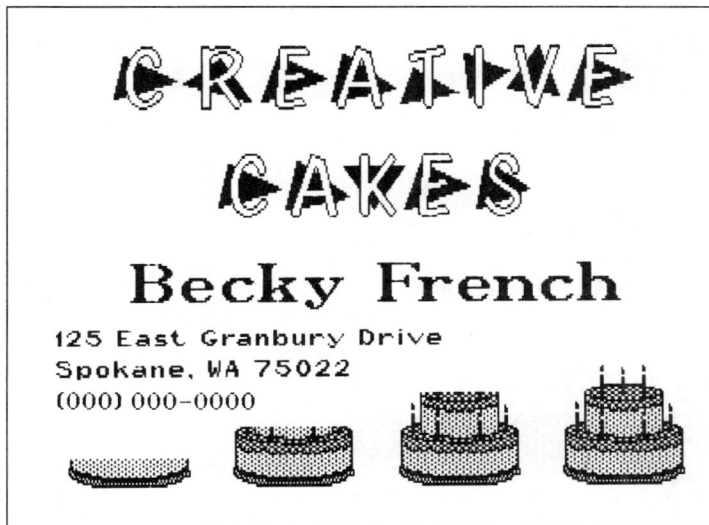

What you do:

GRAPHIC EDITOR;
GRAPHIC:PARTY(CAKE);
DELETE:Y=13 and above;
SAVE(CAKE 1); DELETE:Y=26
and above; SAVE(CAKE 2);
DELETE:Y=39 and above;
SAVE(CAKE 3)

CARD FRONT; DYO; TOP FOLD;
LAYOUT:SM ROWS II;
GRAPHIC:PARTY(CAKE);
CHANGE:(ROW 2) 1 to
MOD(CAKE 3), (ROW 2) 2 to
MOD(CAKE 2), ROW 2) 3 to
MOD(CAKE 1); FONT:MARIN;
MESSAGE:L1,L2(CENTER,SOLID)
text; FONT:SIERRA; MESSAGE:
L3(CENTER,SOLID)text;
FONT:TINY; MESSAGE:L4-L6
(LEFT,SOLID)text

Make the exact same choices for
CARD INSIDE and then PRINT.
Cut out your cards.

Design Notes:

Business cards created in the greeting card mode have impact due
to their oversized design. They're great as handouts on store
counters or exhibits. You can use your original artwork for
reproduction at a local print shop.

With the Graphic Editor, save various sections of a graphic.
Incorporate into a design to generate interest. Here a "building
effect" was used. Choose a graphic appropriate for your profession.

Graphic Alternatives:
For developers or architects: SCH/BUS(BUILDINGS).
For baby-sitters, party planners or day care: NEW(JACK-
IN-THE-BOX, PAGE 181.)
For restaurants or caterers: PROG(PICNIC).

Calendar/WEEKLY

What you need:

What you do:

GRAPHIC EDITOR; draw
NEW(GAME BOX, PAGE 170)
without the inside horizontal and
vertical line; SAVE as BOX

CALENDAR TOP; WEEKLY;
LAYOUT:SM TILED;
GRAPHIC:NEW(HANGER, PAGE
179); DELETE:(ROW 1) 1,3,5,7,9,
(ROW 2) 2,4,6,8,10;
FONT:VENTURA;
MESSAGE:(CENTER TOP TO
BOTTOM)text; RULED
LINE:THICK; INSERT
GRAPHIC:NEW(BOX)(insert for
each day of the week);

CALENDAR BOTTOM;
FONT:SMALL;
MESSAGE:L2(CENTER,SOLID,CH
SIZE:L)text; FONT:VENTURA;
MESSAGE:(CENTER;SOLID)text;
RULED LINE:THIN; PRINT

May, 1991

Sunday 12	
Monday 13	
Tuesday 14	
Wednesday 15	
Thursday 16	
Friday 17	
Saturday 18	

Check Off a Clean Week!
Stanley's Dry Cleaners

Design Notes:

This design works best with a bold graphic. Clean and simple
graphics work well in repetition. A calendar created with The New
Print Shop can be decorated with a unique graphic for each day of
the week.

Graphic Alternatives:
Try using PROG(TELEPHONE, LETTER, PENS) or
SCH/BUS(QUOTE, CLOCK).

Card 1/ANNOUNCEMENT

What you need:

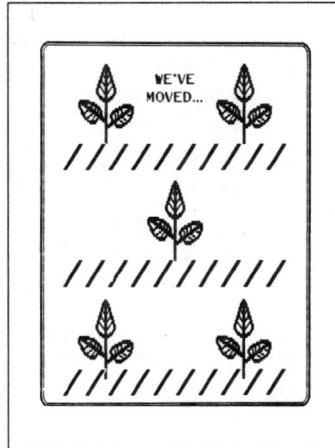

Card Front

What you do:

CARD FRONT; DYO; SIDE FOLD;
BORDER:ROUNDED;
LAYOUT:MED STAGGERED;
GRAPHIC:NEW(PLANT, PAGE
183); FONT:AMADOR;
MESSAGE:L3,L6,L7(CENTER,
SOLID)(slashes); CHANGE TEXT
TO GRAPHIC (IBM
only)/MOVE:L6 up 1 key press, L7
down 2 key presses (*Apple Users:*
Use Quick Print feature to insert
Lines 6 and 7, see page 27);
FONT:SMALL;
MESSAGE:L1,L2(CENTER,SOLID)
TEXT;

CARD INSIDE; FONT:AMADOR;
MESSAGE:L2-L6(CENTER,SOLID)
text; FONT:SMALL;
MESSAGE:L8(CENTER,SOLID,CH
SIZE:L)text; FONT:TINY;
MESSAGE:L9(CENTER,SOLID)
text; PRINT

Card Inside

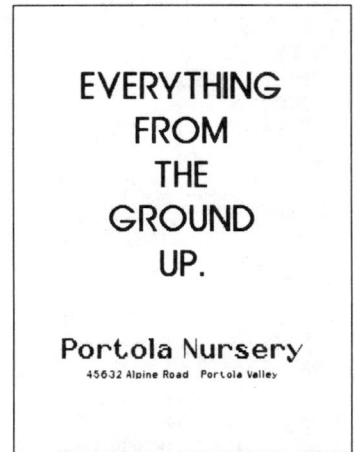

Design Notes:

Often "less is more." A good design idea is as powerful on The New
Print Shop as it is in any other design form. Here a simple Card
Front layout is complemented by an all-type Card Inside.

Graphic Alternatives:

Choose graphics appropriate for your message that are simple, yet
decorative.

Card 2/MOVED

What you need:

What you do:

CARD FRONT; DYO; TOP FOLD;
BORDER:RIBBON; LAYOUT:SM
TILED; GRAPHIC:MOD(BOTTLE,
PAGE 193); DELETE:(ROW 3)
2,3,4; CHANGE:(ROW 3) 1 to
MOD(NO SYMBOL,PAGE 213);
MOVE:(ROW 3) 1 right
2(IBM)/8(APP) key presses;
FONT:TINY;
MESSAGE:L7-L9(IBM)/L9-L11
(APP)(LEFT,SOLID)text

CARD INSIDE; BORDER:NEON;
LAYOUT:SM ROWS II;
GRAPHIC:PROG(BUBBLY);
CHANGE:(ROW 2)ALL to
MOD(ROW HOUSES,PAGE 185);
MOVE:(ROW 1)ALL down
1(IBM)/4(APP) key press;
FONT:SMALL;
MESSAGE:L1-L4(blank);
FONT:MERCED;
MESSAGE:L5(CENTER,SOLID)
text; FONT:TINY;
MESSAGE:L6,L7(CENTER,SOLID)
text; CHANGE TEXT TO
GRAPHIC (IBM only)/MOVE:L5
down 1 key press (*Apple Users:* Use
Quick Print feature to add all text,
see page 27); PRINT

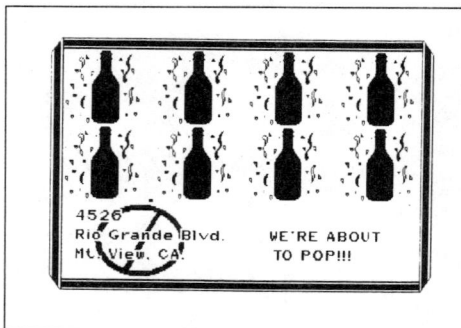

Card Front

Card Inside

Design Notes:

Juxtapose a graphic with a statement for a more clever
announcement or invitation. Printing a graphic over text is no
problem with The New Print Shop. Repetitious patterns of several
graphics work well in rows or a checkerboard pattern.

Graphic Alternatives:

For BOTTLE use SCH/BUS(CLOCK): "Time's Up!", SAMP(TIME
FLIES): "It's about time!", SCH/BUS(TROPHY): "We deserve it!";
for BUBBLY use SCH/BUS(MOVING VAN) or NEW(HOUSE,
PAGE 180).

Flyer 1/RECRUITMENT

What you need:

What you do:

To create CROSS graphic at top:

GRAPHIC EDITOR; draw vertical lines from top to bottom at X=38 - X=50, draw horizontal lines from right to left at Y=22 - Y=30; SAVE as CROSS

SIGN; DYO; TALL; BORDER:SAMP(CUT CORNERS); LAYOUT:MED MIX; GRAPHIC:SCH/BUS(POINTER); DELETE:(ROW 1) 1,3, (ROW 2)ALL, (ROW 4)ALL, (ROW 5)ALL; CHANGE:(ROW 1) 2 to NEW(CROSS), (MED-CTR) to SCH/BUS(CLOCK); FLIP HORIZ:(ROW 3) 3; FONT:SONOMA; MESSAGE:L2,L3(CENTER, OUTLINE)text; FONT:MADERA; MESSAGE:L8,L9(CENTER,SOLID) text; FONT:SMALL; MESSAGE:L10(CENTER,SOLID, CH SIZE:L)text; PRINT

Design Notes:

Highlight a center graphic with flipped images both directed towards a center graphic. Many graphics are appropriate for your message . Leave white space above and below central images. Varying fonts helps create design interest when text areas are almost equal in size.

Graphic Alternatives:

For POINTER use NEW(POINTING FINGER, PAGE 184), for CLOCK use SAMP(TIME FLIES).

Flyer 2/SALE

What you need:

NP

What you do:

SIGN; DYO; TALL;
BORDER:MAZE; LAYOUT:SM
DIAMOND;
GRAPHIC:NEW(HOUSE,PAGE
180); DELETE:(ROW 3) 2;
FONT:AMADOR;
MESSAGE:L1(CENTER,OUTLINE)
text; FONT:SMALL;
MESSAGE:L2(indent 4
spaces)(LEFT,SOLID)enter text at
left,(leave 16-IBM/19-APP spaces),
enter text at right; L3(indent 4
spaces)(LEFT,SOLID)enter text at
left,(leave 18-IBM/23-APP spaces),
enter text at right;
FONT:IMPERIAL;
MESSAGE:L8(CENTER,OUTLINE)
text; FONT:SMALL; MESSAGE
L9-L11,L15-L16(CENTER,SOLID)
text; PRINT

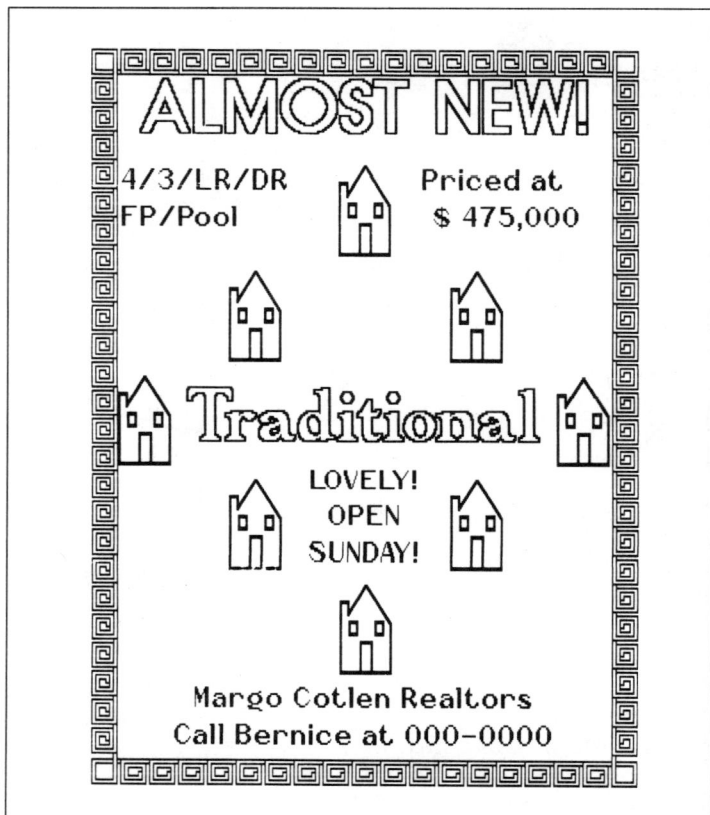

ALMOST NEW!

4/3/LR/DR   Priced at
FP/Pool $ 475,000

Traditional

LOVELY!
OPEN
SUNDAY!

Margo Cotlen Realtors
Call Bernice at 000-0000

Design Notes:

A flyer with several levels of information requires a layout with
one dominant pattern such as the diamond pattern created by the
graphics in this design. A border holds all the elements together.

Graphic Alternatives:
Try using MOD(LARGE HOUSE, PAGE 211) or PARTY(OPEN
HOUSE).

Flyer 3/SERVICE

What you need:

NP **S**

What you do:

SIGN; DYO; TALL;
BORDER:SAMP(FLEUR);
LAYOUT:BRICKS;
GRAPHIC:DAISIES;
DELETE:(ROW 1)ALL, (ROW
2)ALL, (ROW 3) 1,2,4,5, (ROW 4)
1,4, (ROW 5) 1,5; FONT:MERCED;
MESSAGE:L1(CENTER,SOLID)
text; FONT:SMALL;
MESSAGE:L2,L3(CENTER,SOLID)
text; PRINT

Design Notes:

Repeating the same graphic in this pyramid design produces a
clean and simple yet very powerful communication of a message.
Choose a graphic that links well together either through an outline
like the Daisies graphic or through its symmetry.

Graphic Alternatives:

For FLEUR border use PROG(NAVAJO) border. Pick a graphic
appropriate for your service: SCH/BUS(SWITCH)—Electrician,
SCH/BUS(TENNIS)—Tennis instructor, PROG(PIANO)—Piano
teacher, PARTY(GINGERBREAD)—Bakery,
NEW(JACK-IN-THE-BOX, PAGE 181)—Babysitter.

Flyer 4/SERVICE

What you need:

What you do:
SIGN; WIDE;
BORDER:PARTY(BALLOONS);
LAYOUT:FULL PANEL;
GRAPHIC:PROG(PARTY);
FONT:LASSEN;
MESSAGE:L1,L2(CENTER,SOLID)
text; CHANGE TEXT TO
GRAPHIC (IBM only)/MOVE:L1
down 1 key press; FONT:TINY;
MESSAGE:L1,L7(CENTER,SOLID)
text (*Apple Users:* Use Quick Print
feature to add all lines of text, see
page 27); PRINT

Design Notes:
The New Print Shop allows for full panels of many various designs
and messages. Full panels can be combined with borders as shown
here. IBM users can choose the Wide Balloons border instead.

Graphic Alternatives:
For BALLOONS border try using PROG(DECO) border.

Interoffice 1/MEMO

What you need:

What you do:

SIGN; DYO; TALL; LAYOUT:SM
STAGGERED III;
GRAPHIC:NEW(HANDS, PAGE
178); DELETE:(ROW 1)ALL,
(ROW 3)ALL, (ROW 4)ALL, (ROW
5)ALL; FONT:IMPERIAL;
MESSAGE:L1(CENTER,SOLID,
CH SIZE:L)text; FONT:SMALL;
MESSAGE:L4(approx.
40-IBM/48-APP spaces between
words)(LEFT,SOLID)text,
L5(LEFT,SOLID)text; PRINT

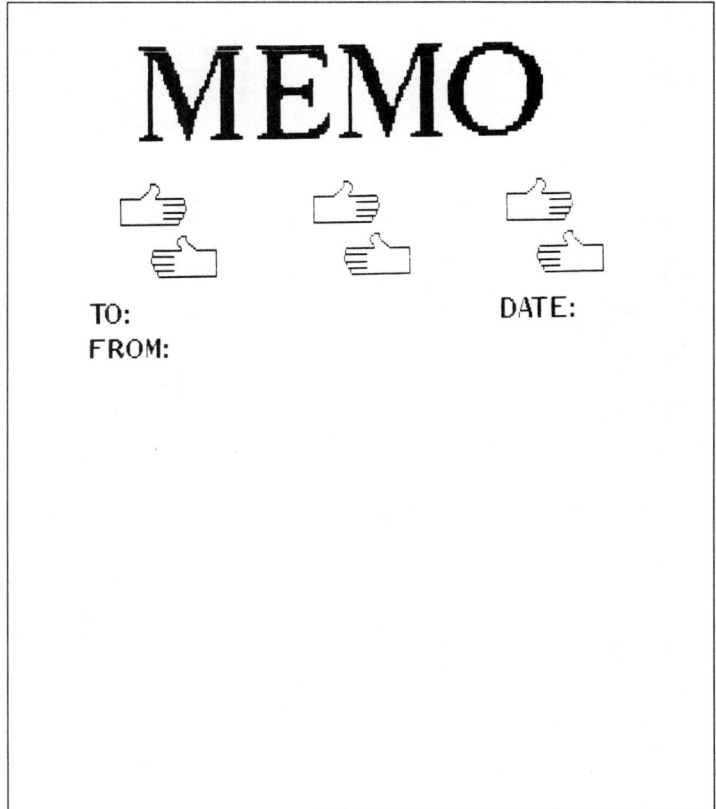

Design Notes:

For casual correspondence in the office use this "cooperation"
design to get your message across. If a more formal correspondence
is required, print NEW(NOTE LINES, PAGE 182) on the bottom
half of your page.

Graphic Alternatives:
Try using SCH/BUS(POINTER), NEW(POINTING FINGER,
PAGE 184), or PROG(IN BOX, FOLDERS).

Interoffice 2/SIGN-OFF SHEET

What you need:

What you do:

SIGN; DYO; WIDE;
BORDER:RIBBON; LAYOUT:SM
TILED; GRAPHIC;NEW(NOTE
LINES, PAGE 182);
DELETE:(ROW 1) 1,2,3;
CHANGE:(ROW 1) 4 to
NEW(BOOK, PAGE 159);
MOVE:(ROW 1) 4 to left
1(IBM)/4(APP) key press, down
1(IBM)/4(APP) key press;
FONT:LASSEN;
MESSAGE:L1(LEFT,RAISED)text;
FONT:SMALL;
MESSAGE:L2(LEFT,SOLID)text;
FONT:TINY;
MESSAGE:L3(LEFT,SOLID)(14
spaces between words 1 & 2, 12
spaces between words 2 & 3)text
(Apple Users: Use Quick Print
feature to add Line 3, see page 27);
PRINT

Design Notes:

Stationery, memo paper and lists can all be created using the
NOTE LINES graphic from the New Art section.

Graphic Alternatives:
For BOOK use PROG(PENS, INK BOTTLE) or
SCH/BUS(POINTER).

Letterhead 1/BUSINESS

What you need:

NP

kohler & leedom
CERTIFIED PUBLIC ACCOUNTANTS

What you do:

LETTERHEAD TOP; DYO;
FONT:SMALL;
MESSAGE:L1(blank);
FONT:IMPERIAL; MESSAGE:L2
(1 space between letters, 3 spaces
between words)(LEFT, SOLID)text;
FONT:SMALL; MESSAGE:L3
(1 space between letters, 3 spaces
between words)(LEFT,SOLID)text;
RULED LINE:THICK

LETTERHEAD BOTTOM;
FONT:TINY;
MESSAGE:L5-L7(LEFT,SOLID)
text; PRINT

6708 San Antonio Road
Santa Barbara, California 45261
000-000-0000

Design Notes:

Typography, properly used, can create interesting designs. For a
different look, try positioning all your text at right or in center.

Letterhead 2/BUSINESS

What you need:

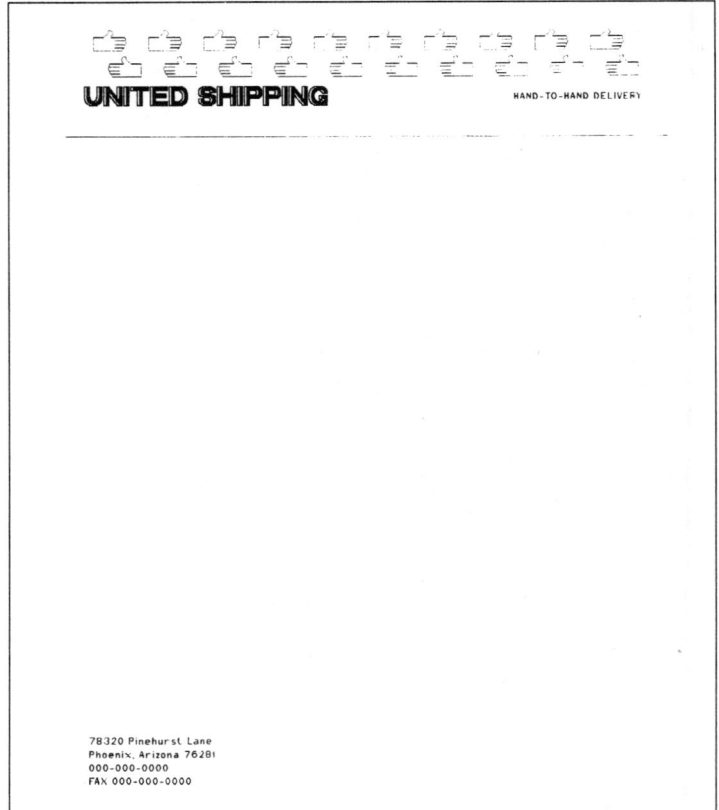

What you do:

LETTERHEAD TOP; DYO;
LAYOUT:SM TILED;
GRAPHIC:NEW(HANDS,PAGE
178); DELETE:(ROW 2)ALL;
FONT:SMALL;
MESSAGE:L1-L4(blank);
FONT:MADERA;
MESSAGE:L5(LEFT,RAISED)text;
FONT:TINY;
MESSAGE:L6(RIGHT,SOLID);
CHANGE TEXT TO GRAPHIC
(IBM only)/MOVE:L5 right 2 key
presses, L6 up 1 key press and left 2
key presses *(Apple Users:* Use
Quick Print feature to insert L5 and
L6 in position, see page 27);
RULED LINE:THIN

LETTERHEAD BOTTOM;
FONT:TINY;
MESSAGE:L3-L6(LEFT,SOLID)
text; CHANGE TEXT TO
GRAPHIC (IBM only)/MOVE:
L3-L6 right 2 key presses *(Apple
Users:* Use Quick Print feature to
insert L3-L6 in position, see page
27); PRINT

Design Notes:

A repeat pattern is effective for a "linking" message as well as a
decorative element. The thin rule helps to balance the left justified
text and hold the design together. If no right justified message is
used, center top and bottom text for a more pleasing layout.

Graphic Alternatives:
For HANDS use SCH/BUS(MOVING) or PARTY(BON VOYAGE).

Letterhead 3/RETAIL

What you need:

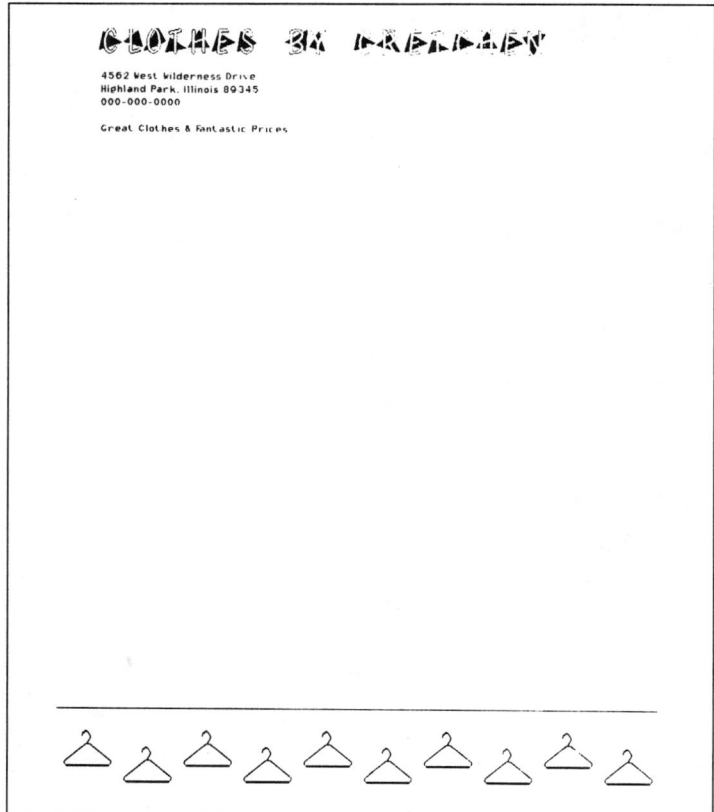

What you do:

LETTERHEAD TOP; DYO;
FONT:MARIN;
MESSAGE:L1(LEFT,SOLID)text;
FONT:TINY;
MESSAGE:L2-L4,L6(LEFT,SOLID)
text; CHANGE TEXT TO
GRAPHIC (IBM only)/MOVE:
L1-L7 to right 4(IBM)/16(APP) key
presses (Apple Users: Use Quick
Print feature to add text, see page
27)

LETTERHEAD BOTTOM;
LAYOUT:SM STAGGERED II;
GRAPHIC:NEW(HANGER,PAGE
179); MOVE:(ROW 1) 1,3,5,7,9 up
1(IBM)/4(APP) key press; RULED
LINE:THIN; PRINT

Design Notes:

A playful look is accomplished with the Marin font. Use a simple
design in conjunction with a busy font and layout. The simplicity
of the graphic and the solidity of the repeat pattern balance or
"ground" the multiple design elements.

Graphic Alternatives:
Select graphics appropriate for your business. For finance:
NEW(DOLLAR, PAGE 167). For teaching or performing:
PROG(MUSIC). For performing or costumes: NEW(CLOWN,
PAGE 163). For fitness: SAMP(MAN), SAMP(WOMAN), or
NEW(SPORTS SYMBOL, PAGE 187).

Letterhead 4/RETAIL

What you need:

NP

What you do:

SIGN; DYO; TALL; LAYOUT:SM
FRAME;
GRAPHIC:NEW(SOUTHWEST
PATTERN,PAGE 186);
DELETE:(L-COL) 2,3,4,5,6,(R-COL)
2,3,4,5,6; FONT:LASSEN;
MESSAGE:L1(1 space between
letters)(CENTER,SOLID)text;
FONT:TINY;
MESSAGE:L2-L12(IBM)/L2-L15
(APP)(blank), L13-L14(IBM)/L16-
L17(APP6)(CENTER,SOLID)text;
PRINT

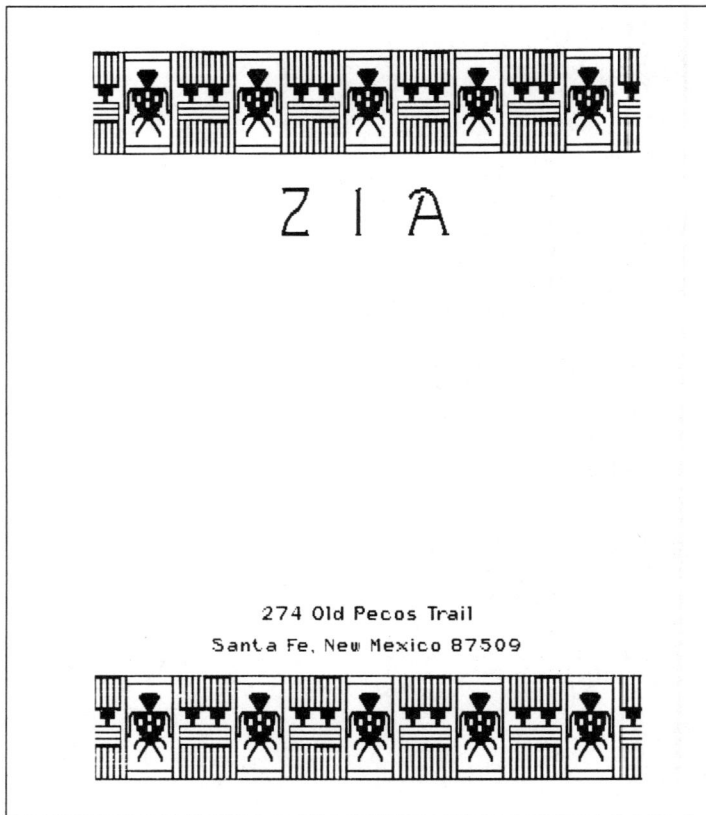

```
Z I A

                274 Old Pecos Trail
            Santa Fe, New Mexico 87509
```

Design Notes:

A linking graphic is one that fills the Graphic Editor box and has
elements of symmetry. This Design's impact is from the repetition
of the graphic as well as the repetition of the rows. A short text
treatment with a more delicate font is best suited to balance the
weight of the design.

Graphic Alternatives:
For SOUTHWEST use NEW(GRAPHIC TILE PATTERN 1, PAGE
173).

Letterhead 5/SMALL BUSINESS

What you need:

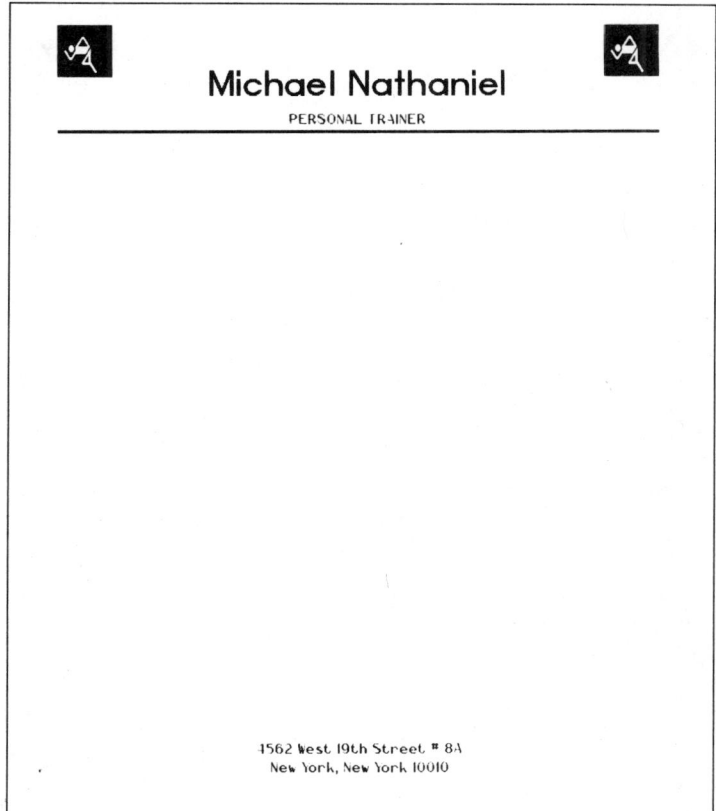

Michael Nathaniel

PERSONAL TRAINER

1562 West 19th Street # 8A
New York, New York 10010

What you do:

LETTERHEAD TOP; DYO;
LAYOUT:SM ENDS II;
GRAPHIC:NEW(SPORTS
SYMBOL,PAGE 187);
FONT:AMADOR;
MESSAGE:L2(CENTER,SOLID)
text; FONT:SMALL;
MESSAGE:L3(CENTER,SOLID)
text; RULED LINE:THICK

LETTERHEAD BOTTOM;
FONT:SMALL;
MESSAGE:L3,L4(CENTER,SOLID)
text; PRINT

Design Notes:

A centered and simple layout communicates a straightforward yet sophisticated and strong personality. A simple sans serif font works well with this design.

Graphic Alternatives:
Try using SAMP(MAN) or SAMP(WOMAN).

Letterhead 6/SMALL BUSINESS

What you need:

NP

What you do:

LETTERHEAD TOP; DYO;
LAYOUT:SM STAGGERED;
GRAPHIC:NEW(GEOMETRICS:
TRIANGLE, PAGE 172);
DELETE:(ROW 1) 3,4;
INSERT:MED/MOD(EMBLEM,
PAGE 195) to right
24(IBM)/96(APP) key presses;
FONT:MADERA;
MESSAGE:L1(approx.
19-IBM/23-APP spaces between
words)(CENTER,SOLID)text

LETTERHEAD BOTTOM; DYO;
FONT:TINY;
MESSAGE:L1,L3-L5(CENTER,
SOLID)text; PRINT

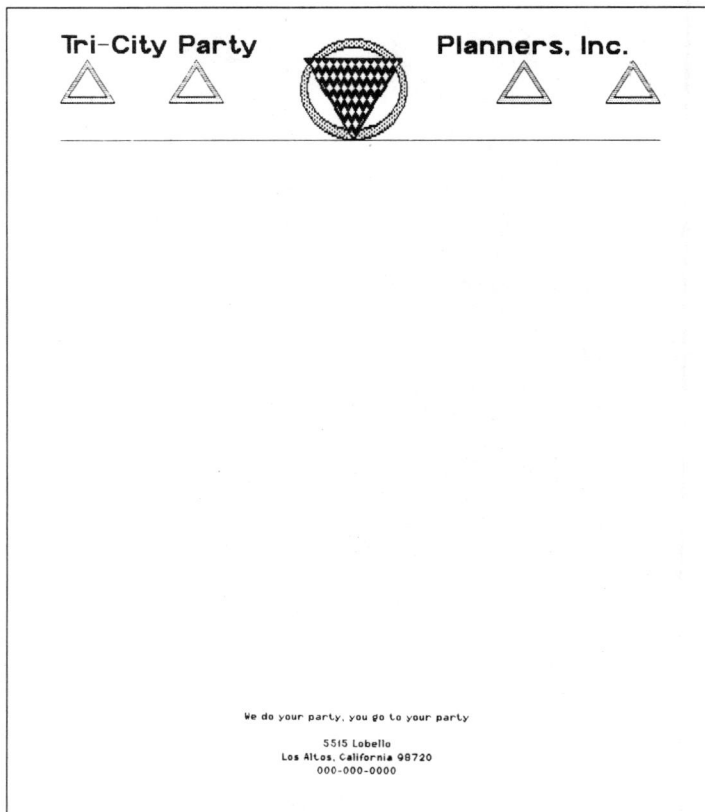

Tri-City Party   Planners, Inc.

We do your party, you go to your party

5515 Lobello
Los Altos, California 98720
000-000-0000

Design Notes:

Letterheads have more flair with 2 sizes of graphics. The center
graphic is nicely balanced with the small-size repeat graphics. By
keeping a centered text design, a more formal look is
accomplished. This image is important for services requiring
efficiency and professionalism.

Graphic Alternatives:

Depending on your service, there are many appropriate Print Shop
graphics. Look for symmetrical graphics to maintain this formal
look.

List 1/DAILY TO DO

What you need:

NP

What you do:

SIGN; DYO; TALL; BORDER:THIN LINE; LAYOUT:SM TILED; GRAPHIC:NEW(NOTE LINES, PAGE 182); DELETE:(ROW 1)ALL, (ROW 2)ALL, (ROW 3) 1, (ROW 4) 1, (ROW 5) 1, (ROW 6) 1, (ROW 7) 1; INSERT:SM/MOD (PENCIL,PAGE 196) down 7(IBM)/28(APP) key presses; INSERT:SM/MOD (PUSHPIN RIGHT,PAGE 198) to right 19(IBM)/76(APP) key presses, down 1(IBM)/4(APP) key press; FONT:MADERA; MESSAGE:L1(2 spaces before word)(LEFT,SOLID, CH SIZE:L)text, L2(5 spaces before words)(LEFT,SOLID)text; FONT:SMALL; MESSAGE:L3(RIGHT,SOLID)text; PRINT

Daily To Do:

DATE:

Design Notes:

By erasing a graphic on one side as well as at the top, a more dynamic layout is created. Personalize and print at your local print shop for your own use. Glue pads are easy to make if desired.

Graphic Alternatives:
For PENCIL use PROG(INK BOTTLE), NEW(POINTING FINGER, PAGE 184), SCH/BUS(CLOCK), or SAMP(TIME FLIES).

List 2/WEEKLY TO DO

What you need:

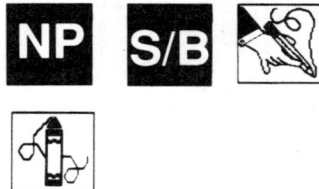

What you do:

SIGN; DYO; TALL;
BORDER:ROUNDED;
LAYOUT:SM TILED;
GRAPHIC:NEW(NOTE
LINES,PAGE 182);
DELETE:(ROW 1) 2,3,4,5, (ROW
2)ALL; CHANGE:(ROW 1) 1 to
MOD(PENCIL,PAGE 196);
MOVE:(ROW 1) 1 down
2(IBM)/8(APP) key presses, right
2(IBM)/8(APP) key presses;
FONT:SCH/BUS(BLIPPO);
MESSAGE:L1,L2(RIGHT,SOLID)
text; FONT:TINY;
MESSAGE:L4,L6,L8,L10,L12,L14,
L16,L18(LEFT,SOLID)text;
CHANGE TEXT TO GRAPHIC
(IBM only)/MOVE:L4,L6,L8,L10,
L12,L14,L16,L18 up 1 key press
(*Apple Users:* Use Quick Print
feature to insert each day of the
week, see page 27); PRINT

WEEK AT A GLANCE

monday:

tuesday:

wednesday:

thursday:

friday:

saturday:

sunday:

NOTES:

Design Notes:

By erasing an area of an overall graphic layout, text can be
emphasized and a layout made more interesting. Small text can
drop out of NOTE LINES without any distraction.

Graphic Alternatives:
For PENCIL use PROG(PENS, COFFEE) or
SCH/BUS(POINTER).

Mailing Label

What you need:

NP

What you do:

CARD FRONT; DYO; TOP FOLD; BORDER:THIN; LAYOUT:SM TILED; GRAPHIC:MOD(KITTY CAT SOLID, PAGE 205); DELETE:(ROW 1) 2,3,4, (ROW 2)ALL, (ROW 3)ALL, MOVE:(ROW 1) 1 to right 1(IBM)/4(APP) key press; FONT:SMALL; MESSAGE: L4,L5(LEFT,SOLID)text; FONT: TINY; MESSAGE:L6-L9(LEFT, SOLID)text

Make same choices for CARD INSIDE and then go to PRINT.

SELECT SIZE:MEDIUM(75%); PRINT

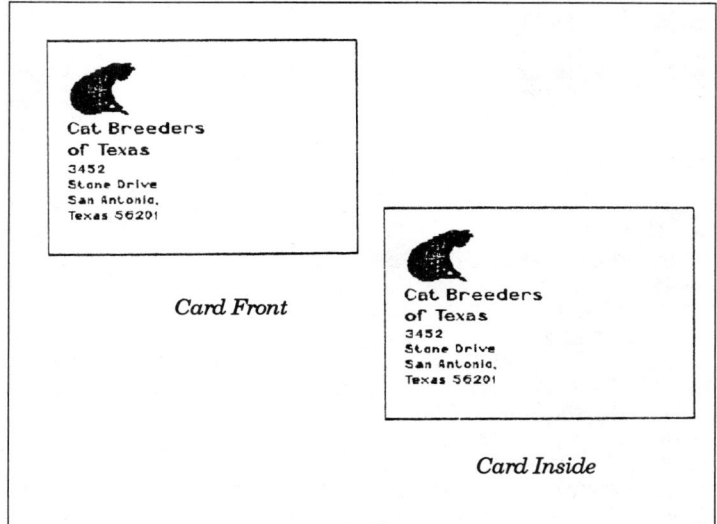

Cat Breeders
of Texas
3452
Stone Drive
San Antonio,
Texas 56201

Card Front

Cat Breeders
of Texas
3452
Stone Drive
San Antonio,
Texas 56201

Card Inside

Design Notes:

Choose a thin border and either use as a cutting line or, using a cutting board or x-acto knife, trim 1/4" beyond the border. Choose any size desired at the Print Menu. For small packages or large packages a size appropriate to your needs is available.

Graphic Alternatives:
Any symbolic graphic will work here. Choose one appropriate to your business.

Masthead/NEWSLETTER

What you need:

NP **S/B**

What you do:

SIGN; DYO; TALL; LAYOUT:SM
FRAME; GRAPHIC:SCH/BUS
(FLOPPY DISK); DELETE:(T-ROW)
ALL, (L-COL) 4,5,6, (R-COL) 4,5,6,
(B-ROW)ALL; CHANGE:(L-COL) 3
to SCH/BUS(QUOTE), (R-COL) 3
to SCH/BUS(QUOTE); FLIP
HORIZ:(R-COL) 3; INSERT:
SM/PROG(COMPUTER) to right
11(IBM)/44(APP) key presses,
down 7(IBM)/28(APP) key presses;
Mark your original print starting
point and then PRINT

To add text at top, roll back paper
to original print starting point.

LETTERHEAD; DYO; FONT:
AMADOR; MESSAGE:L1(2 spaces
between letters, 4 spaces between
words)(CENTER,SOLID)text,
L2(CENTER,SOLID)text;
FONT:SMALL; MESSAGE:L3
(1 space between letters, 2 spaces
between words)(CENTER,SOLID)
text; PRINT

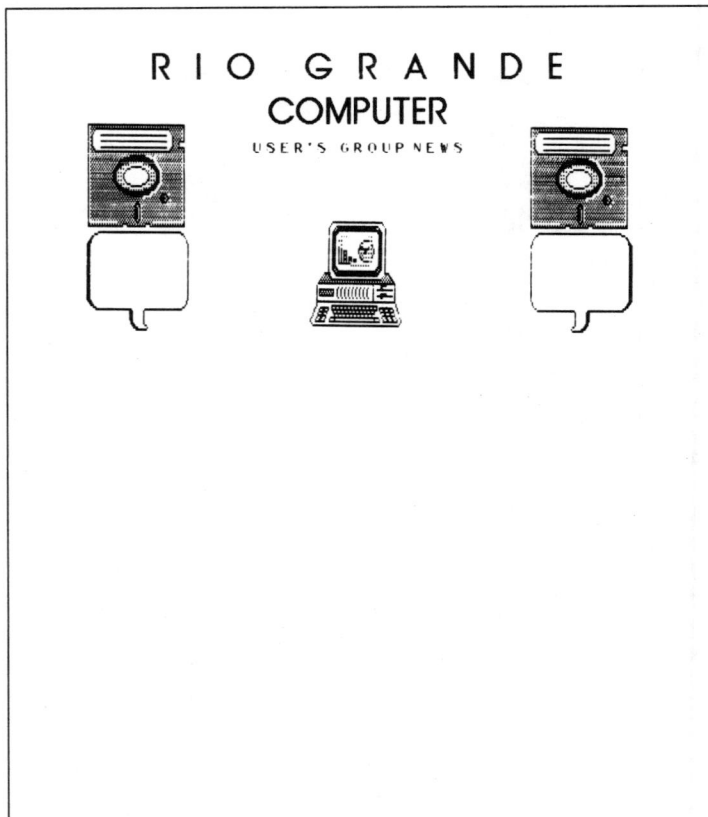

RIO GRANDE
COMPUTER
USER'S GROUP NEWS

Design Notes:

A multi-element design makes a strong statement. This layout is
useful for short letters for organizations or even invoices or signs
for small businesses.

Graphic Alternatives:
For QUOTE use NEW(POINTING FINGER, PAGE 184). Try
other combinations for FLOPPY DISK/COMPUTER:
PROG(PRINTER)/PROG(COMPUTER), PROG(CASH
BOX)/NEW(DOLLAR, PAGE 167),
PROG(PIANO)/PROG(MUSIC),
PROG(LETTERS)/PROG(FOLDERS).

Meeting Ideas/BRAINSTORMING

What you need:

What you do:

SIGN; DYO; TALL; LAYOUT:MED STAGGERED; GRAPHIC:NEW(NOTE LINES, PAGE 182); INSERT:MED/SAMP(LIGHT BULB) as follows: to right 2(IBM)/8(APP) key presses, down 1(IBM)/4(APP) key presses, to right 15(IBM)/60(APP) key presses, down 1(IBM)/4(APP) key presses, to right 8(IBM)/32(APP) key presses, down 9(IBM)/36(APP) key presses, to right 2(IBM)/8(APP) key presses, down 16(IBM)/64(APP) key presses, to right 15(IBM)/60(APP) key presses, down 16(IBM)/64(APP) key presses; PRINT

Design Notes:

Sometimes what a brainstorming session needs most is inspiration. Print and make cards with handwritten or typed thoughts on back. See suggestions below. You may want to eliminate the light bulbs and use entire sheet for participants to jot down their 5 strongest ideas.

Brainstorm Card Ideas:

1. Are you making the big issues little and little issues big? Rank the issues.
2. Look at your problem and "think something different."
3. How would a 5-year-old look at this?
4. Stop! Discuss the solutions, not the problems.
5. Can you state the problem in one paragraph?

Menu

What you need:

What you do:

CARD FRONT; DYO; TOP FOLD;
BORDER:PARTY(FIESTA);
LAYOUT:MED CENTER;
GRAPHIC:PROG(PICNIC);
FONT:SMALL; MESSAGE:L1
(1 space between letters)
(CENTER,RAISED,CH SIZE:L)
text, L8(1 space between letters, 2
spaces between words)(CENTER,
RAISED)text

CARD INSIDE;
BORDER:PROG(DECO);
LAYOUT:SM TILED;
GRAPHIC:PROG(COFFEE);
DELETE:(ROW 1) 2,3, (ROW 2)
1,2,3,4, (ROW 3) 2,3;
CHANGE:(ROW 3) 1 to
PARTY(SANDWICH), (ROW 3) 4
to SAMP(PIE SLICE); INSERT:SM/
NEW(SUNSHINE,PAGE 189) to
right 1(IBM)/4(APP) key presses,
down 4(IBM)/16(APP) key presses;
to right 16(IBM)/64(APP) key
presses, down 4(IBM)/16(APP) key
presses; FONT:VENTURA;
MESSAGE:L1,L4(CENTER,SOLID)
text; PRINT

Card Front

Card Inside

Design Notes:

If your restaurant's specials require more space than allowed in
this design, simply delete the middle row of graphics. If you need
even more space, select a smaller font at top. Try printing on
colored paper or on white paper with your restaurant name in a
bright color! Red or blue are good choices. If you don't have a color
printer you can have the menu printed at a quick print shop
instead.

Graphic Alternatives:

For PICNIC use PARTY(PENGUIN), for SANDWICH use
PARTY(PIZZA), for COFFEE use PARTY(COOL DRINK), for
SUNSHINE use PROG(DESERT).

Notepaper/ (IBM ONLY)

What you need:

What you do:

SIGN; DYO; TALL; BORDER:
PROG(WIDE/CLIPBOARD—IBM
only); LAYOUT:SM TILED;
GRAPHIC:NEW(NOTE LINES,
PAGE 182); DELETE:(ROW
1)ALL, (ROW 2)ALL, (ROW
3)ALL; FONT:AMADOR;
MESSAGE:L1(LEFT,SOLID)text;
FONT:SMALL;
MESSAGE:L2,L3(LEFT,SOLID)
text; (Note: For dotted line, use
"dash" key with Shift); PRINT

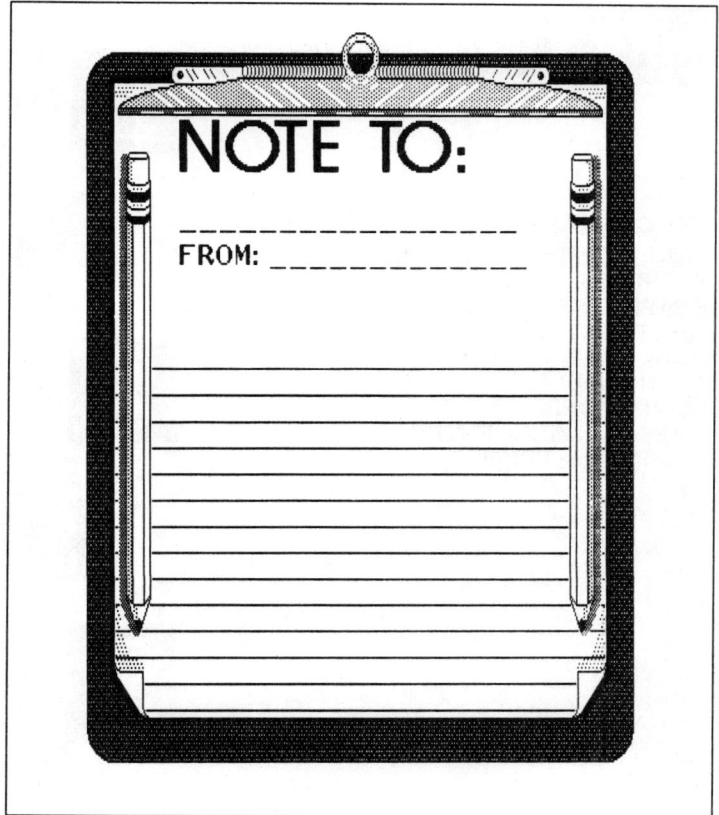

Design Notes:

Apple Users: For CLIPBOARD border use RIBBON border.

Sign 1/CHECKOUT

What you need:

NP

What you do:

SIGN; DYO; TALL; LAYOUT:SM
STAGGERED;
GRAPHIC:NEW(DOLLAR,PAGE
167); DELETE:(ROW 2)ALL,
(ROW 4)ALL; FONT:SMALL;
MESSAGE:L1-L3(blank);
FONT:MADERA;
MESSAGE:L4-L8(CENTER,
RAISED)text; PRINT

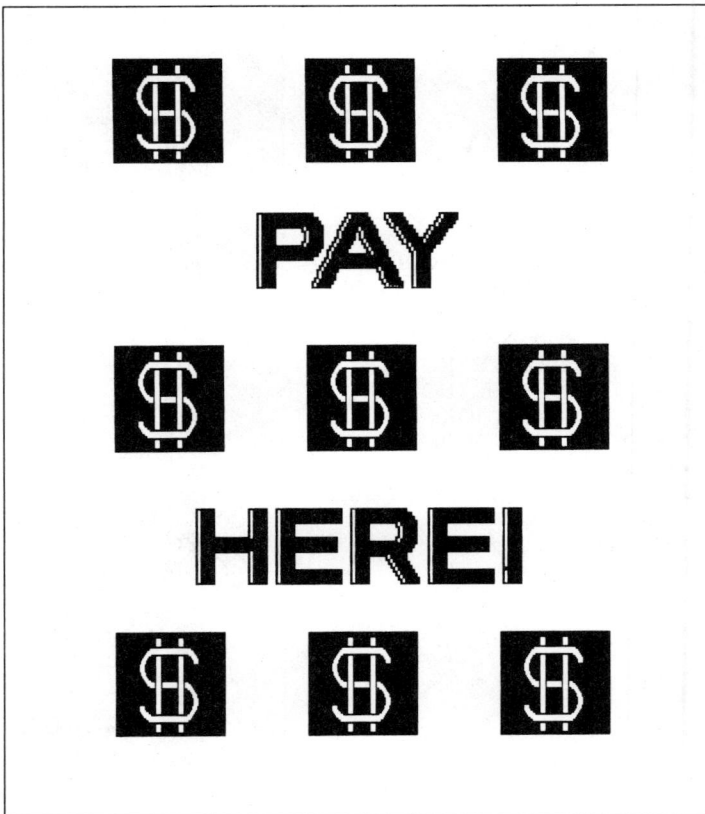

Design Notes:

A simple repeat pattern design using a bold graphic is effective for
a sign. For a different look, try using the font in outline and then
fill in with a brightly colored marker for a commanding message.

Graphic Alternatives:
Try using SCH/BUS(DOLLARS) or PROG(CASH BOX).

Sign 2/DIRECTIONS (IBM ONLY)

What you need:

What you do:

SIGN; DYO; TALL;
BORDER:PROG(WIDE/COLUMNS
—IBM only); LAYOUT:MED
CENTER;
GRAPHIC:SCH/BUS(POINTER);
FONT:SIERRA;
MESSAGE:L1,L2(CENTER,SOLID,
CH SIZE:L)text,
L7,L8(CENTER,SOLID)text;
PRINT

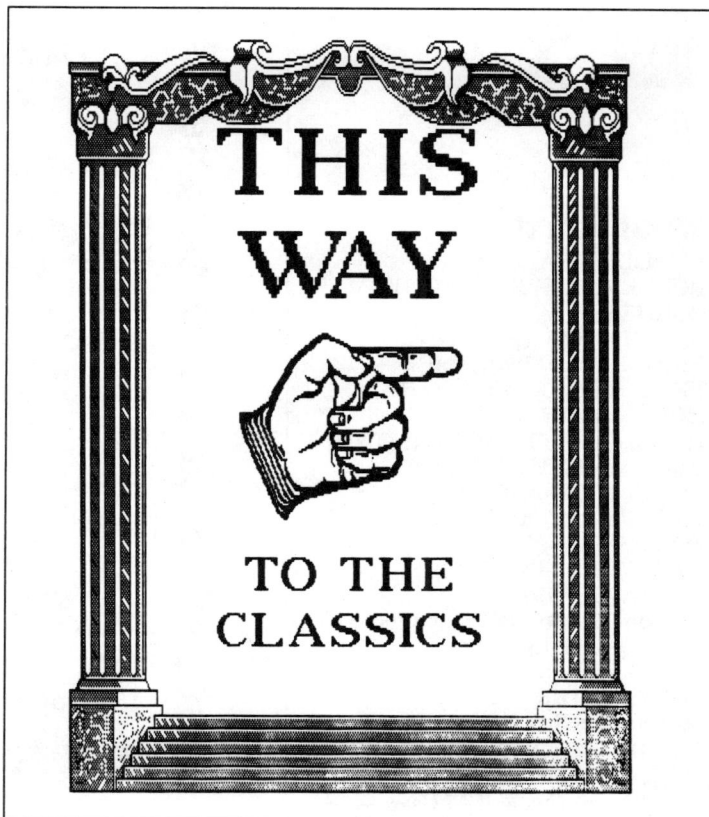

Design Notes:

Apple Users: Substitute NAVAJO border for COLUMNS border.

A large pointing finger or arrow is effective for any kind of directional sign. Color in with brightly colored markers for added emphasis.

Graphic Alternatives:
Try using NEW(ARROW 1, PAGE 157), NEW(ARROW 2, PAGE 158), or NEW(POINTING FINGER, PAGE 184).

Sign 3/HELP WANTED

What you need:

What you do:

SIGN; DYO; TALL;
BORDER:NAVAJO; LAYOUT:SM
CORNERS;
GRAPHIC:NEW(POINTING
FINGER,PAGE 184); FLIP
VERT:(ROW 1) 1; FLIP VERT &
HORIZ:(ROW 1) 2; FLIP
HORIZ:(ROW 2) 2; MOVE:(ROW 2)
1 to left 1(IBM)/4(APP) key
presses, (ROW 2) 2 to right
1(IBM)/4(APP) key presses;
FONT:SMALL;
MESSAGE:L1-L4(blank);
FONT:VENTURA;
MESSAGE:L5(CENTER,OUTLINE)
text; FONT:SMALL;
MESSAGE:L6(blank);
FONT:SUTTER;
MESSAGE:L7,L8(CENTER,
SOLID)text; FONT:SMALL;
MESSAGE:L9-L14(CENTER,
SOLID)text; (Note: IBM Users—
CHANGE TEXT TO
GRAPHIC/MOVE Lines 7 & 8 up 1
key press); PRINT

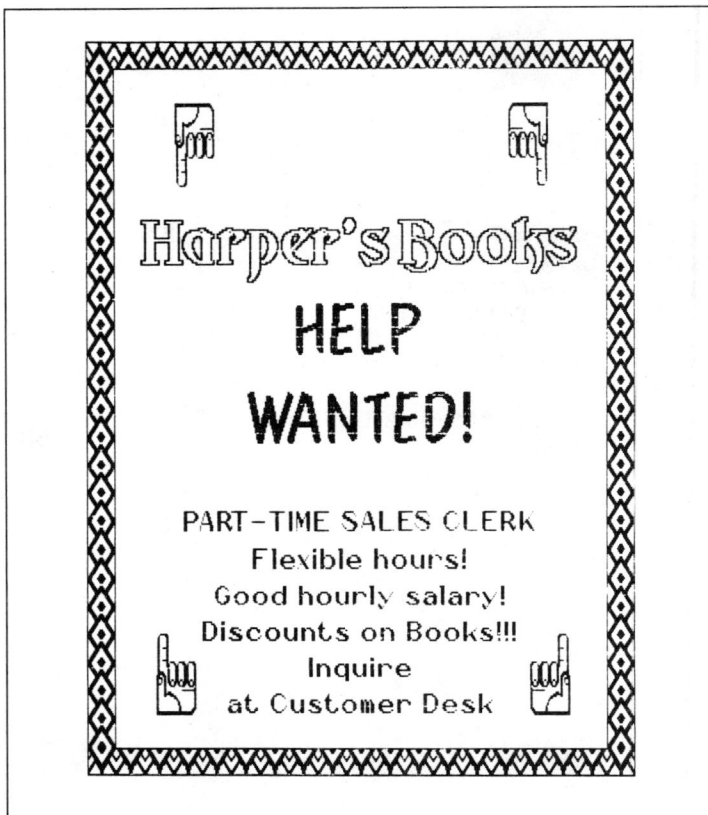

Design Notes:

Stimulate your logo with a more decorative New Print Shop font in
outline, shadow or raised. Experiment with varying sizes from line
to line. A straightforward centered text layout works well if
contained by a strong border.

Graphic Alternatives:
For POINTING FINGER use SCH/BUS(POINTER).

Sign 4/HOURS 1 (IBM ONLY)

What you need:

NP **S/B**

What you do:

SIGN; DYO; WIDE;
BORDER:PROG(WIDE/LILIES—
IBM only); LAYOUT:SM
CENTERED;
GRAPHIC:SCH/BUS(BUILDINGS);
MOVE:SM-CTR down
3(IBM)/12(APP) key presses, left
5(IBM)/20(APP) key presses;
FONT:VENTURA;
MESSAGE:L1,L2(CENTER,
SHADOW)text; FONT:SMALL;
MESSAGE:L3,L4(RIGHT,SOLID)
text; (Note: Add 2 spaces at end of
Line 4 to align with Line 3); PRINT

Design Notes:

Apple Users: For LILIES border use DECO border.

Choose a graphic that communicates your message. Use a small graphic for punctuation, and a larger font to create a strong message.

Graphic Alternatives:

Choose a graphic appropriate for your business. For copywriting: PROG(PENS). For word processing: PROG(COMPUTER). For music school: PROG(PIANO). For catering: PROG(PICNIC, SANDWICH) or PARTY(PENGUIN). For bakery: PARTY(CAKE). For hardware or electrician: SAMP(LIGHT BULB).

Sign 5/HOURS 2

What you need:

NP **S/B**

What you do:

SIGN; DYO; TALL; BORDER:THIN
LINE; LAYOUT:MED CENTERED;
GRAPHIC:SCH/BUS(CLOCK)(*Apple
Users:* Move graphic up 4 key
presses); FONT:SONOMA;
MESSAGE:L1,L2(CENTER,SOLID,
CH SIZE:L)text; FONT:SIERRA;
MESSAGE:L7-L10(IBM)/L6-L9
(APP) (CENTER,RAISED)text;
PRINT

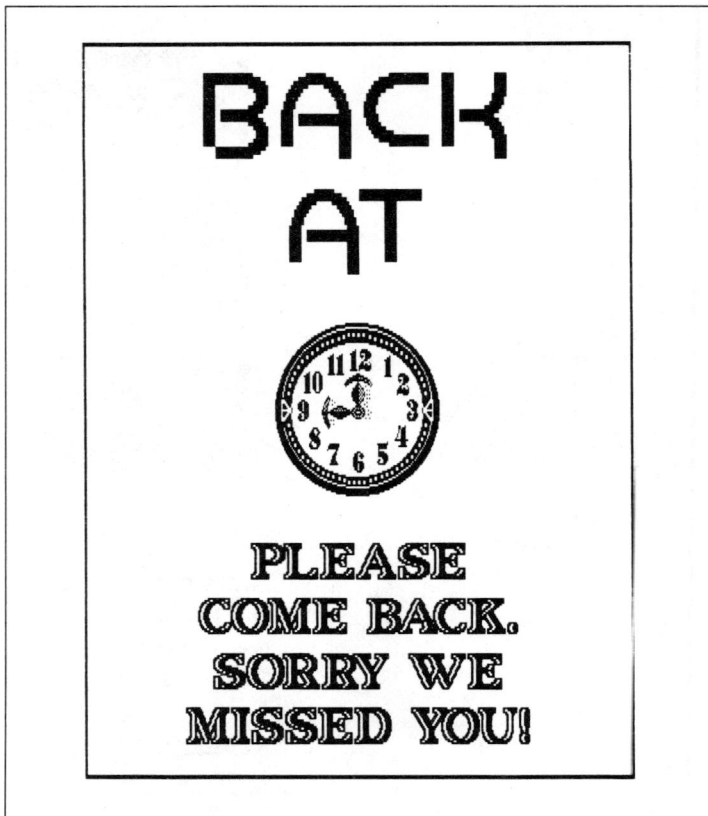

Design Notes:

To change time on clock, simply copy CLOCK graphic on a copying
machine and cut out hands. White out hands on original design
and attach xeroxed hands in new position with rubber cement or
spray mount. You may want to leave hand area completely blank
on original design and fill in with red-colored marker. For best
results, erase hands in Graphic Editor mode.

Sign 6/INVITATION

What you need:

NP

What you do:

SIGN; DYO; TALL; LAYOUT:FULL PANEL; GRAPHIC:PROG(SANTA); FONT:IMPERIAL; MESSAGE:L6,L7(CENTER, OUTLINE)text; Mark your original print starting point and then PRINT. (Note: Turn off printer after the last side panels are printed.)

To add message at bottom, roll back paper to original print starting point.

SIGN; DYO; TALL; FONT:SMALL; MESSAGE:L19,L20(CENTER, SOLID) text; PRINT

CLUB PARTY! 6:00 SUNDAY THE 23RD
BYO-PRESENT! IN FELLOWSHIP HALL

Design Notes:

Outline type drops out of even a varied background if the font is of a uniform thickness. Besides a full panel, many graphics are appropriate when printed in a layout covering the page. Erase the last row for your message.

Graphic Alternatives:

Use an overall pattern of PROG(POINSETTIA). IBM users can try the HOLLY wide border.

Sign 7/SHELF

What you need:

What you do:

For TRAVEL BOOKS sign:
SIGN; DYO; WIDE; LAYOUT:SM ROWS II; GRAPHIC:MOD(ARROW LEFT,PAGE 209); DELETE:(ROW 2) 2,3; CHANGE:(ROW 2) 1 to SCH/BUS(GLOBE), (ROW 2) 4 to MOD(BOOKS,PAGE 192); FONT:AMADOR; MESSAGE:L2,L3(1 space between letters)(CENTER,RAISED,CH SIZE:L)text, L5-L6(1 space between letters) (CENTER, RAISED)text; PRINT

For COMPUTER BOOKS sign:
SIGN; DYO; WIDE; LAYOUT:SM ROWS II; GRAPHIC:MOD(ARROW LEFT,PAGE 209); DELETE:(ROW 2) 2,3; CHANGE:(ROW 2) 1 to PROG(COMPUTER), (ROW 2) 4 to MOD(BOOKS,PAGE 192); FLIP HORIZ:(ROW 1)ALL; FONT:AMADOR; MESSAGE:L2(CENTER,RAISED, CH SIZE:L)text, L3(1 space between letters)(CENTER, RAISED,CH SIZE:L)text, L5-L6(1 space between letters)(CENTER, RAISED)text; PRINT

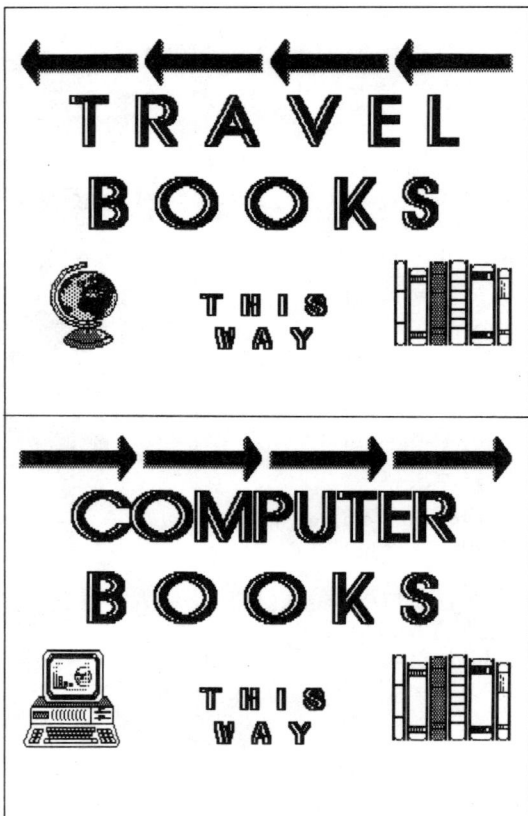

Design Notes:

Switch text and arrows and print as a banner for a larger sign. Arrows and pointing fingers coupled with graphics meaningful to your message create a bold and clear design.

Graphic Alternatives:

For other categories use: SCH/BUS(FILM, ART, BEAKER, MATH), PROG(PIANO), SCH/BUS(APPLE) for education, PROG(NIGHT SKY) for romance novels, or the many sports symbols.

Sign 8/DAILY SPECIALS

What you need:

NP

What you do:

SIGN; DYO; TALL; LAYOUT:SM
TILED; DELETE:(ROW 1)ALL,
(ROW 2)ALL, (ROW 3) 1,2,3,4,
(ROW 4) 1,2,3,5, (ROW 5) 1,2,4,5,
(ROW 6) 1,3,4,5, (ROW 7) 2,3,4,5;
FONT:VENTURA;
MESSAGE:L1,L2(LEFT,SOLID,CH
SIZE:L)text; FONT:SMALL;
MESSAGE:L4(LEFT,SOLID)text,
L7(3 spaces after word)(RIGHT,
SOLID)text; CHANGE TEXT TO
GRAPHIC (IBM only)/MOVE:L2 up
1 key press (*Apple Users:* Use Quick
Print feature to add L2, see page
27); PRINT 3 times

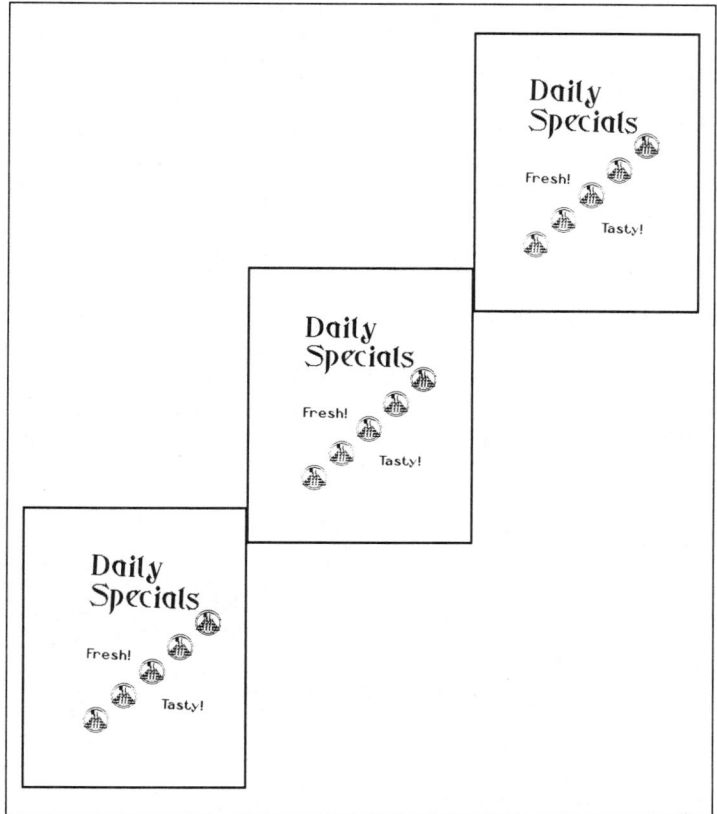

Design Notes:

A repeated design is very powerful if kept simple with a strong
linear statement. This concept is effective for a "wallpaper" design.
Try stacking these printouts diagonally for greatest impact or in
an "X-shaped" arrangement.

Graphic Alternatives:
Try using PARTY(PENGUIN, SANDWICH, DINNER NITE) or
SAMP(HOT DOG, BURGER).

New and Modified Art

What's in This Section

This is a section of alternatives—art alternatives. There is new art you can copy easily, alternative looks for the existing Print Shop art, and techniques you can use to create an alternative graphic library of your own. It's the section to turn to when you're thinking about a New Print Shop design and need to find a new art idea—or need to freshen up an old one.

Highlighted here is an overview of what you'll find in this section.

New Art: Easy-to-create original art—more pictures, more symbols.

Modified Print Shop Art: Many Print Shop graphics with an entirely new look, or transformed into a completely different object.

Art Techniques: Easy-to-copy techniques you can use when you want to give your graphic choices a new look or identity.

Design Ideas: Suggestions and applications to give you a sense of the look and feel each graphic can contribute to a design.

Art Overview: Reduced samples of every piece of Handbook art all in one place—on the art overview page.

Using This Section

The art overview page is an excellent place to begin. At a glance you'll see every piece of new and modified art and you'll know exactly what lies ahead. Well, almost. As in Designs, Designs, Designs, the printed samples are a key element of the section. Yet, they represent only a portion of what's included.

To get the most out of New and Modified Art, look beyond the printed samples. Throughout the section are many ideas not found elsewhere in the Handbook. Many techniques for inputting and modifying art are sure to come to mind for your own work.

Highlighted here are suggestions for using this section.

Suggestion #1: Always keep the art overview page in mind. It's a great place to start thinking about a look for your design.

Suggestion #2: Copy, adapt, embellish! When you find a piece of art you like, by all means copy it. If the art is not exactly right for your design, add your own personal touch and adapt it for your own special purpose.

Suggestion #3: Modify any New Print Shop graphic. The Handbook's techniques for modifying art are easy to copy and can be applied to any Print Shop graphic. In many cases, a particular graphic was selected simply to illustrate an art modification technique.

Suggestion #4: The New and Modified Art pages show how a piece of art can be used to create a certain look or convey a special message. Use the design ideas—copy or adapt them.

Suggestion #5: If a modified art example uses a Print Shop package you don't have, don't flip past it. There are likely to be ideas and techniques on the page that you can easily apply to other graphics. And if you're really in love with the graphic, simple treat it as new art—copy the graphic and input it from scratch!

Suggestion #6: Let the Handbook's art be a springboard for new art ideas of your own.

Symbols: A Review

Every art sample is clearly marked with the following easy-to-recognize symbols to let you know immediately if more than The New Print Shop program was used to create it. (If you're in the Modified Art section and see a graphic you'd like to use but don't have the appropriate Print Shop package, remember, you can treat the graphic as new art and copy it from scratch.)

NP   The New Print Shop

S   Sampler Edition

P   Party Edition

S/B   School & Business Edition

About the Art Grid

Every new and modified art sample is positioned on an art grid. The grid looks just like graph paper, composed of many small boxes. The grid is used to represent the Graphic Editor drawing area. Each small box represents a dot that can be filled in with the Graphic Editor. The Handbook grid shows the position of every possible dot on the Graphic Editor drawing surface. Every tenth box on the grid is labeled and highlighted to make it easy to identify the position of a box.

In the Graphic Editor, the position of every dot is identified on screen by an x-coordinate and a y-coordinate. The position of the dot from left to right is called the x-coordinate. The position of the dot from top to bottom is called the y-coordinate. For example, if you want to fill in a dot that is 25 dots across and 30 dots down, just move your cursor on the Graphic Editor drawing surface to the position labeled $x = 25$, $y = 30$ and you're all set.

The numbers on the art grid correspond to the numbers on screen. A box on the art grid that is 25 boxes across and 30 boxes down corresponds to the dot on screen that is 25 dots across and 30 dots down. The box corresponds to the dot labeled $x = 25$, $y = 30$.

Inputting the Handbook Art

Fill in the dots on screen in the same positions as shown on the art grid. To input art from the New Art section, go to the Graphic Editor and fill in dots on screen from scratch. To input art from the Modified Art section, go to the Graphic Editor and call up the graphic to be modified. Keep or add all the dots shown in black on the art grid. Erase all the dots shown in light grey. You'll have a new piece of art at your disposal—save it to use again and again. *(Note:* Try to copy the same pattern of dots on screen as shown on the art grid. But don't be concerned if you don't copy every single dot. Even if 90% of the dots match up, your art will probably look just like the Handbook's!)

If you don't have the appropriate Print Shop package for a modified art sample, don't rush past that page. Treat the sample as new art and input it from scratch. Just fill in the dots on screen in the same positions as the black boxes on the art grid. (Ignore the light grey boxes—they represent the positions of dots to be erased when modifying.)

Inputting Your Original Art

Print Shop users can take advantage of the Graphic Editor to create original graphics. With the blank art grid on page 298 of the Planning Tools section, you can sketch your creation in pencil ahead of time (just copy the grid on a copying machine), fine tune your artwork, and then head for your computer. Use your art grid drawing as a guide to filling in the appropriate dots on the Graphic Editor drawing surface.

About Modified Art Resolution

The New Print Shop offers most graphics in three different sizes. When creating a design and calling up a graphic in the large size, a very detailed, high resolution version of the graphic appears (see School & Business/Switch, page 285). This is the version shown on the Graphic Reference card. In the medium and small sizes, a less detailed version of the graphic appears. The graphic has been adapted to best fit the amount of space allotted for each graphic size.

In the Graphic Editor, graphics appear in the grid in their simplest form. The version of the Switch that appears in the Graphic Editor grid is the same version that appears in a design when the small size is used (see page 210). Therefore, it is this version that appears in the Before position under the heading Before & After on the Modified Art page. It's the version of a graphic that is the easiest to work with and quickest to modify.

The New Art Page

The reduced page shown here provides an explanation of the various elements you'll find with every piece of new art.

Sunshine: Art Sample Name—identifies the specific item shown.

What You Need: The New Print Shop symbol always appears here—you'll never need more in the New Art section!

Category Symbol: Symbol on top right tells you if you're in the New Art or Modified Art section.

Ideas: A variety of information including alternative suggestions for modifying and using the art may appear here.

Applications: Samples in Designs, Designs, Designs that use the art are shown here. Turn to the page indicated for step-by-step design instructions.

Sunshine

What you need:

NP

Ideas:
Cute children's designs aren't the only application for whimsical graphics such as this. A garden shop, swimwear store or even a pool maintenance firm can use the graphic as a logo on stationery or flyers. Also, use in repetition as part of an illustration.

Applications:
See pages 65 and 82.

The Art: An actual printout of the art is shown in position on the art grid. Just call up the Graphic Editor on your New Print Shop disk. Fill in the dots on the Graphic Editor drawing surface in the same positions as shown on the art grid, save your work, and you'll have a new piece of art at your disposal. (*Note:* Try to copy the same pattern of dots on the screen as shown on the art grid. But don't be concerned if you don't copy every single dot. Even if 90% of the dots match up, your art will look just like the Handbook's!)

The Modified Art Page

The reduced page shown here provides an explanation of the various elements you'll find with every piece of modified Print Shop art.

Emblem: Art Sample Name—identifies the specific item shown.

What You Need: Easy-to-recognize symbols (shown on page 11) tell you what Print Shop programs were used to create the art.

Before & After: Shows what the art looks like before and after the changes are made.

Special Instructions: Instructions for manipulating a graphic (e.g., flipping) appear here.

Category Symbol: Symbol at top right tells if you're in the New Art or Modified Art section.

Ideas: A variety of information including alternative suggestions for modifying and using the art may appear here.

Applications: Samples in Designs, Designs, Designs that use the art are shown here. Turn to the page indicated for step-by-step instructions.

NEW AND MODIFIED ART   195

Emblem

What you need:

NP

Before & After:

(Picnic)

Special Instructions:
To begin, VERTICALLY FLIP the Picnic graphic inside the grid.

Ideas:
Filling in and erasing becomes simple when a pattern is embedded in Print Shop art. This emblem is a good example of looking at a graphic and "seeing something different."

Applications:
See pages 60 and 130.

The Art: An actual printout of the art is shown in position on the art grid. Every tenth box is labeled for easy identification. All boxes to be kept from the original graphic or to be added by you are shown in black. All boxes to be erased by you are shown in light grey. (*Note:* Try to copy the same pattern of dots on the screen as shown on the art grid. But don't be concerned if you don't copy every single dot. Even if 90% of the dots match up, your art will look just like the Handbook's!)

Art Overview

All the Handbook's new and modified art is shown here. Use these pages for quick reference to find a graphic with the right look for your design.

New Art

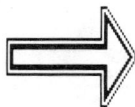
Arrow 1

Arrow 2

Book

Butterfly

Cactus

Cake

Clown

Crown

Cube

C-Type Logo

Dollar

Dots

Flower

Game Box

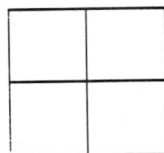
Geometrics: Square

Geometrics: Triangle

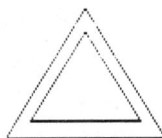
Graphic Tile Pattern 1

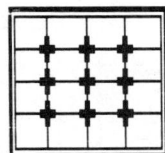
Graphic Tile Pattern 2

Graphic Tile Pattern 3

Graphic Tile Pattern 4

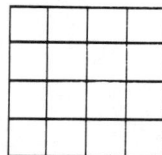
Grid

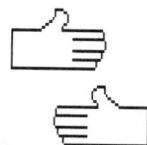
Hands

Hanger

House

Jack-in-the-Box

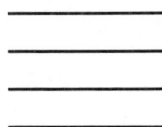
Note Lines

Plant

Pointing Finger

Row Houses

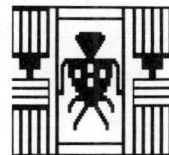
Southwestern Pattern

Sports Symbol

Star

Sunshine

Teddy Bear

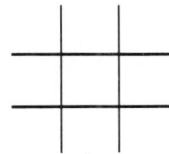
Tic-Tac-Toe

Modified Art

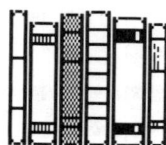

Book Logo

Bottle

Christmas Tree

Emblem

Pencil

Pushpin/Left

Pushpin/Right

Ribbon/First Place

Sun Crest

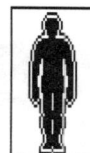

Stars & Stripes

Airplane Solid

Creature
Maker/Giraffe

Creature
Maker/Rabbit

Kitty Cat Solid

Man Symbol

Man of Strength Symbol

Piggy Bank Graphic

Arrow Left

Graphic Pattern

Large House

Man Profile

No Symbol

Please Write Chalkboard

Rubber Stamp

Crest Frame

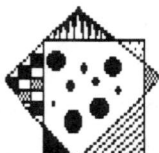

Festive Graphic

Pumpkin

Waiter

Arrow 1

What you need:

NP

Ideas:

A large graphic arrow makes an excellent communicative symbol. This arrow is designed in outline form for design interest and to allow for highlighting with brightly-colored markers. Try using the arrow on a banner in a hallway or as a door sign for directions. Printed large and colored in, the arrow will quickly deliver your message. The thickness of the inside black border provides safety for coloring in smaller arrows on a card or wrapping paper design.

For a left facing arrow, simply use the FLIP function in the customize section of your program.

Applications:

See pages 75 and 104.

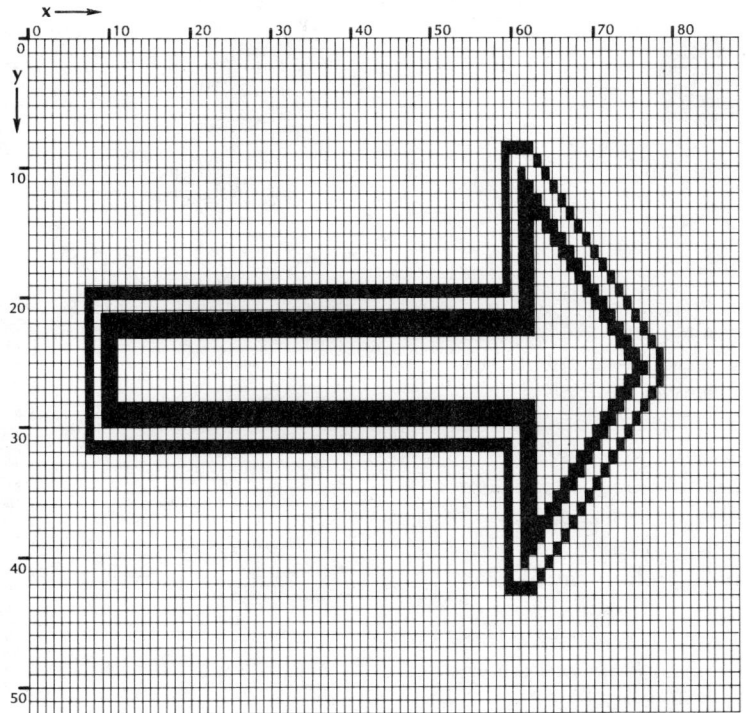

Arrow 2

What you need:

NP

Ideas:

A large graphic arrow makes an excellent communicative symbol. This arrow is designed in outline form for design interest and to allow for highlighting with brightly colored markers. Try using the arrow on a banner in a hallway or as a door sign for directions. Printed large and colored in, the arrow will quickly deliver your message. The thickness of the inside black border provides safety for coloring in smaller arrows on a card or wrapping paper design.

For a downward pointing arrow, use the FLIP function in the customize section of your program.

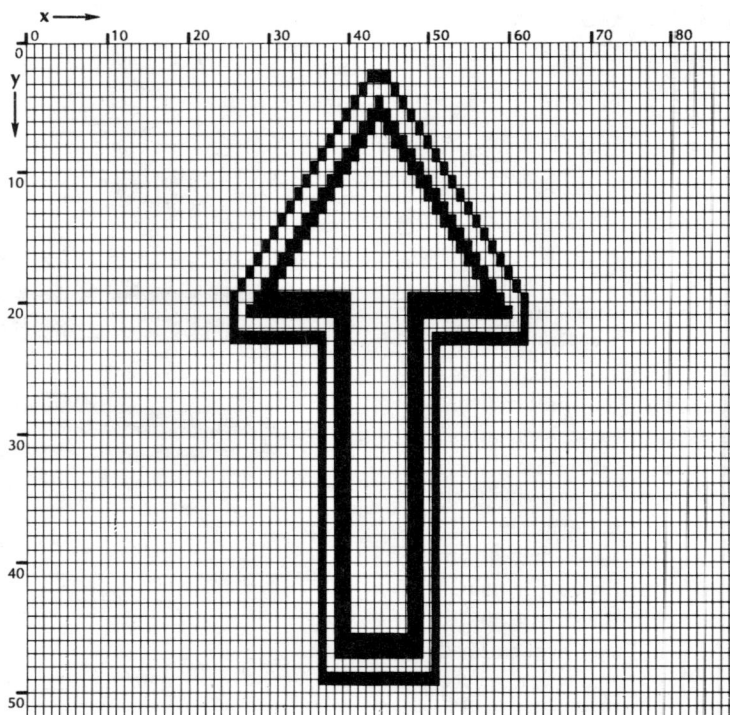

Book

What you need:

NP

Ideas:

Writers, schools, clubs, bookstores, and publishers can all benefit from a simple open book symbol. This graphic works both as a symbol and decorative piece of art. It's also the perfect graphic to use for book gift wrap.

Applications:

See page 124.

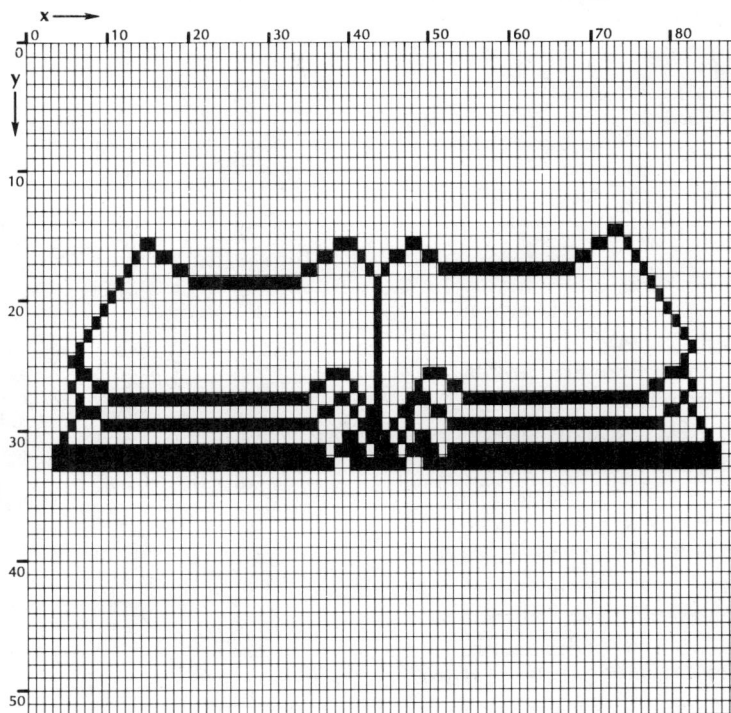

Butterfly

What you need:

NP

Ideas:

An image that is graphic, yet realistic, is appropriate for personal and professional letterheads and cards. There are many concepts a symbol from nature can represent. These types of symbols can be easily adapted for posters and greeting cards. Other elements from nature are simple to produce with The New Print Shop. Note other examples in the New Art section: Cactus, Flower, Plant, and Sunshine.

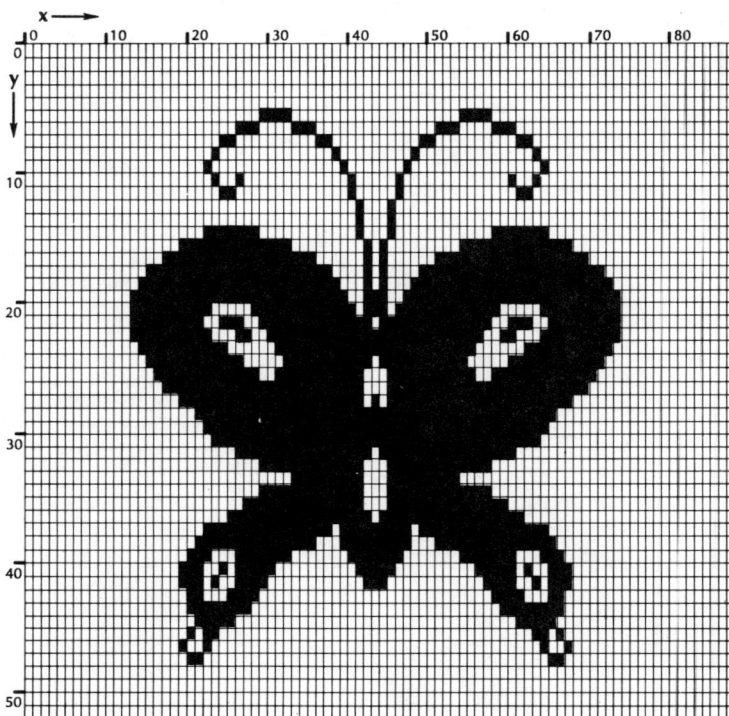

Cactus

What you need:

NP

Ideas:

The fascination with the Southwest allows many applications for a Cactus image. The stylized nature of the design makes it appropriate for professional as well as personal applications. A logo design that is primarily line art is simple to produce with the Graphic Editor. Try starting with the trunk and then moving up to the top right hand corner.

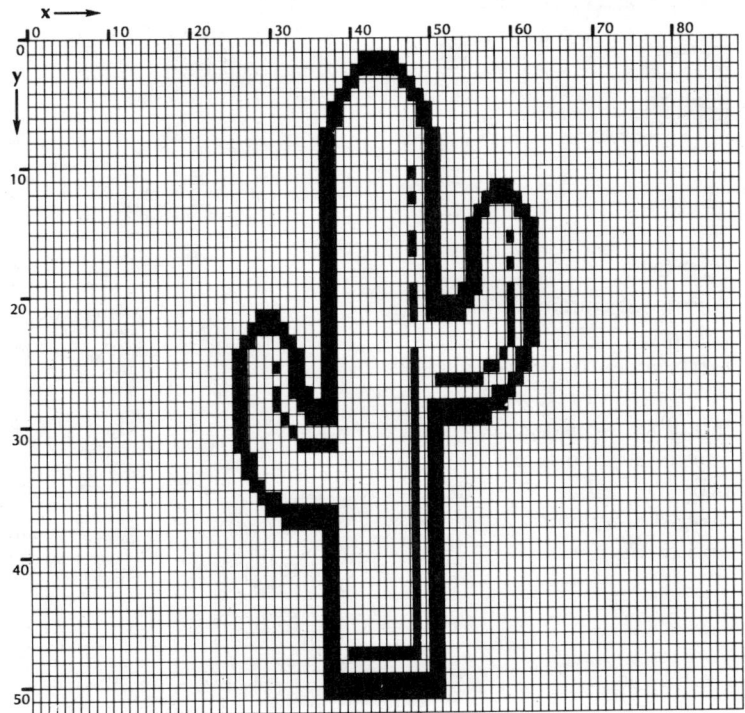

Cake

What you need:

NP

Ideas:

A graphic cake such as this one can be used on birthday cards or party invitations, for a food-related business logo, or customized with the proper number of candles for birthday party banners and cards.

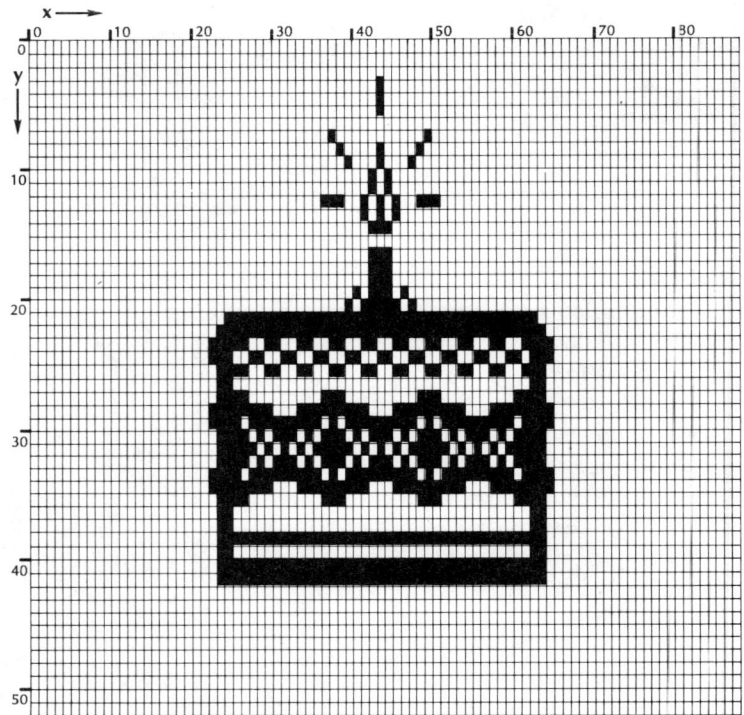

Applications:

See page 68.

Clown

What you need:

NP

Ideas:

A simple representative graphic is often much more powerful than a more illustrative piece. Using the Graphic Editor, a simple logo is quite easy to produce. Try animal faces or hats to symbolize different occupations. A few changes to the art, plus various messages, add whimsy to the more dramatic with this clown art.

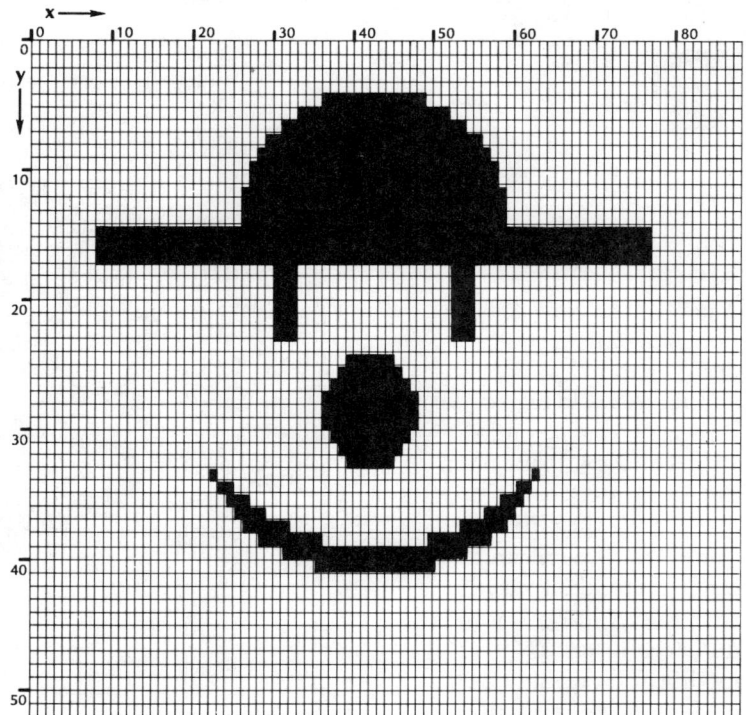

Applications:

See pages 71 and 82.

Crown

What you need:

NP

Ideas:

A goal of the New Art section is to enable you to design a more graphic and simple, yet bold logo style. This contrasts strongly with The New Print Shop illustration style. Both styles have their applications. The Crown can be made more illustrative with the addition of jewels and decoration. This modification would be useful for a large printout. Try pasting the art on a piece of heavier cardboard for a play crown.

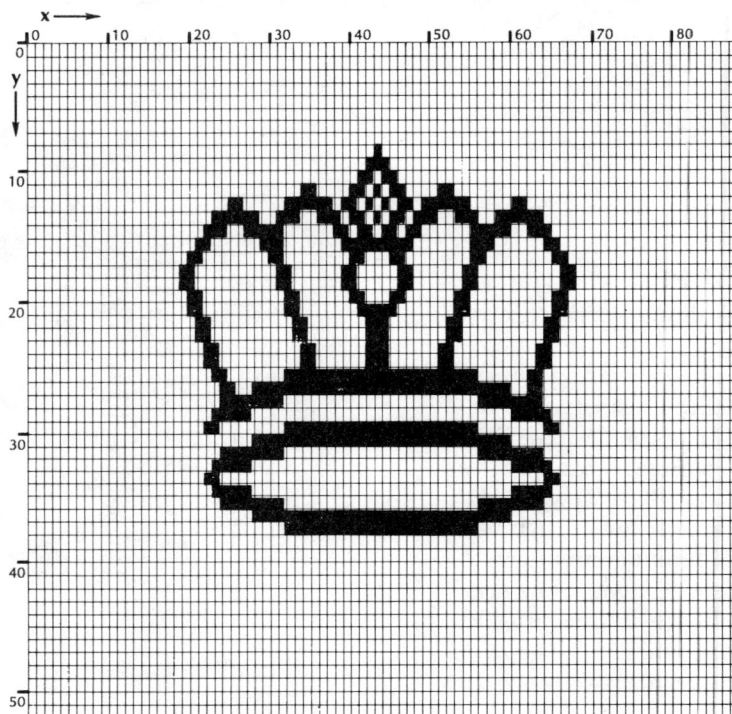

Cube

What you need:

NP

Ideas:

The cube is a strong basic shape for many applications. Try putting your personal, company or organization initials inside for a crest look. Print large- or medium-sized cubes in the sign mode and use the frames for children's drawings. Print multiple copies, or copy on a copying machine and keep children busy on car trips!

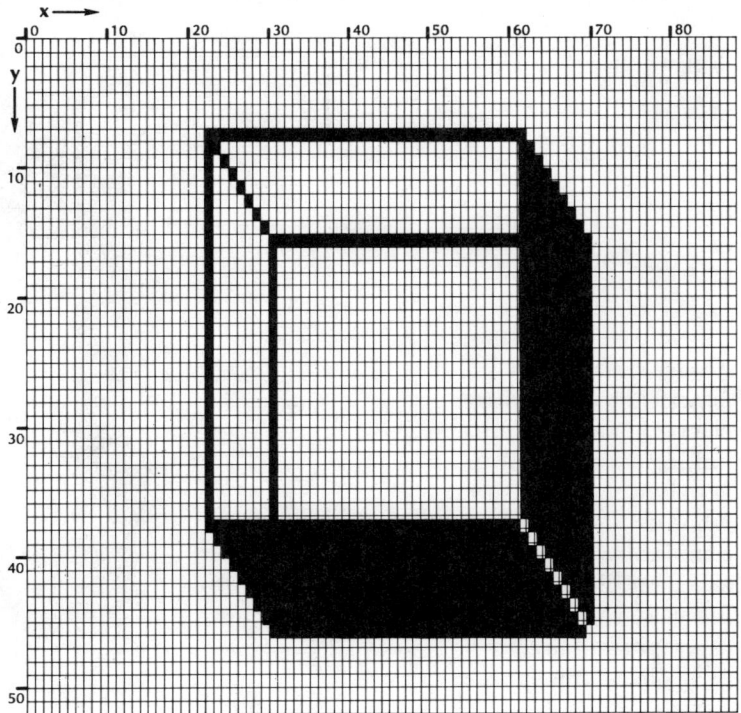

C-Type Logo

What you need:

NP

Ideas:

Logos are often used symbolically as well as literally. Use this graphic generically to symbolize strength, momentum, or a linking concept. The trick is in how it is used—whether alone or in repetition. It also makes an excellent tile pattern. Literally used, the "C" logo can represent architecture, development or an initial.

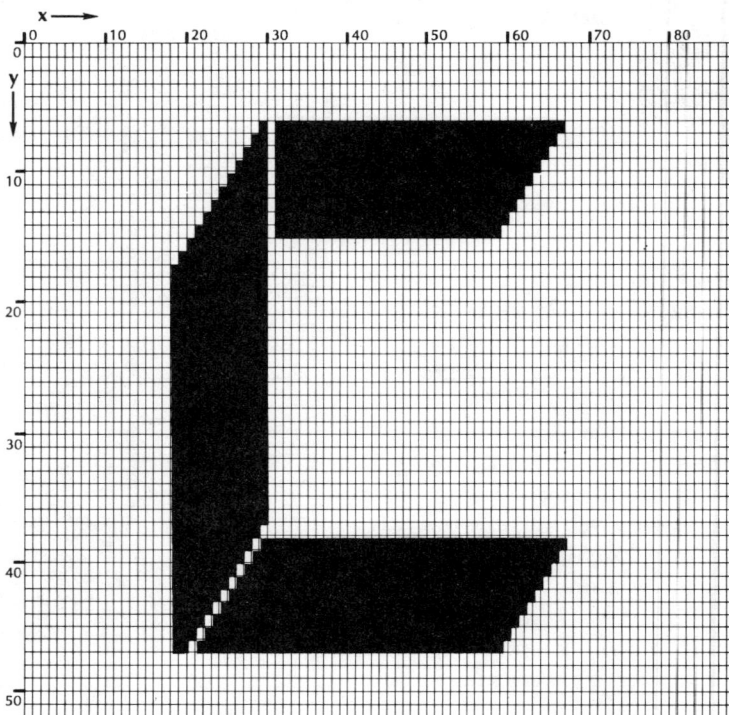

Dollar

What you need:

NP

Ideas:

A dollar sign becomes a bold and professional symbol when the surrounding Graphic Editor box is filled in. The solid black boxes work extremely well in a tiled layout as they form a new graphic by butting up to one another.

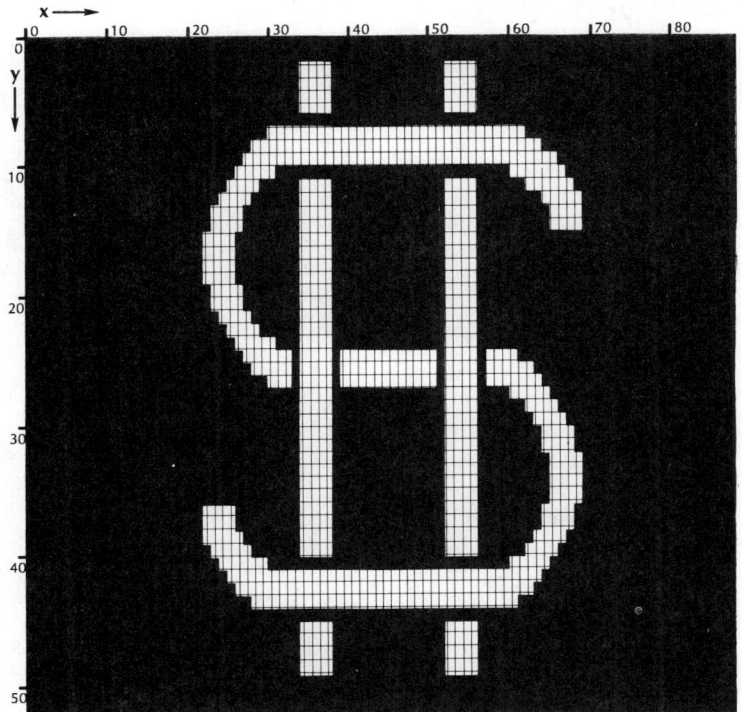

Applications:

See pages 75 and 138.

Dots

What you need:

NP

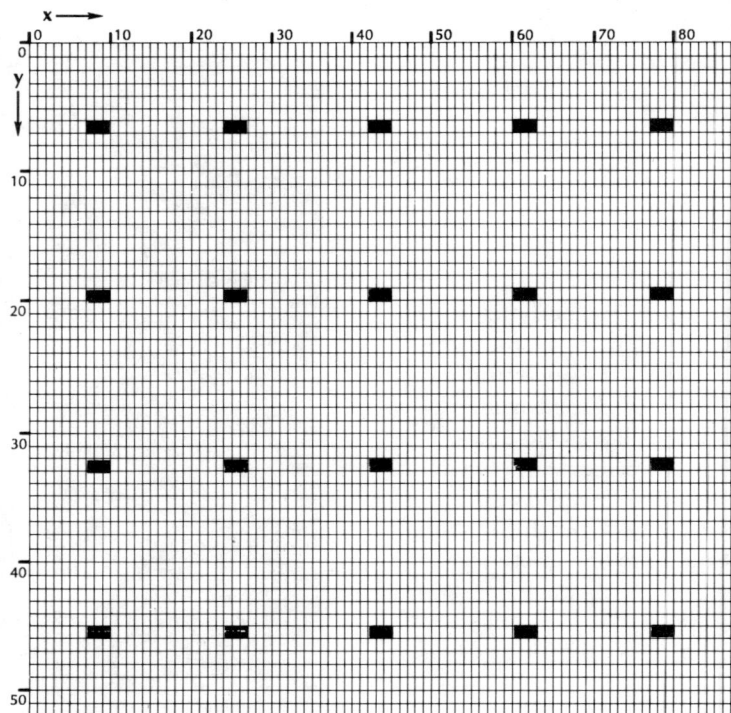

Ideas:

Repeating dots make a great pattern behind other Print Shop graphics. Just call up the dots in one of the tiled layouts and then insert another graphic over the dots. This graphic can also be used as the "game board" of a fun dot-connecting game. For more about this, see page 91.

Applications:

See page 91.

Flower

What you need:

NP

Ideas:

The Flower symbol works well as a personal symbol or as a representation of natural ingredients or respect for nature in a product or service. In repetition the message is more decorative. Try creating a border at top and bottom of a sign or letterhead, or make a full frame for a child's drawing. For a child's party, a full frame printout with each guest's name serves well for stickers and drawing entertainment. Or, hand out personalized frames to paste instant photos of arriving guests.

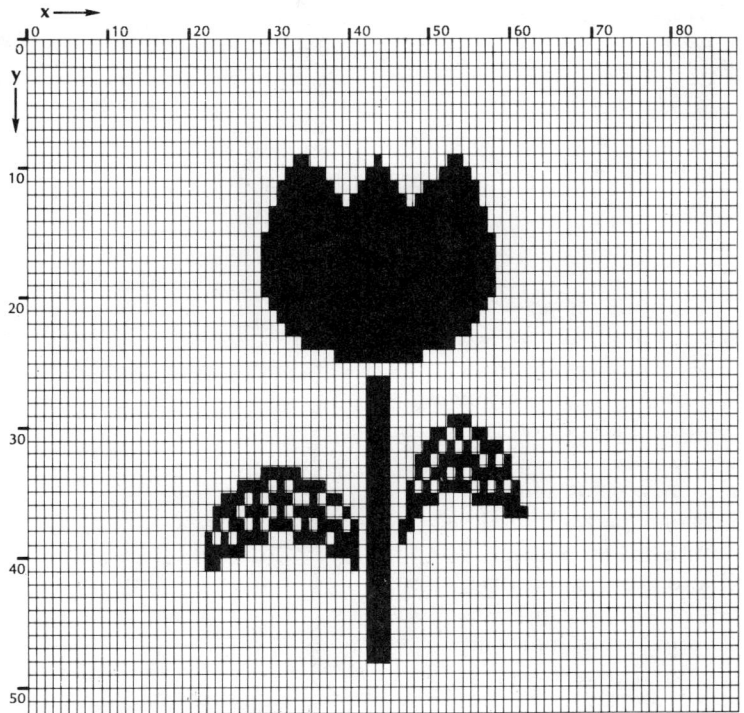

Applications:

See pages 43 and 80.

Game Box

What you need:

NP

Ideas:

This graphic is used to create the puzzle/game box shown on page 86. Insert the game box directly over another Print Shop graphic such as an animal, and then print and cut into four pieces to make a child's jigsaw puzzle. The Game Box graphic also works well in repetition for a letterhead, as a sign background or wrapping paper design.

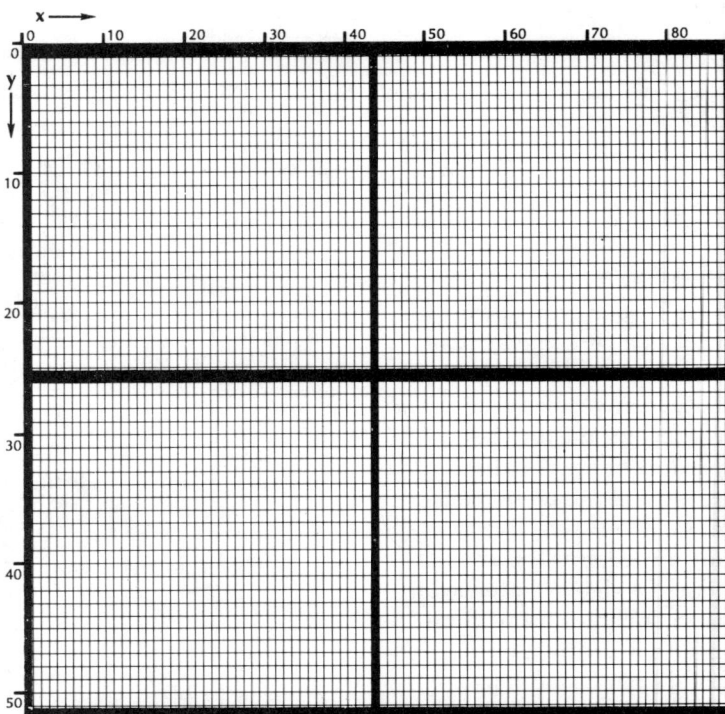

Applications:

See page 86.

Geometrics: Square

What you need:

NP

Ideas:

Tile patterns are very graphic and easy to produce in the Graphic Editor and are easy to apply to multiple uses. A graphic such as this is bold and decorative. Try using it in an overall tile pattern for wrapping paper or as an asymmetrical design on the Father's Day card example.

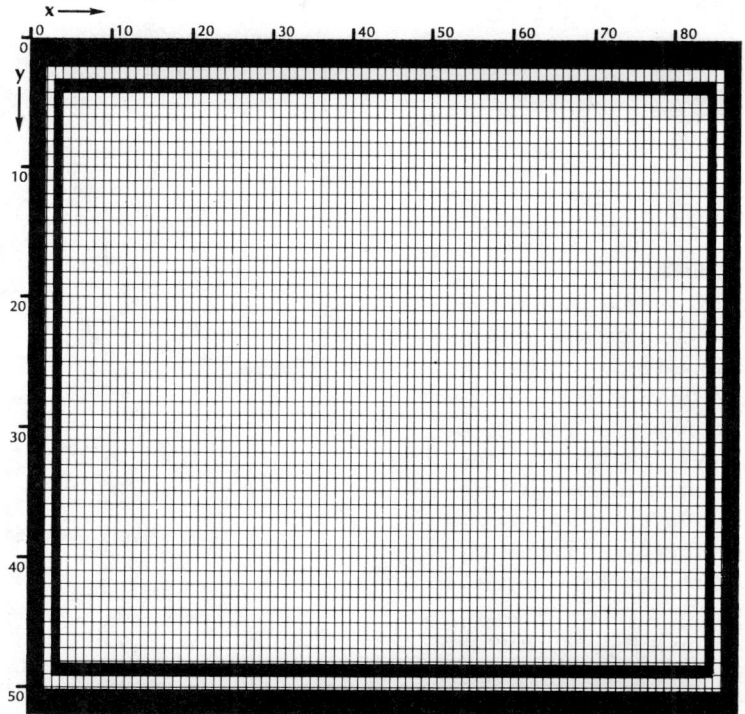

Geometrics: Triangle

What you need:

NP

Ideas:

This simple graphic works well in repetition and in a flipped pattern where four graphics with all four triangle points converge. A row of triangle graphics all pointing inward in a border format is also very decorative and sophisticated. Try a row of triangles with every other triangle flipped, or where every third graphic forms a more illustrative piece. The beauty of geometrics is in their many applications and their contrast with "busy" pieces of art.

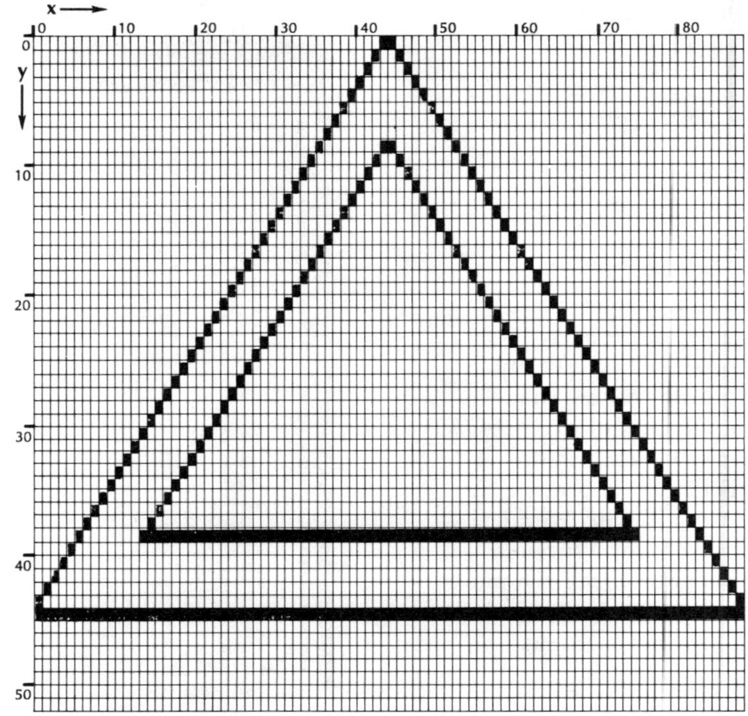

Applications:

See page 130.

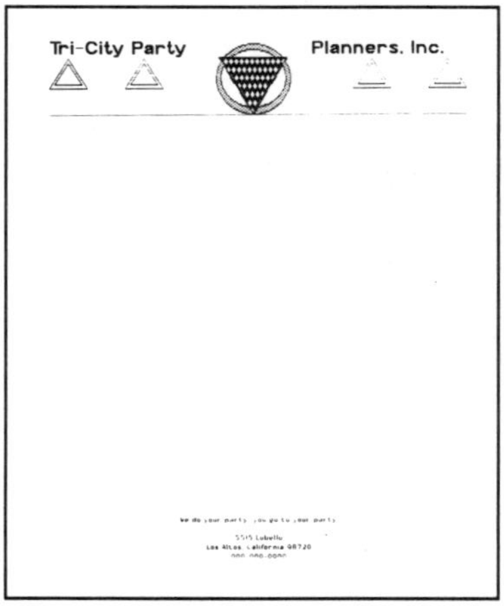

Graphic Tile Pattern 1

What you need:

NP

Ideas:

A geometric design has many applications. The use of the full square in the Graphic Editor allows for an interesting pattern when butted together in an overall design. Try drawing only the vertical or horizontal lines for a more open look.

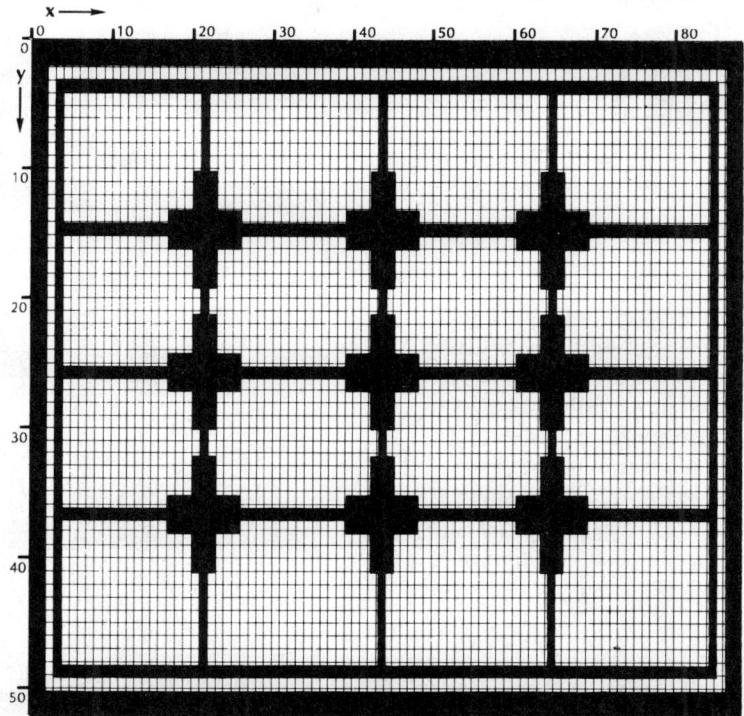

Applications:

See pages 44 and 46.

Graphic Tile Pattern 2

What you need:

NP

Ideas:

An open geometric design allows for a more sophisticated statement when used in a solid tile pattern. For a more delicate statement, create a checkerboard layout by simply erasing every other graphic position of your design.

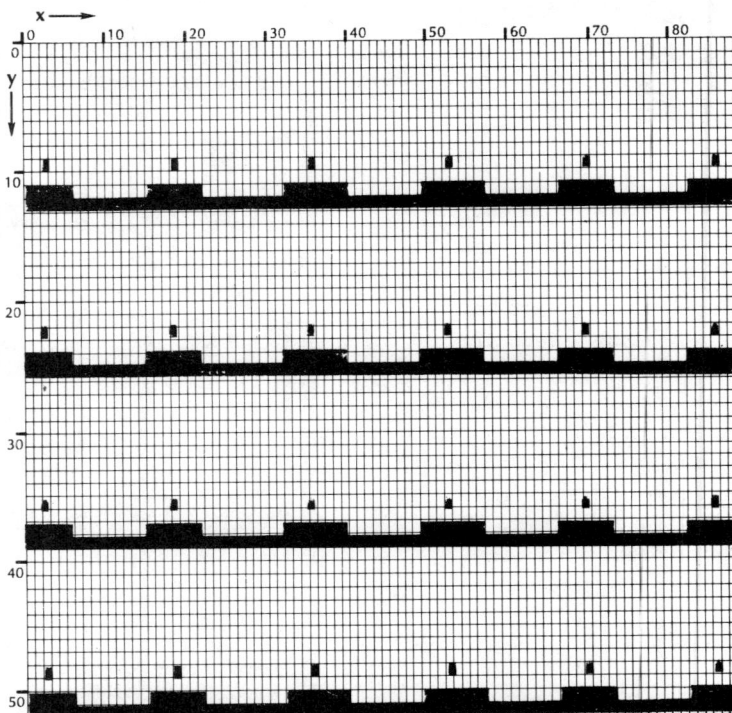

Graphic Tile Pattern 3

What you need:

NP

Ideas:

A diamond-style multi-faced graphic makes an excellent tile pattern and can be modified easily. Try using this graphic in a tiled layout and then vertically flipping every other graphic. Felt tip markers can be used to enhance the negative spaces.

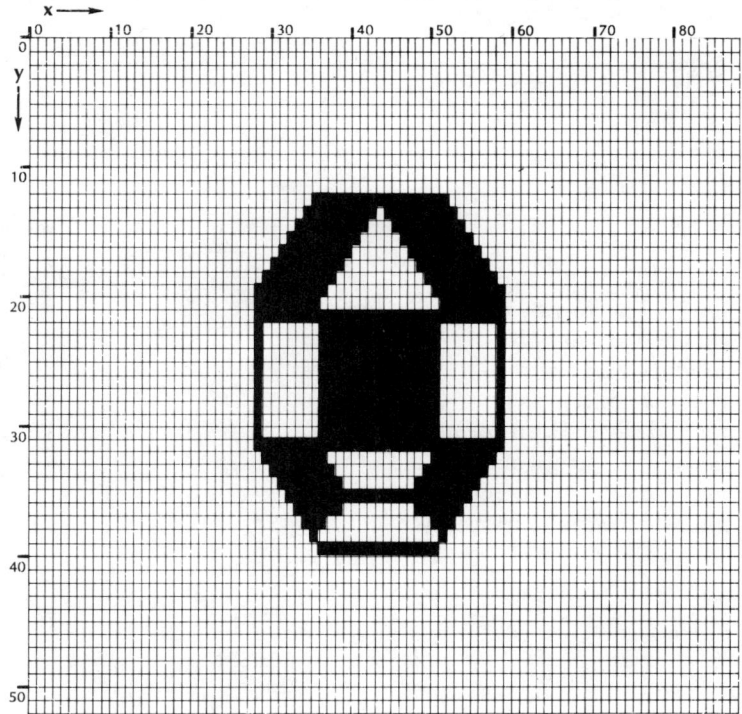

Graphic Tile Pattern 4

What you need:

NP

Ideas:

Quilted patterns such as this one are easy to produce and are very reusable either as intended tile patterns or as decorative pieces of spot art. Vary this design only slightly for greater variety.

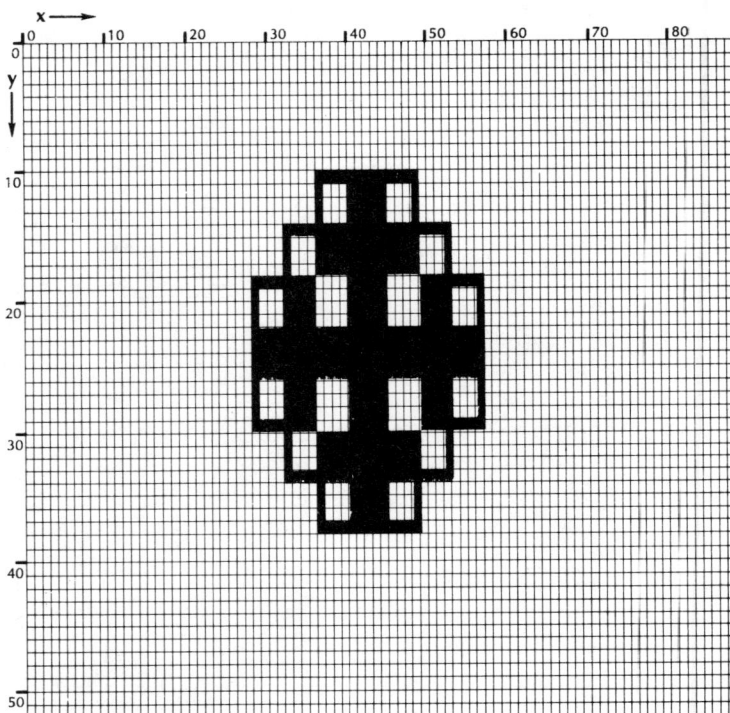

Grid

What you need:

NP

Ideas:

A Grid is a good basic design element which can be used in infinite ways. Try filling in every other square in a checkerboard manner for a bolder look. The Grid also makes a great background pattern in the sign mode. Simply choose a tiled pattern.

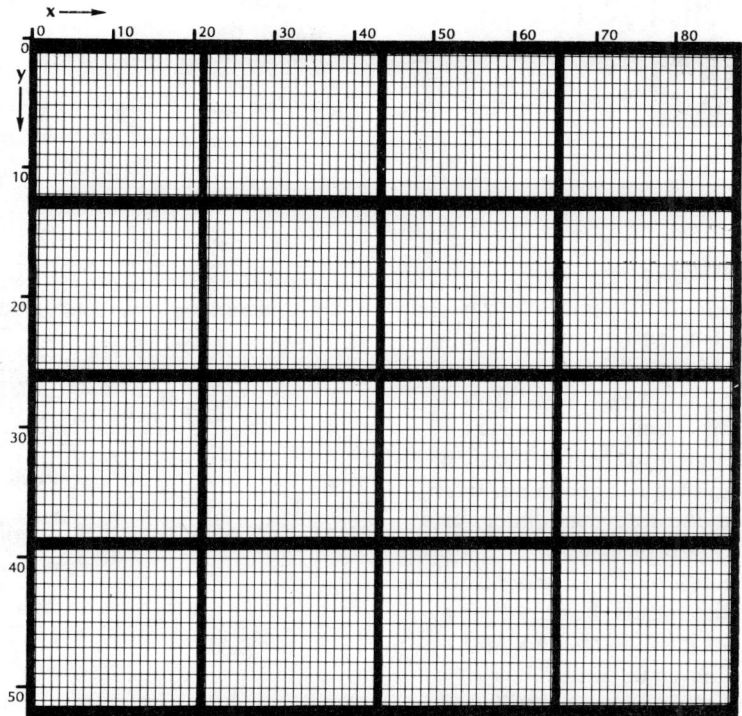

Hands

What you need:

NP

Ideas:

The message of unity and cooperation implied by this graphic makes it applicable to many different situations. Its generic quality of friendship also makes it a good choice for a decorative graphic. For a different look, draw a large outline box around the hands. For another look, fill in the box as shown in the Dollar graphic on page 167.

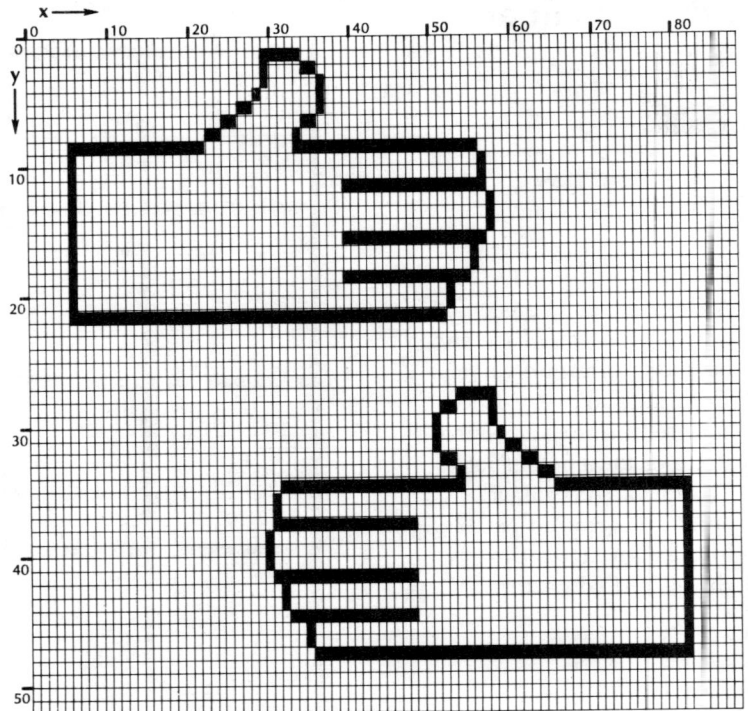

Applications:

See pages 43 and 126.

Hanger

What you need:

NP

Ideas:

This graphic is easy to create and can be used as a logo for clothing stores, dry cleaners, charity drives, or closet signs. It's also a fun graphic to repeat in the sign mode for gift wrap for any clothing related gifts such as shirts and ties.

Applications:

See pages 116 and 127.

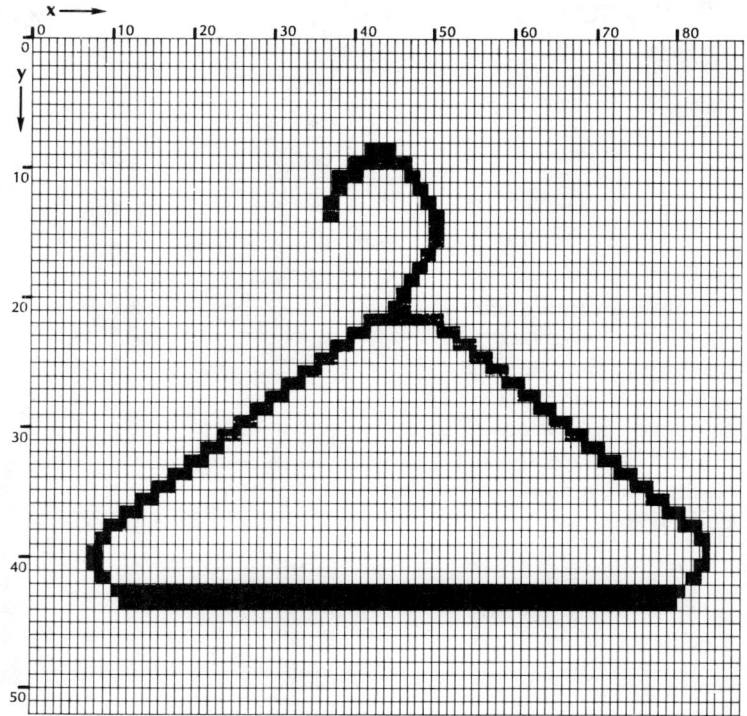

Check Off a Clean Week!
Stanley's Dry Cleaners

House

What you need:

NP

Ideas:

A simple graphic such as the House is very easy to produce in the Graphic Editor, and is transferable to many applications. The art can be made solid, if desired, for a more symbolic look.

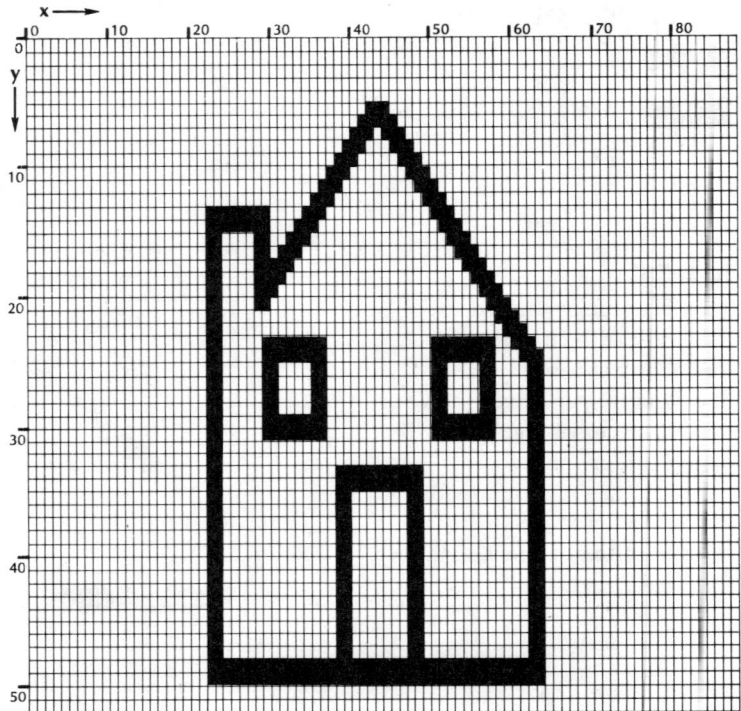

Applications:

See pages 53 and 120.

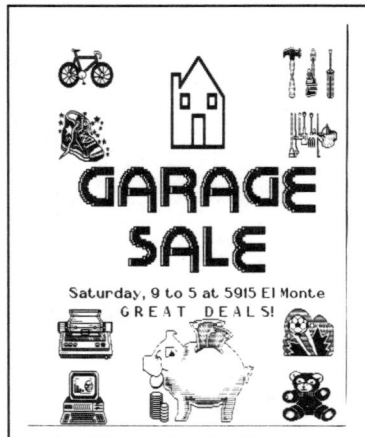

Jack-in-the-Box

What you need:

NP

Ideas:

Toy stores, child care centers, and party services are examples of the many potential applications for this graphic. The Jack-in-the-Box graphic also makes a perfect personal symbol for a child or the young at heart. In repetition the graphic is effective for wrapping paper or sign backgrounds. The box with the star inside is a useful decorative graphic by itself!

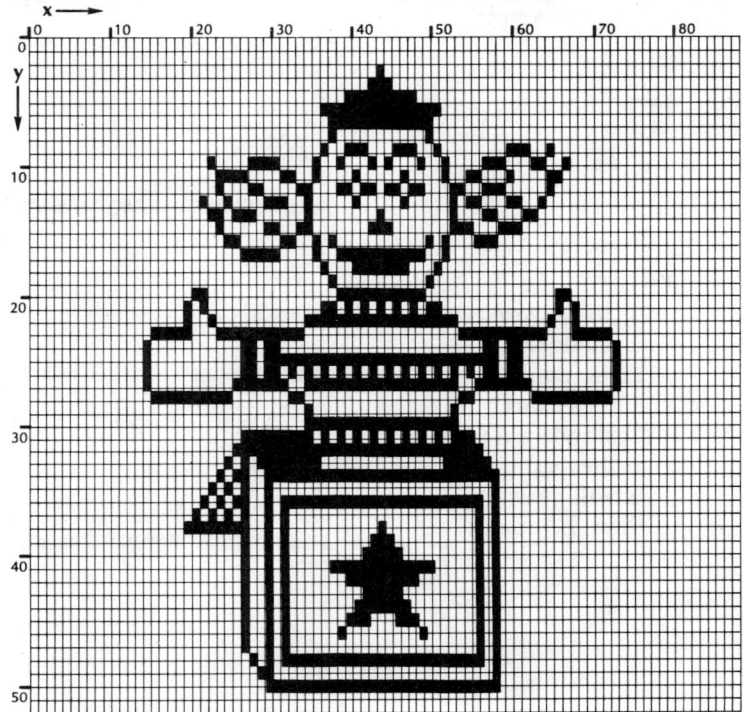

Applications:

See pages 79 and 99.

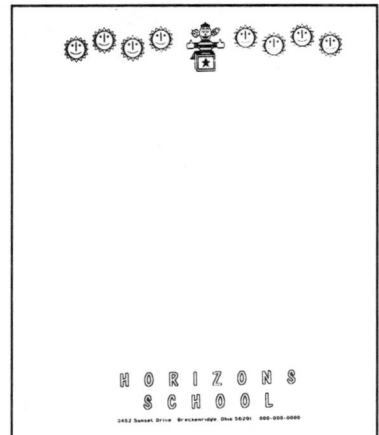

Note Lines

What you need:

NP

Ideas:

These four lines were carefully positioned for creating ruled note paper. Input the lines exactly as shown, then choose a tiled pattern in the sign mode. Your lines will be evenly spaced when they print!

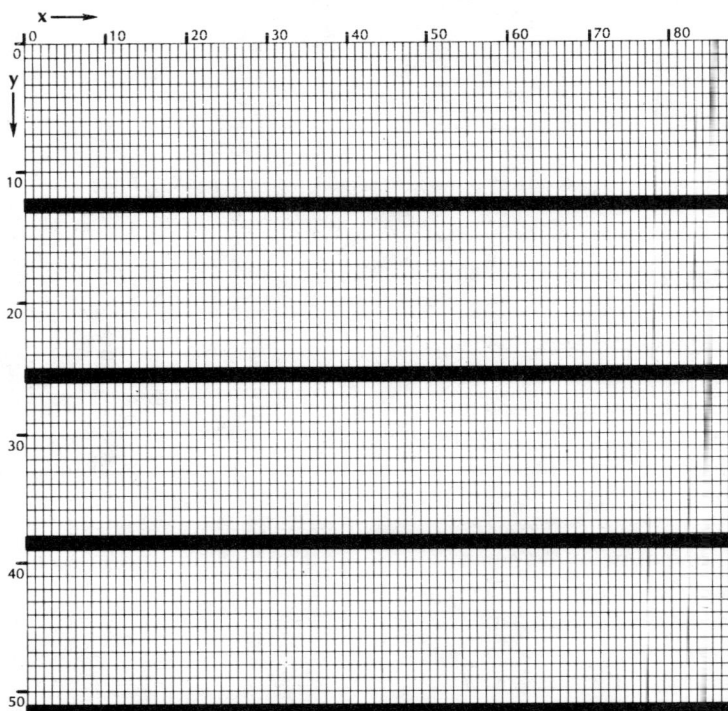

Applications:

See pages 131 and 132.

Plant

What you need:

NP

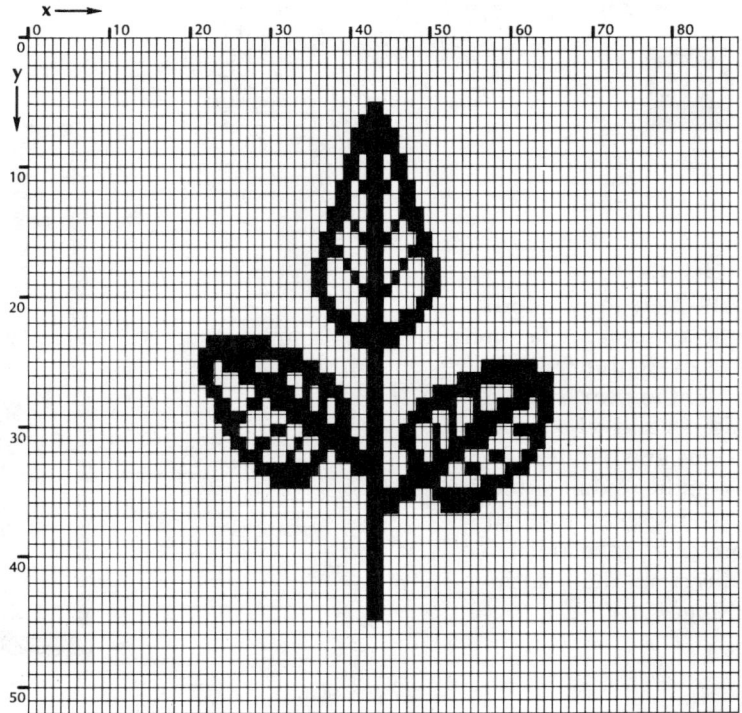

Ideas:

A simple nature graphic can convey many different messages. A border of plant shapes makes a nice picture frame for a child's leaf rubbings or outdoor pictures. For corporate use, try a design with a single graphic in one corner, or two graphics in opposite corners. Other applications include nursery or landscape architecture, personal growth or natural health care.

Applications:

See page 117.

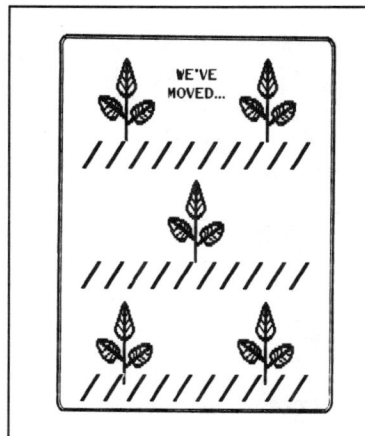

Pointing Finger

What you need:

NP

Ideas:

The New Print Shop's most useful applications (as evidenced by their frequent appearances in stores and schools) are signs and banners. Whether to call attention to a message, another graphic, or to indicate a direction, the Pointing Finger is a must.

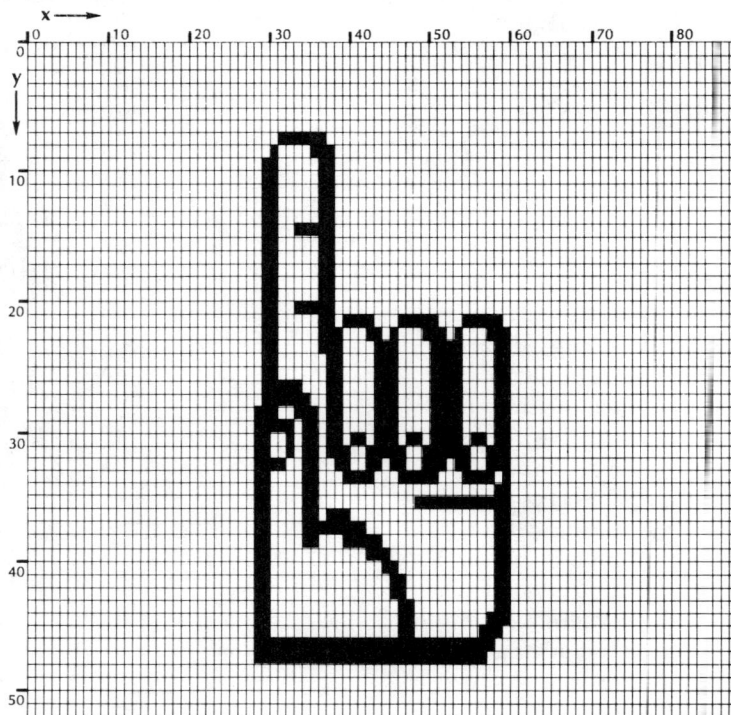

Applications:

See page 140.

Row Houses

What you need:

NP

Ideas:

Boldly designed symbols that are a bit more decorative have many applications. Use Row Houses as a logo for a development company or social services organization, as well as to announce a neighborhood gathering or crime watch. This graphic connects well when used in repetition.

Applications:

See page 38.

Southwestern Pattern

What you need:

NP

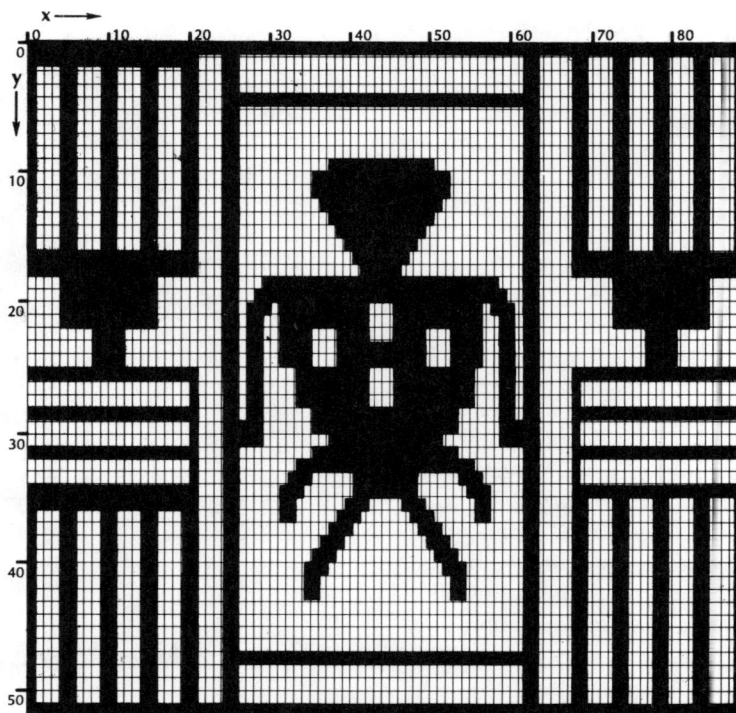

Ideas:

The Southwest has a flavor all its own. This symbol can be modified with your own touches in a variety of ways. The balance of geometric symmetry with decorative embellishments is reflective of this traditional art inspiration.

Applications:

See page 128.

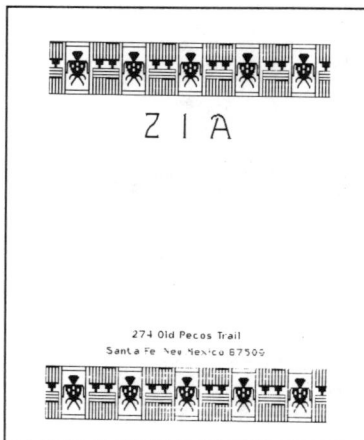

Sports Symbol

What you need:

NP

Ideas:

A simplified Olympic-style runner has application for many retail businesses, service organizations or sport teams. Even individual trainers, athletes or fans can use the graphic as a personal logo. In repetition, a dramatic team image is created. As an overall pattern a good backdrop it creates to sporting events posters or personalized wrapping paper for young athletes.

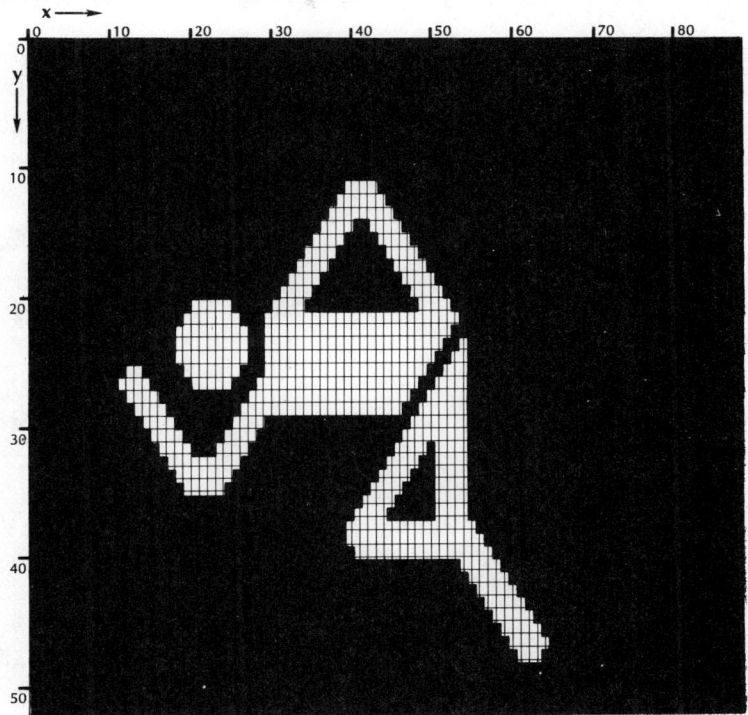

Applications:

See page 129.

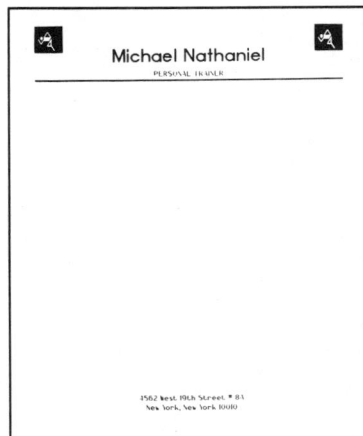

Star

What you need:

NP

Ideas:

Notice how clean this symbol is when produced with The New Print Shop. The Star works well as a stand-alone graphic for a logo or as an attention-getting larger graphic. Use it in repetition in a border or tile pattern. Try filling in the star for a different look.

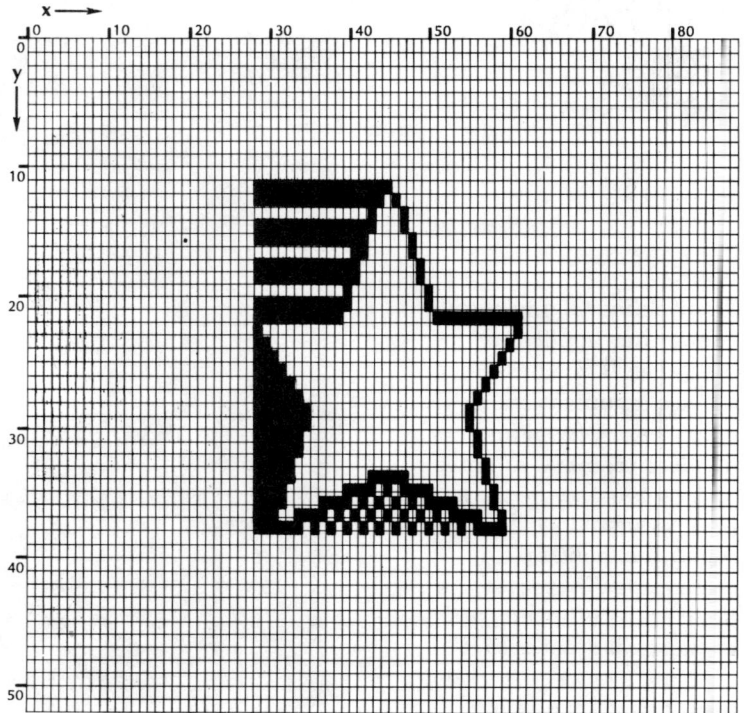

Applications:

See page 101.

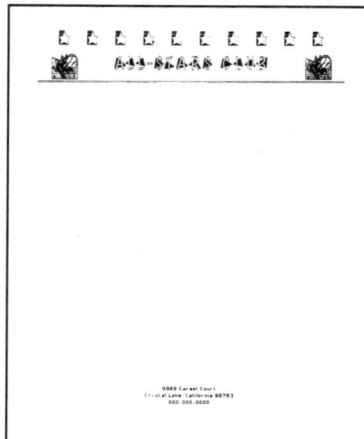

Sunshine

What you need:

NP

Ideas:

Cute children's designs aren't the only application for whimsical graphics such as this. A garden shop, swimwear store or even a pool maintenance firm can use the graphic as a logo on stationery or flyers. Also, use in repetition as part of an illustration.

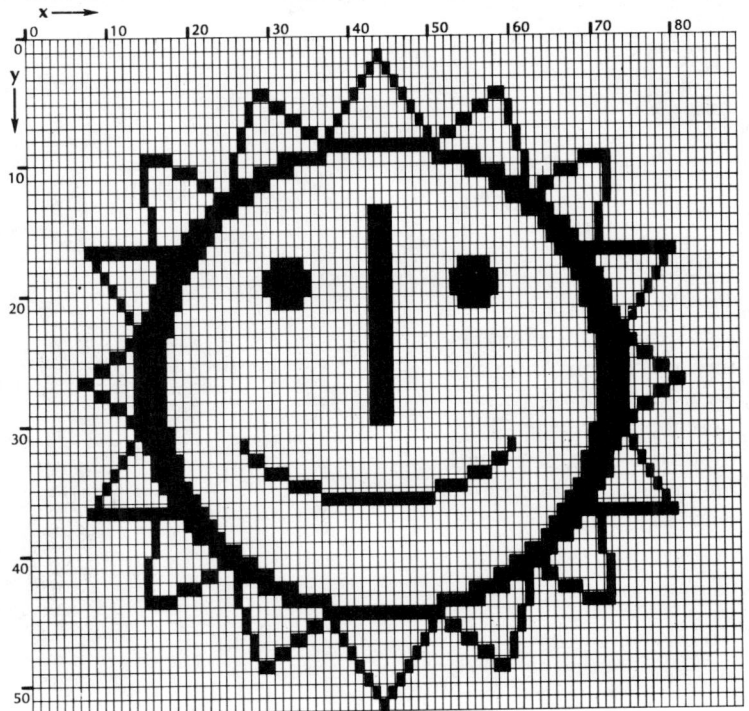

Applications:

See pages 65 and 82.

Teddy Bear

What you need:

NP

Ideas:

This bear makes a terrific logo for a young child, a toy or gift store, or even for a school or organization charity project. To input the bear, start with his arms, and then move on to his body.

Applications:

See page 39.

Tic-Tac-Toe

What you need:

NP

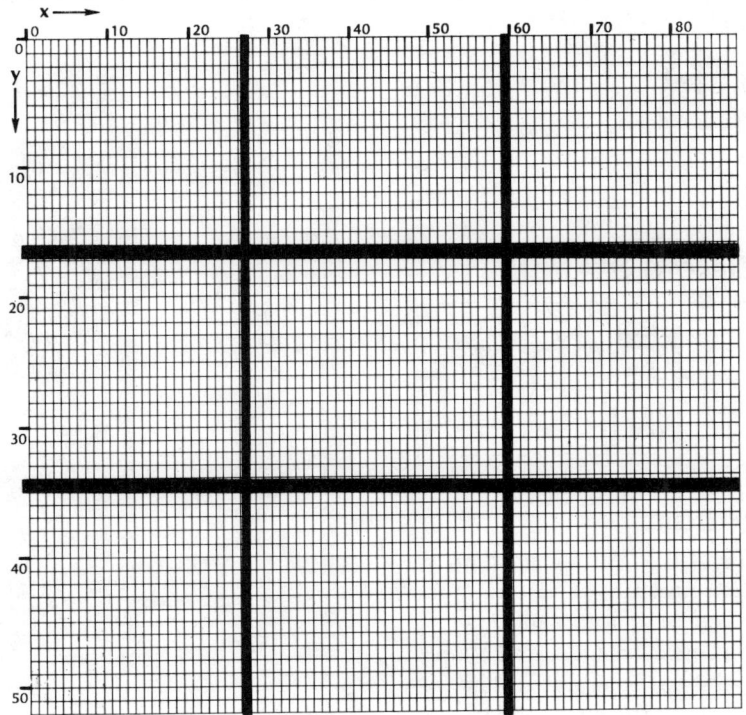

Ideas:

A Tic-Tac-Toe graphic is easy to create with The New Print Shop's Graphic Editor. Print out lots of sheets in the sign mode. Just choose one of the medium staggered or tiled layouts and you have a great travel or waiting game. The graphic can also be used to create an interesting symbol or decorative pattern. Blacken the center box to create a graphic with another look.

Applications:

See page 87.

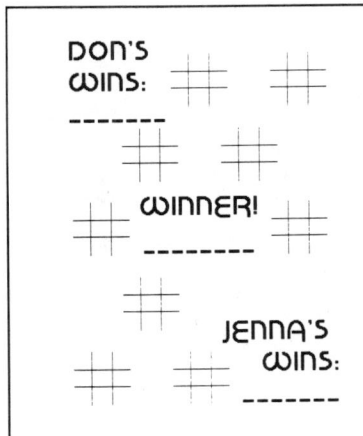

Book Logo

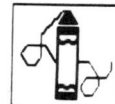

What you need:

NP

Before & After:

(Books)

Ideas:

The Book graphic without text becomes easily applicable to organizations for logos or signs, and even personal bookplates. Try using in the card mode and printing two bookplates per page by repeating the same design for the card front and inside.

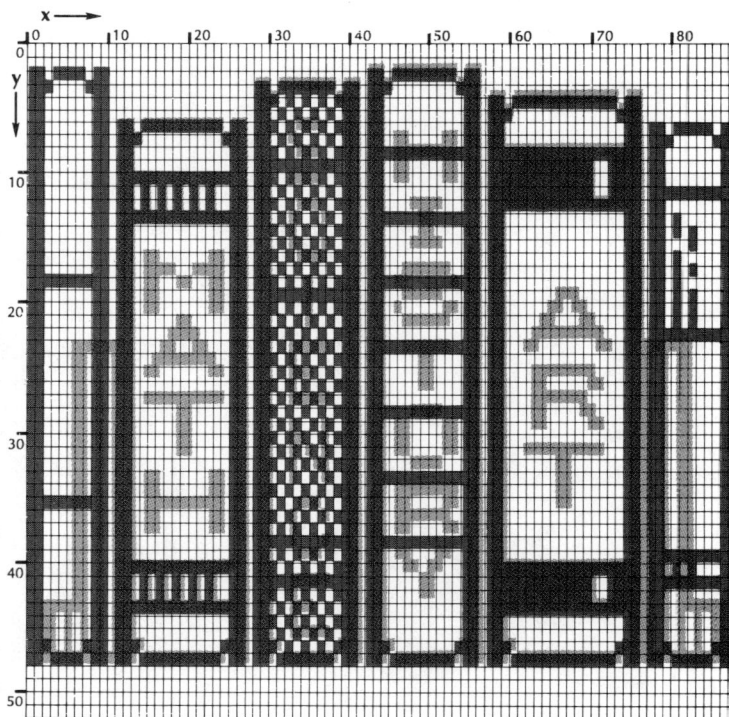

Applications:

See page 144.

Bottle

What you need:

NP

Before & After:

(Bubbly)

Special Instructions:
Center art in grid when
finished.

Ideas:

Blacken in the champagne
bottle for a strong graphic
look. Try erasing all the
decorative flairs and
centering the art for a
more uniform look when
used in repetition. Add a
horizontal rule above or
below the art across the
entire length of the
Graphic Editor grid for a
symbolic look. Then when
your new art is printed in
multiples, either tiled or in
a row, a new statement is
made.

Applications:

See page 118.

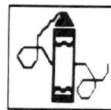

Christmas Tree

What you need:

NP

Before & After:

(Ice Cream)

Special Instructions:
To begin, FLIP ice cream cone in grid both VERTI-CALLY and HORIZON-TALLY. Move graphic down 6 rows erasing bottom portion of graphic. Move graphic to right 8 rows.

Ideas:

Flipping a graphic and then modifying it gives amazing results. It will look as if you spent hours creating this Christmas Tree, but it's really quite simple. Just flip vertically and horizontally and simplify as shown.

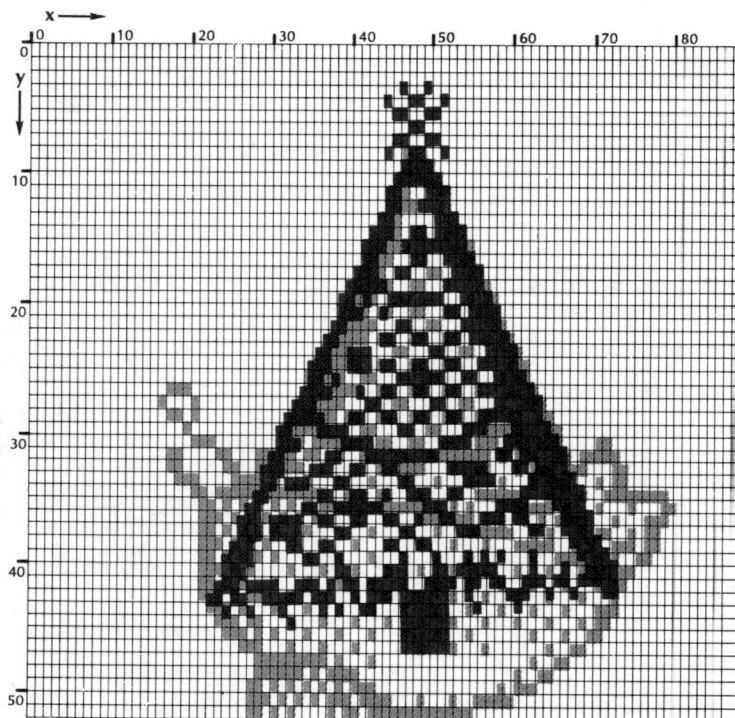

Applications:

See page 42.

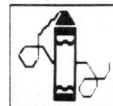

Emblem

What you need:

NP

Before & After:

(Picnic)

Special Instructions:
To begin, VERTICALLY
FLIP the Picnic graphic in-
side the grid.

Ideas:

Filling in and erasing becomes simple when a pat-
tern is embedded in Print
Shop art. This emblem is a
good example of looking at
a graphic and "seeing
something different."

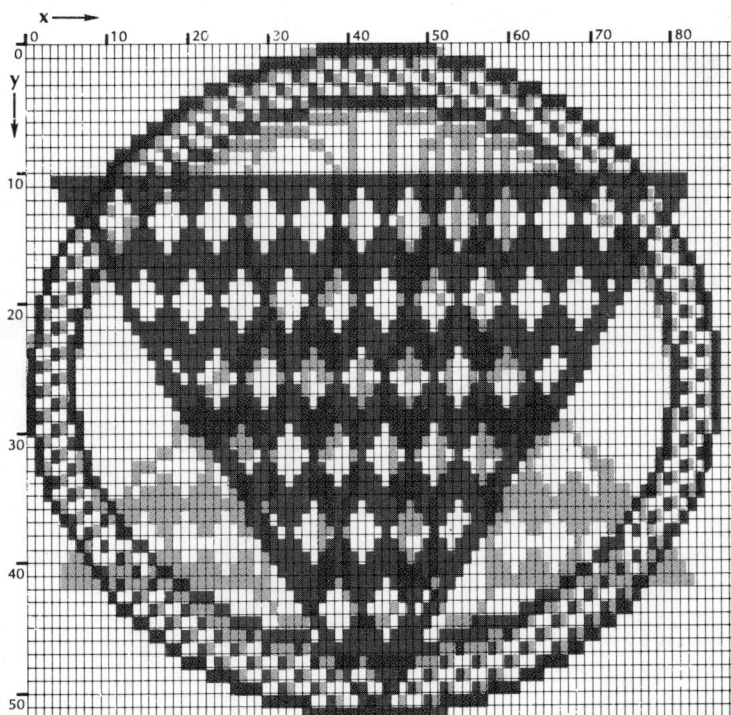

Applications:

See pages 60 and 130.

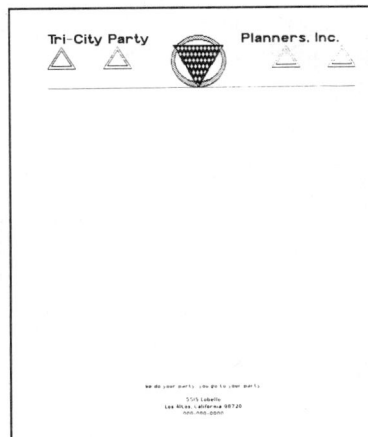

Pencil

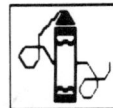

What you need:

NP

Before & After:

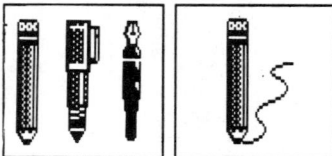

(Pens)

Special Instructions:
Center art in grid when finished.

Ideas:

Many times a message can be made stronger using one writing tool rather than the three in the Pens graphic. Try adding a decorative line or a distinct message emanating from the pencil lead. Try flipping vertically for a more logo-like graphic.

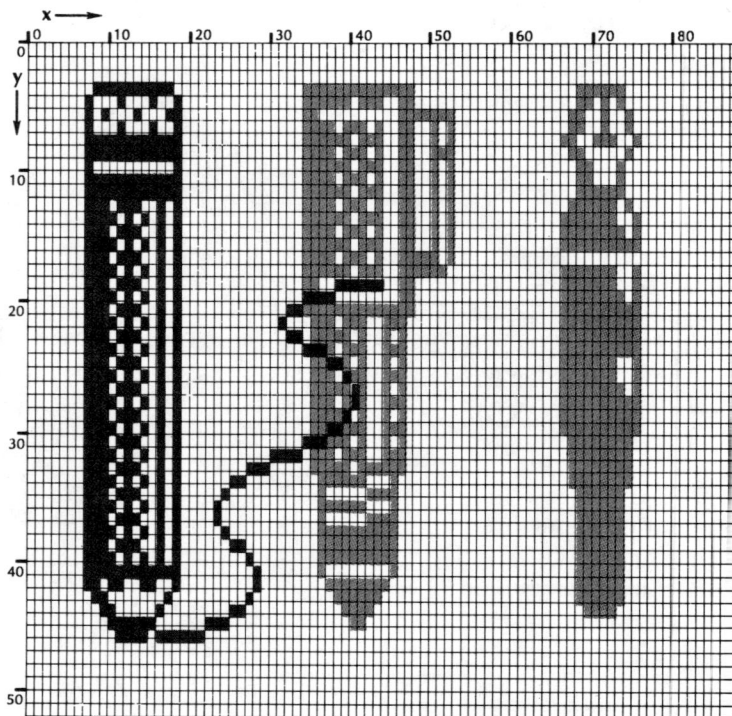

Applications:

See pages 50 and 132.

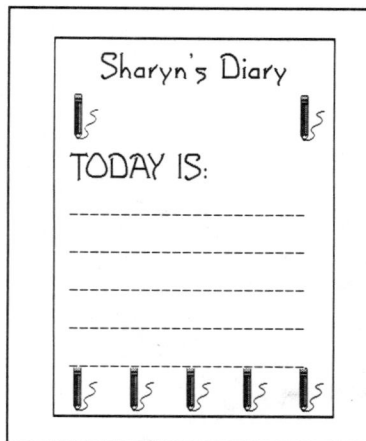

Pushpin/Left

What you need:

NP

Before & After:

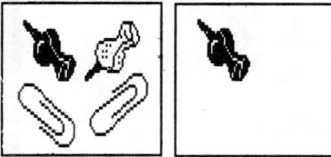

(Pushpins)

Ideas:

By selecting only the left pushpin, this art used in the corner of a sign or card with or without printed borders can add extra flair and whimsy to your message. Try placing the pushpin over a graphic to imply dimensionality.

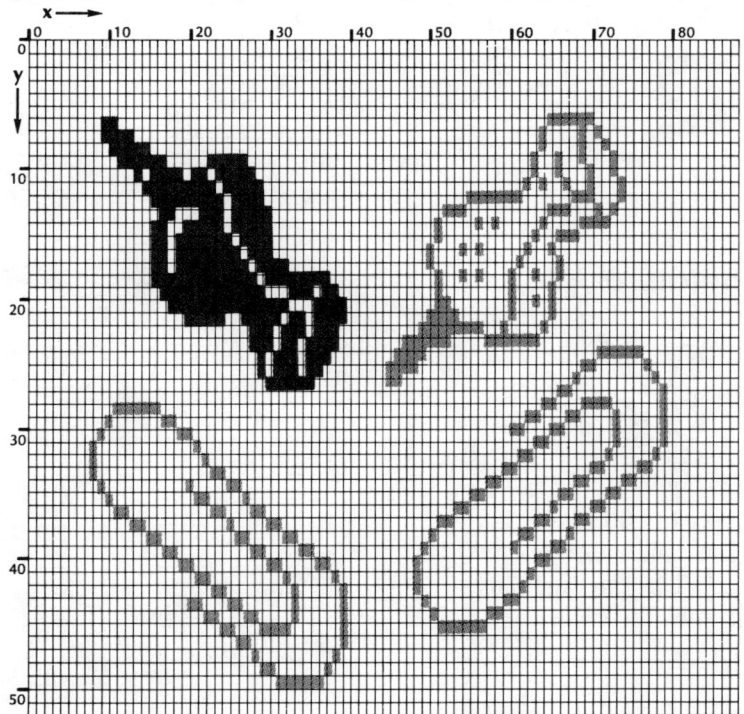

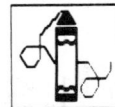

Pushpin/Right

What you need:

NP

Before & After:

(Pushpins)

Special Instructions:
To begin, HORIZONTAL-LY FLIP the Pushpins graphic in the grid.

Ideas:

By selecting only the right pushpin this art used in the corner of a sign or card with or without printed borders can add extra flair and whimsy to your message. Try placing the pushpin over a graphic to imply dimensionality.

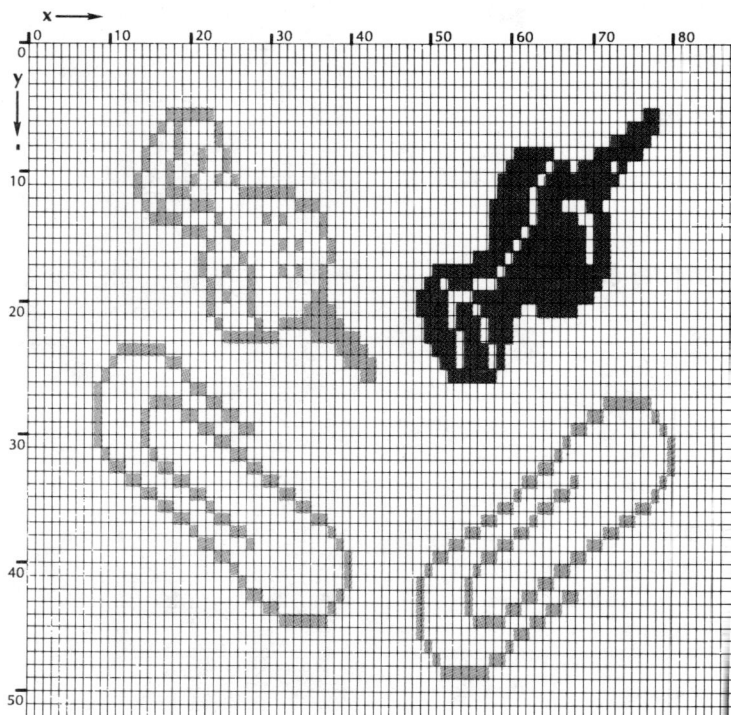

Applications:

See page 131.

Ribbon/First Place

What you need:

NP

Before & After:

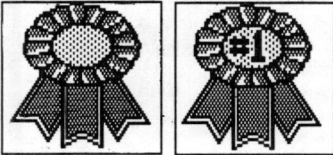

(Ribbon)

Ideas:

The personalization of any New Print Shop graphic always makes a design more powerful. Try adding the initials of the recipient in place of the word "1st."

Applications:

See page 110.

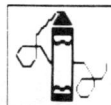

Sun Crest

What you need:

Before & After:

(Coffee)

Ideas:

A simple decorative emblem can be created by erasing this representative cup art. Now, instead of limited application, many variations can be employed. This graphic is very strong when used alone in a medium size and centered.

Applications:

See pages 37 and 74.

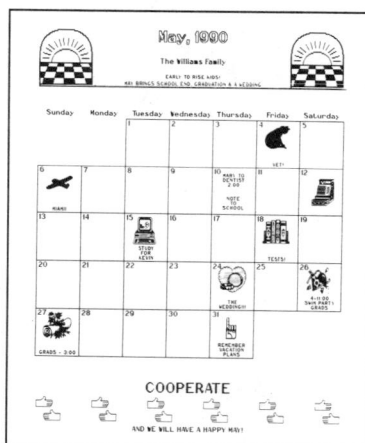

Stars & Stripes

What you need:

NP

Before & After:

(Eagle)

Ideas:

Look for bold and simple images embedded within New Print Shop graphics. Erasing parts of a graphic is easy to do and dramatic effects can be achieved.

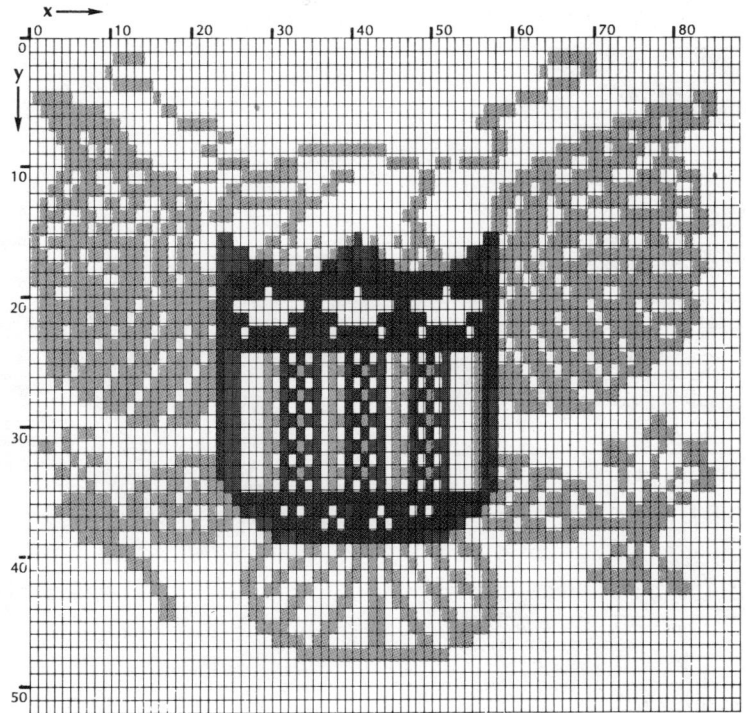

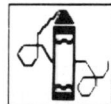

Airplane Solid

What you need:

Before & After:

(Airplane)

Ideas:

Turn an illustrative type graphic into a logo simply by erasing the decorative cloud and the propellers and filling in the plane. In addition to a logo or background pattern, the plane can be used for any travel-related message.

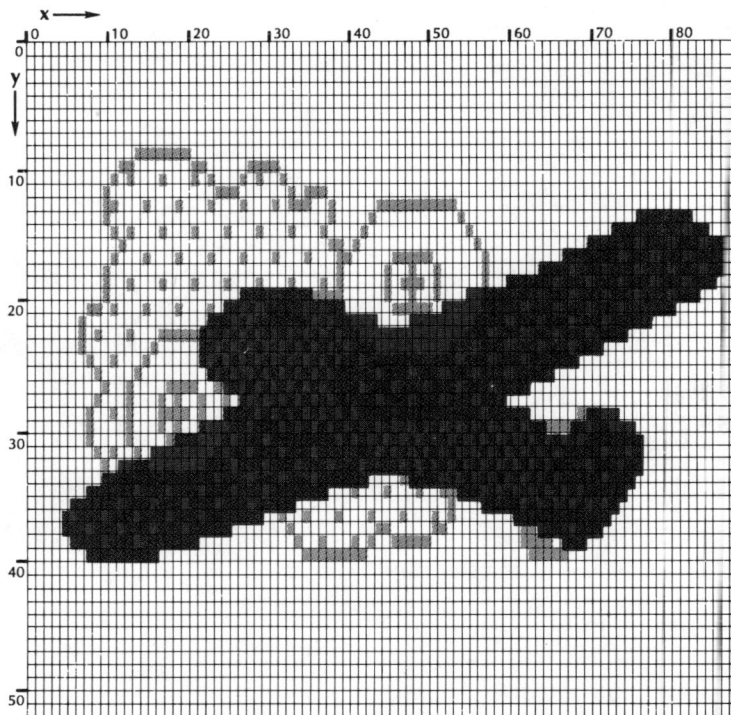

Applications:

See page 54.

Creature Maker/Giraffe

What you need:

Before & After:

(Giraffe)

Ideas:

Kids can play for hours at home, at a restaurant or in the car with headless Print Shop animals! Print out and copy on a copying machine. You can flip the giraffe and print two facing animals in the medium size for a "friendship" drawing or "story making design."

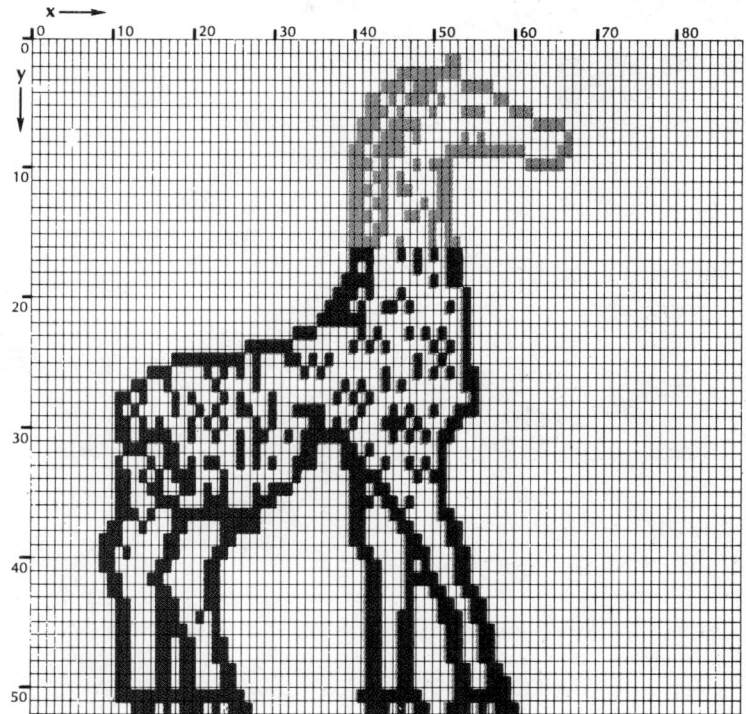

Applications:

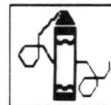

Creature Maker/Rabbit

What you need:

Before & After:

(Rabbit)

Ideas:

Many Print Shop graphics will fill creative playtime hours when modified. Try the Scottie, Baby Dino, Skier, or Man on the Sampler disk, or the Gingerbread on the Party disk for more laughs.

Applications:

See page 83.

Kitty Cat Solid

What you need:

Before & After:

(Kitty Cat))

Ideas:

A strong illustrative graphic becomes bolder and more symbolic for a wider range of uses when filled in using the Graphic Editor.

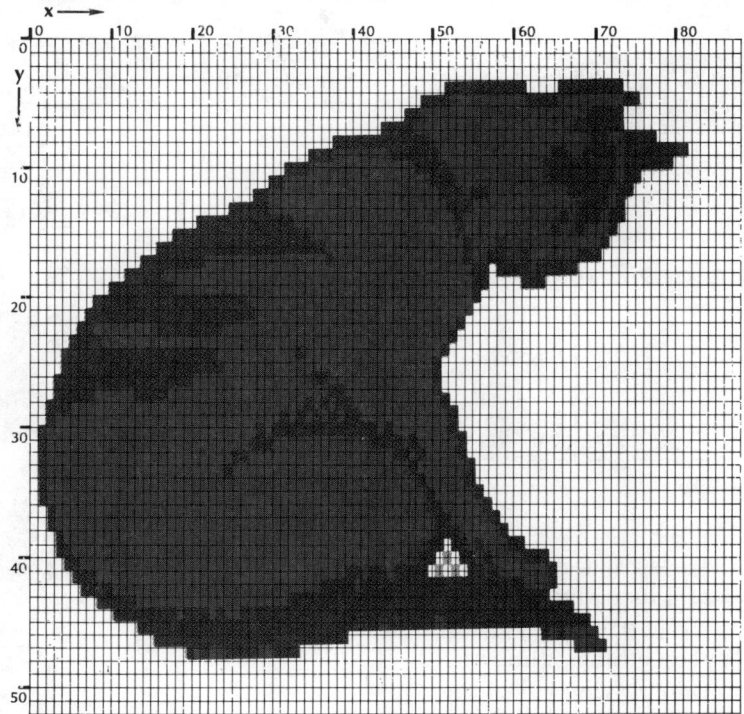

Applications:

See pages 73 and 133.

Pin-the-Tail!

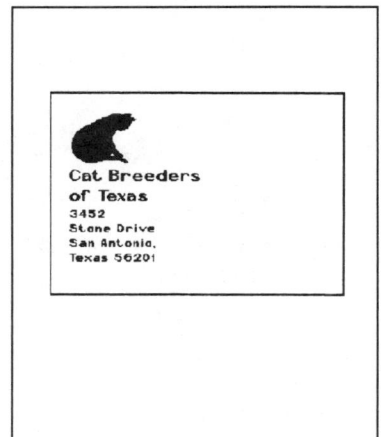

Cat Breeders
of Texas
3452
Stone Drive
San Antonio,
Texas 56201

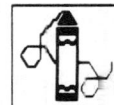

Man Symbol

What you need:

Before & After:

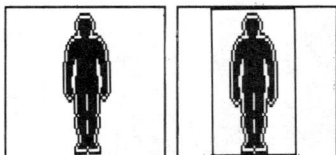

(Man)

Ideas:

A logo is created from a
more illustrative graphic
with just a few alterations.
Try smoothing, filling in
and simplifying any of the
New Print Shop graphics
to create strong symbols.

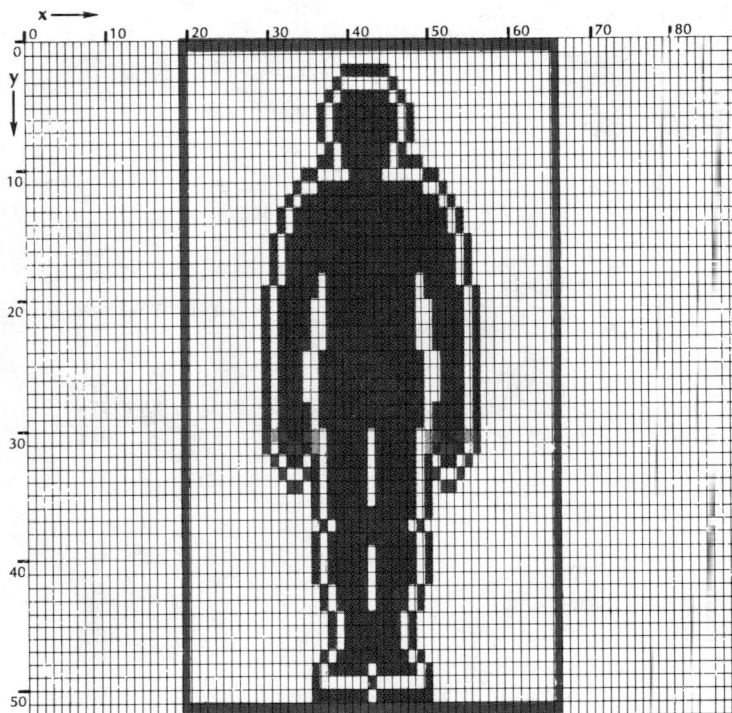

Man of Strength Symbol

What you need:

Before & After:

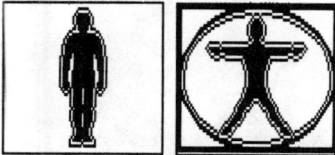

(Man)

Ideas:

With a few simple addi-
tion to a figurative
graphic, a more logo-like
image is created.

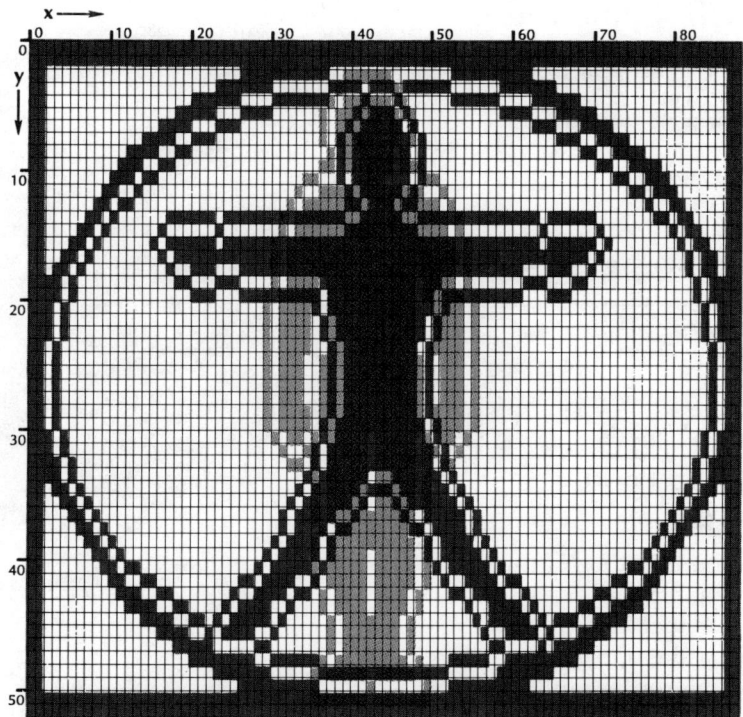

Applications:

See page 92.

Piggy Bank Graphic

What you need:

Before & After:

(Piggy Bank)

Ideas:

Simplification of this graphic makes it a stronger image with broader application. Children, organization fund raisers, bank promotions, and retail businesses at sale time can benefit from this symbol.

Applications:

See page 112.

Arrow Left

What you need:

NP **S/B**

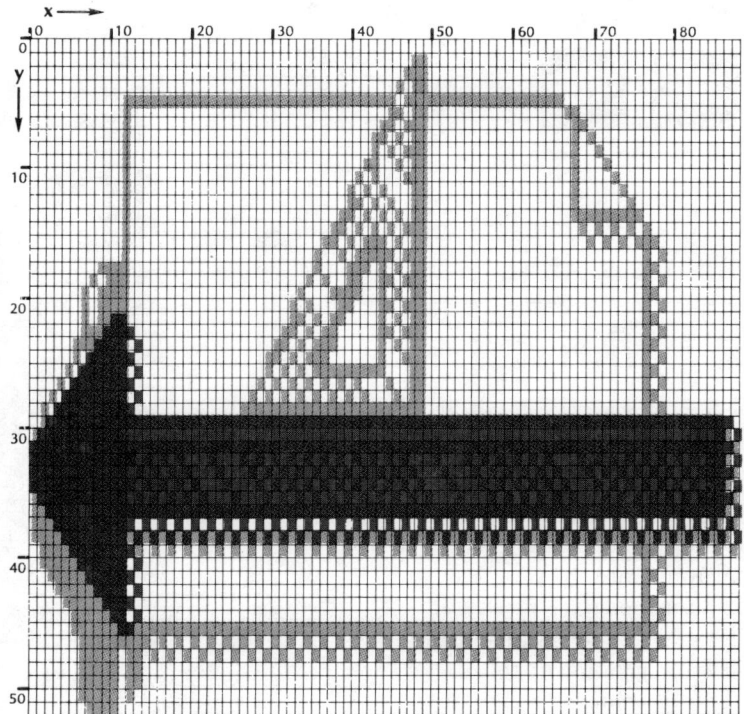

Before & After:

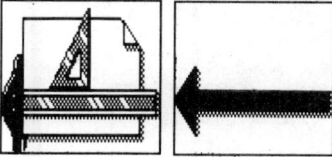

(Drafting)

Special Instructions:
Center arrow from top to bottom in grid when finished. (Move arrow up approximately 8 rows.)

Ideas:

Arrows are simple to create with this image. Flipping horizontally will give you an arrow in the opposite direction. Combine with text in your design for a direction sign or use in repetition for a dynamic pattern.

Applications:

See page 144.

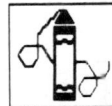

Graphic Pattern

What you need:

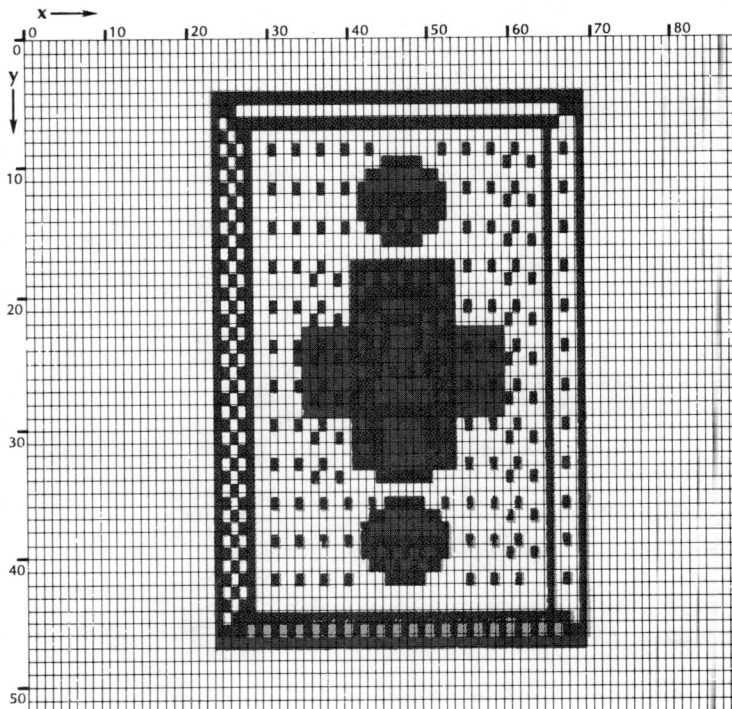

Before & After:

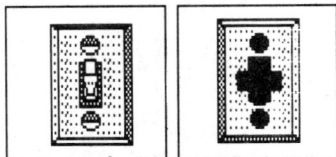

(Switch)

Special Instructions:
When you load the Switch
graphic into the Graphic
Editor mode, a simplified,
less detailed version of the
Switch graphic appears.
This graphic, as shown in
the Before position, con-
verts easily into the
generic pattern shown in
the After position. To see
the actual Switch graphic
as it appears in Print Shop
designs, see page 285.

Ideas:

New Print Shop graphics that
are completely symmetrical
or have embedded elements
that are geometric make excellent candidates for modifying. The Switch is easily
changed into a decorative
design that can be used as a
tile pattern or as spot art.

Large House

What you need:

NP **S/B**

Before & After:

(School)

Ideas:

This original graphic can be modified to become a large home or type of organization headquarters such as a fraternity, sorority, or club. A social services group could benefit from combining this graphic with a more representative image of their service.

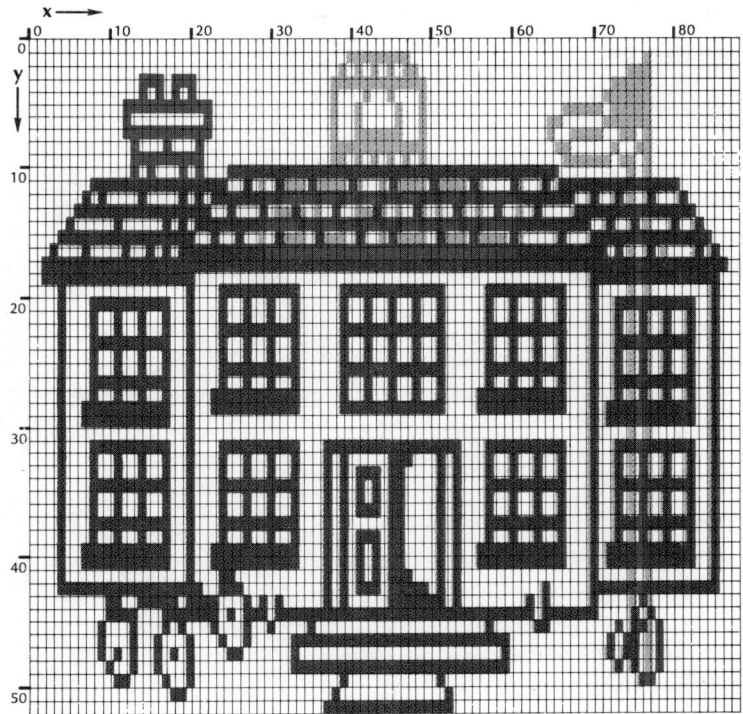

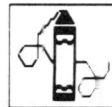

Man Profile

What you need:

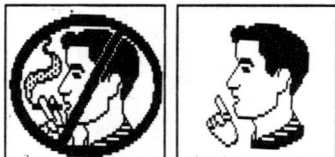

Before & After:

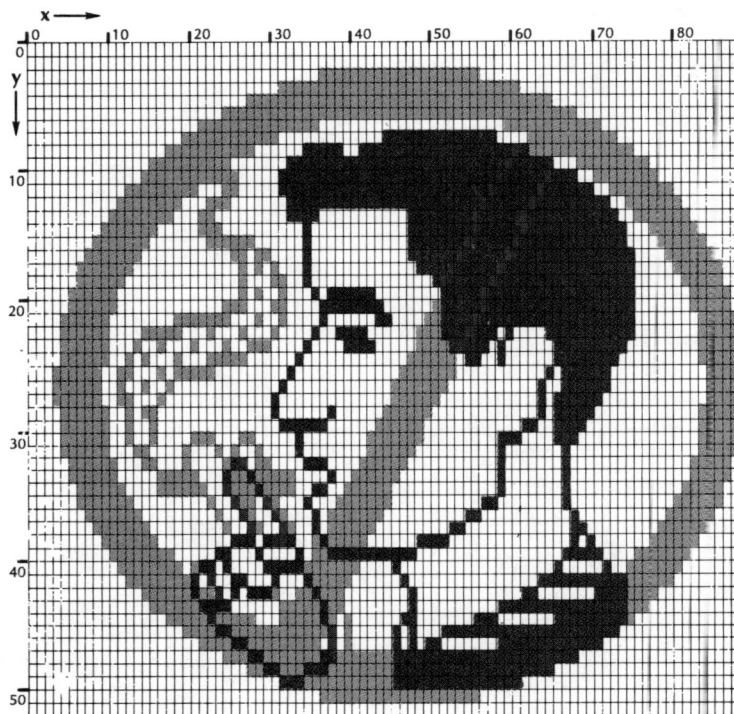

(No Smoking)

Ideas:

Half of a New Print Shop graphic can be very different without its other component. The Man Profile can be used alone or with other graphics such as the Quote balloon with text inside.

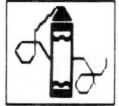

No Symbol

What you need:

NP **S/B**

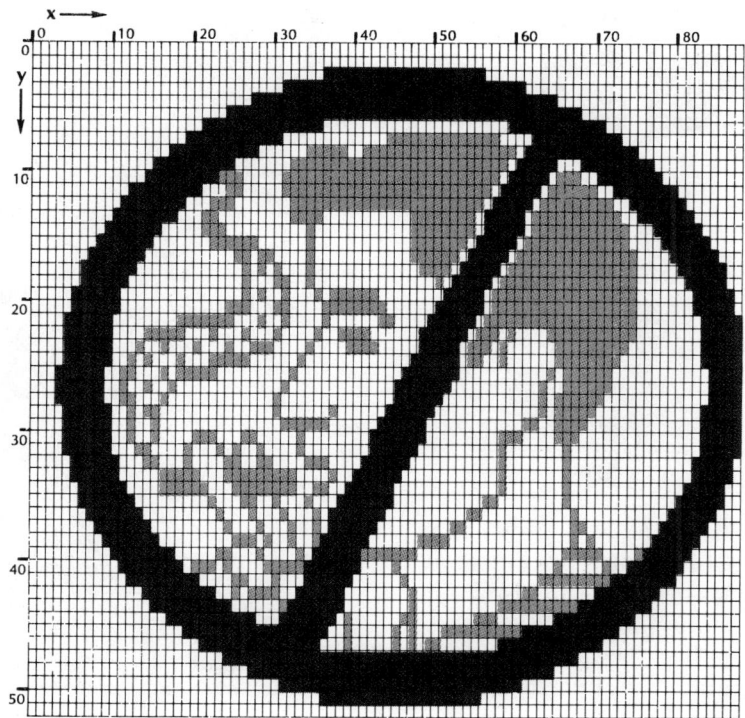

Before & After:

(No Smoking)

Ideas:

Split one New Print Shop graphic into two by first erasing one image and then the other. Print this No symbol over dozens of other graphics or text. For example, use a fish graphic for "No Fishing!"

Applications:

See page 64.

Please Write Chalkboard

What you need:

Before & After:

(Chalkboard)

Ideas:

Chalkboards are meant for messages and New Print Shop graphics are perfect for alteration— and instant personalization! Try other messages such as "I Love You," "I Miss You" or "I (heart symbol) (a friend's name)."

Rubber Stamp

What you need:

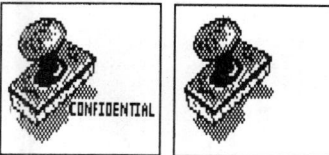

Before & After:

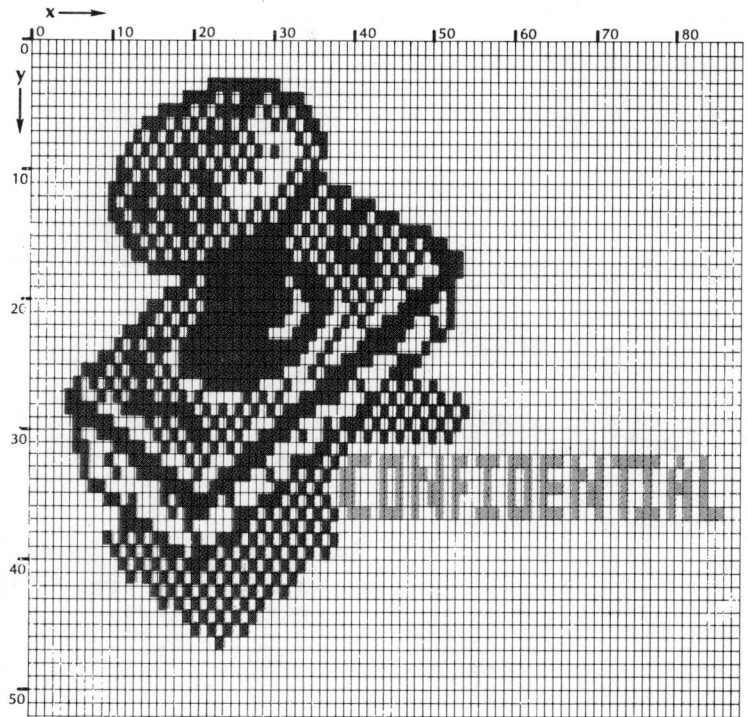

(Stamp)

Ideas:

Any message can be added to this rubber stamp such as "Past Due" or "Time to Write." Or you can type text on your sign, card, or letterhead positioning it near your stamp graphic. Not only is the latter method simpler than adding text with the Graphic Editor, but a longer message can be used.

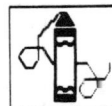

Crest Frame

What you need:

Before & After:

(Open House)

Special Instructions:
Center art in grid when
finished.

Ideas:

By simplifying the Open
House graphic, a versatile
crest is created which can
serve many different pur-
poses. With initials, the
crest can be used on greeting cards or stationery, or
as a lawn sign for a party.
Just print in the banner
mode and reprint your
oversized house numbers
or birthday child's name.

Applications:

See page 95.

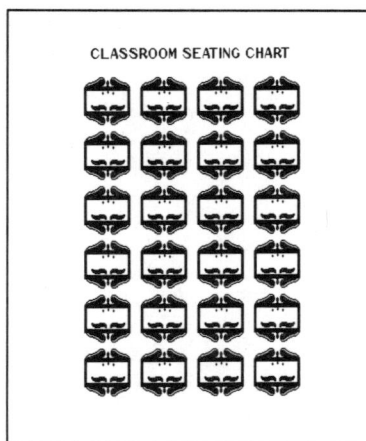

CLASSROOM SEATING CHART

Festive Graphic

What you need:

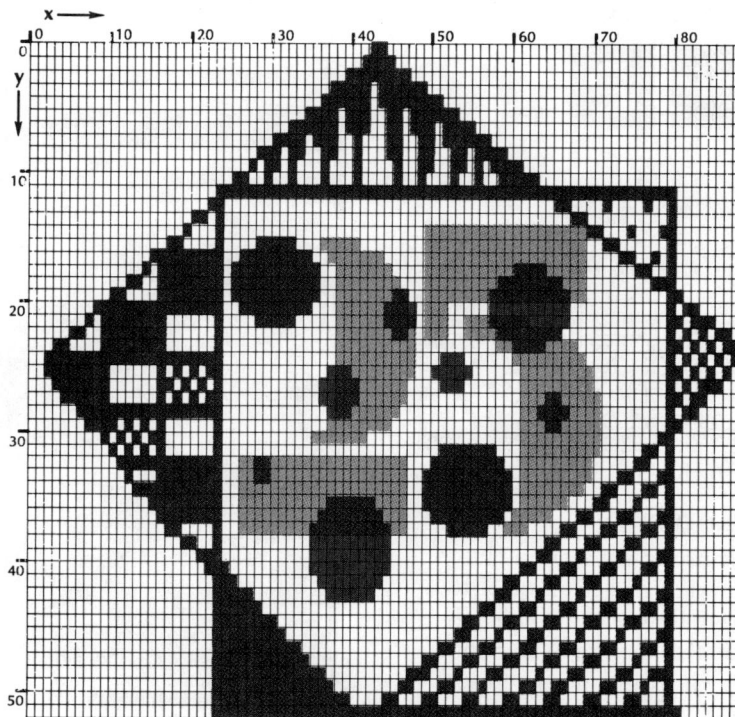

Before & After:

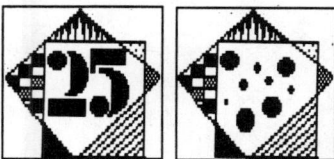

(Twenty-Five)

Ideas:

Many Print Shop graphics lend themselves to simplification resulting in a graphic that can be used as a decorative element. Whether used alone or in repetition, the Festive Graphic has many different applications.

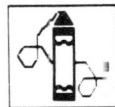

Pumpkin

What you need:

Before & After:

(Black Cat)

Ideas:

Grinning out from a Halloween card or taped onto a window or door, this graphic is sure to be a hit. Try printing oversized and cutting out the eyes, nose, and mouth. Then tape yellow cellophane paper over the holes in the back. Turn on a light behind your pumpkin and watch him glow!

Waiter

What you need:

NP **P**

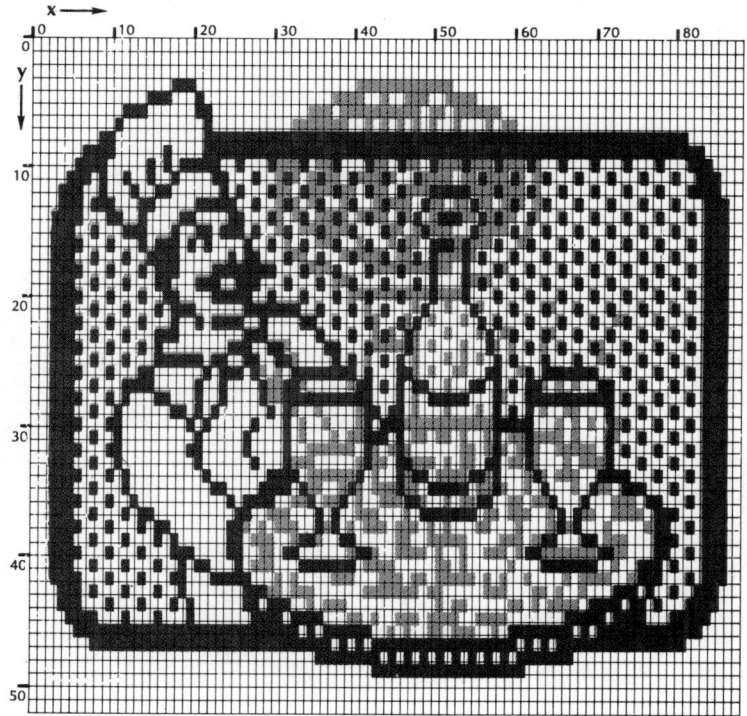

Before & After:

(Pizza)

Ideas:

In addition to symbolic art, bold art can be created by modifying and simplifying New Print Shop graphics. The Waiter emerges bolder, yet remains illustrative when the pizza is erased.

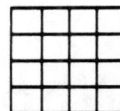

Planning Tools

- THE LAYOUTS

- CUSTOMIZE FEATURES—AT A GLANCE

- THE FONTS

- THE GRAPHICS

- ABOUT THE ART GRID

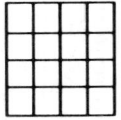

What's in This Section

The planning section is a collections of tools to use when you're working on an original New Print Shop creation. You'll find all New Print Shop fonts, graphics and layouts to help you plan and organize your design ideas. With the planning tools at your side you'll be able to fine tune your design before you even turn on your computer.

Highlighted for you here is an overview of what you'll find in this section:

The Layouts: 58 New Print Shop layout possibilities— the patterns of graphics available for starting your design.

The Fonts: All New Print Shop program fonts with specifications indicating how many letters fit on a line and how many lines fit on a page.

The Customize Features: A "visual" overview of all available options for customizing your design.

The Graphics: Every graphic from *The New Print Shop* program, *The Party Edition, The School & Business Edition* and *The Sampler Edition* all in one place.

The Art Grid: A blank art grid to copy and use for your own original graphics.

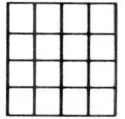

Using This Section

When you're working on an original New Print Shop design, remember the planning tools. Use them to determine the right layout for your pictures and the right font for your words. Use them to eliminate guesswork —know in advance the choices that will best suit your design. Use the planning tools to save time and paper.

Highlighted here are suggestions for approaching this section and getting the most mileage out of the planning tools.

Suggestion #1: Put the handbook layouts to work for you. They're invaluable guides for determining in advance where to place pictures on the page.

Suggestion #2: If a design requires a customized layout, use the handbook layouts to find the best starting point. The quickest way to create your own customized layout is to use the New Print Shop layout requiring the fewest number of changes.

Suggestion #3: Use the font specifications to find the font or fonts best suited for the look of your design and the amount of test you want to include. If you have a lot to say, try mixing a large font with a smaller one.

Suggestion #4: When you're thinking of a new design idea, look at the patterns created by the placement of graphics in the handbook layouts. The pattern possibilities may trigger ideas.

Suggestion #5: Expand your creativity. Use the customize features section to consider new ways to manipulate graphics and add excitement to your designs.

Suggestion #6: Plan ahead! Use the tools to organize your thoughts before you even boot up your disk.

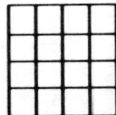

The Layouts

The New Print Shop offers more than 50 layout possibilities. And all of them can be customized to meet the exact needs of your design.

When you're planning a new design, call on the Handbook layouts. They show the variety of graphic patterns available in the sign, greeting card, letterhead and calendar top modes.

If you're about to begin working on a new design but are not certain of the graphic pattern best suited to your needs flip through the Handbook layouts. Looking at the possibilities may help focus your ideas.

If you know what size graphics you want to include in a design and where you want to place them, first check to see if that layout already exists. If not, select the layout closest to what you have in mind. Then use the customize feature to make the necessary modifications.

With the Handbook layouts by your side you'll know the quickest way to get the job done—before you even turn on your computer.

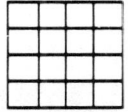

Layouts/FOR SIGN/WIDE AND CARD/TOP FOLD

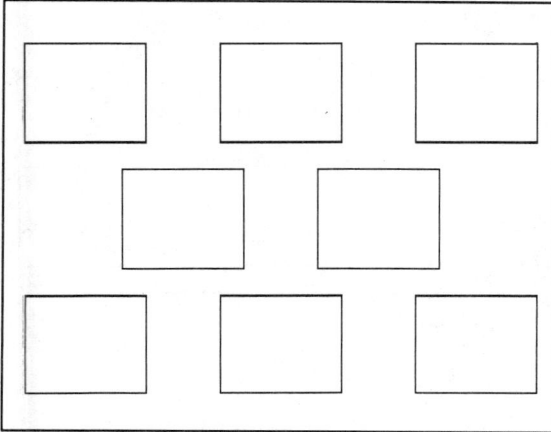

Small Staggered

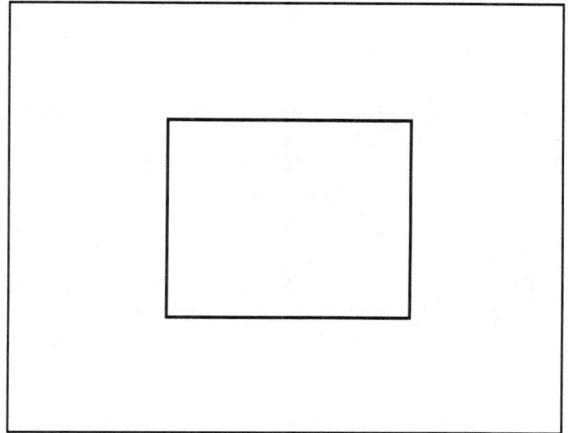

Medium Centered

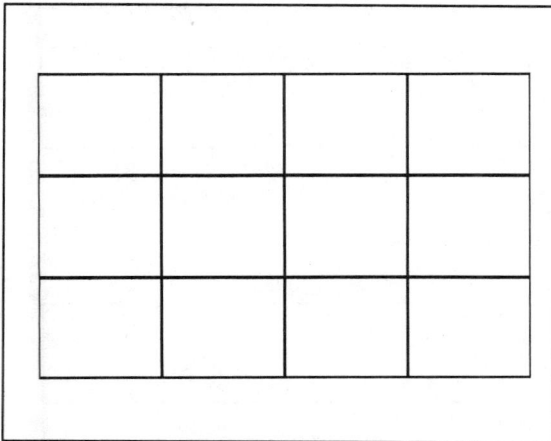

Small Tiled

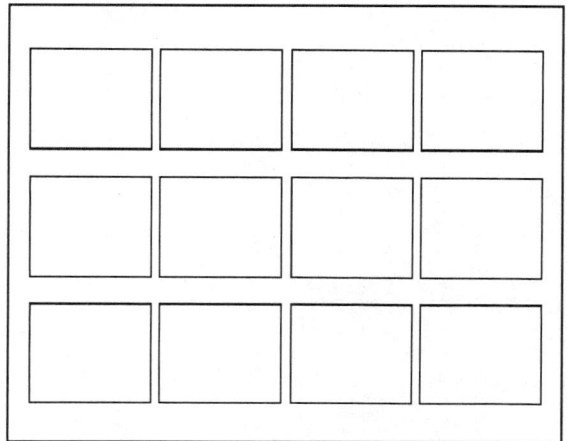

Small Tiled II

Layouts/FOR SIGN/WIDE AND CARD/TOP FOLD

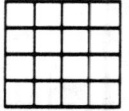

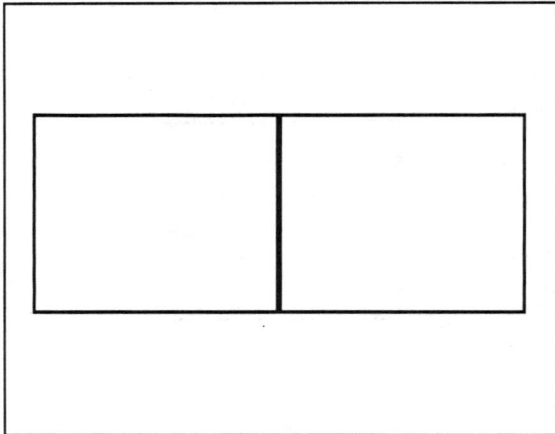

Medium Pair

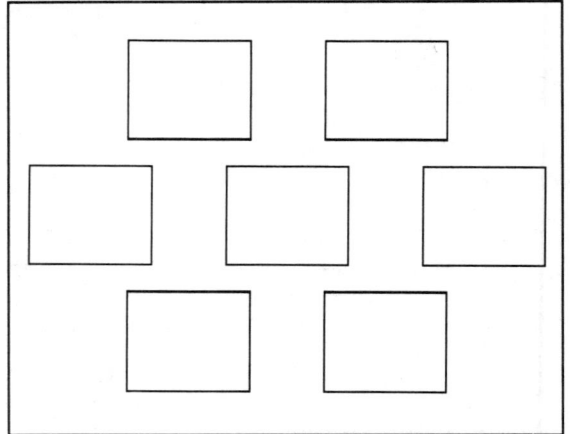

Small Staggered II

Small Rows

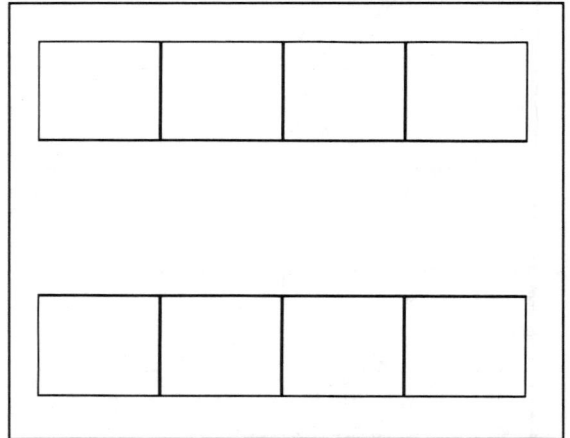

Small Rows II

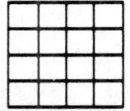

Layouts/FOR SIGN/WIDE AND CARD/TOP FOLD

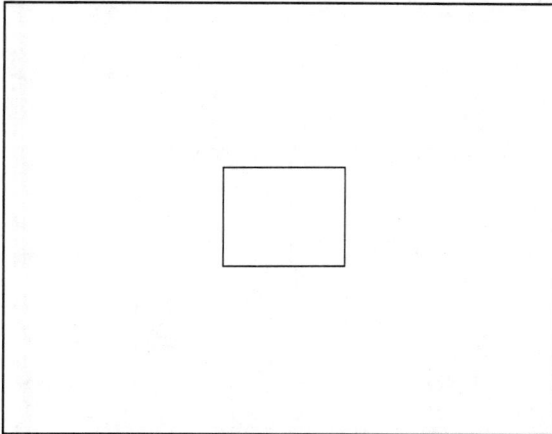

Small Centered

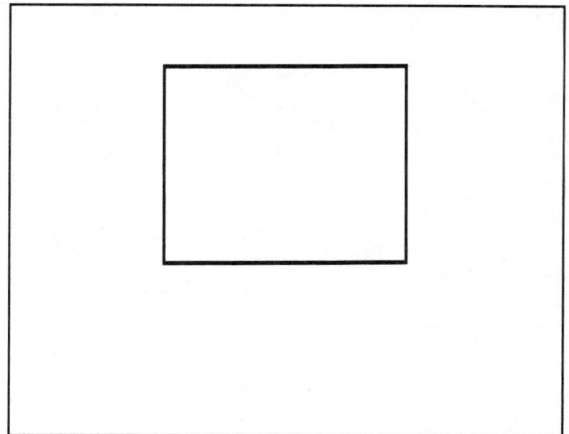

Medium Top

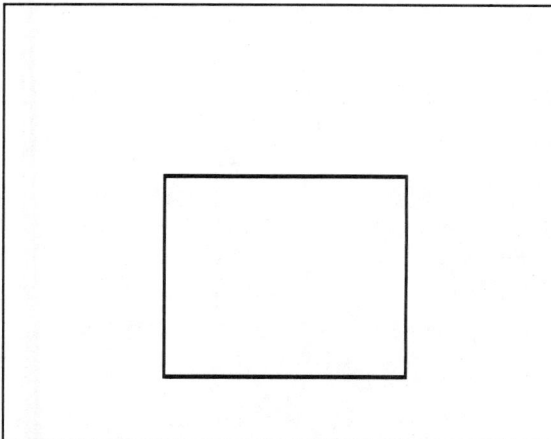

Medium Bottom

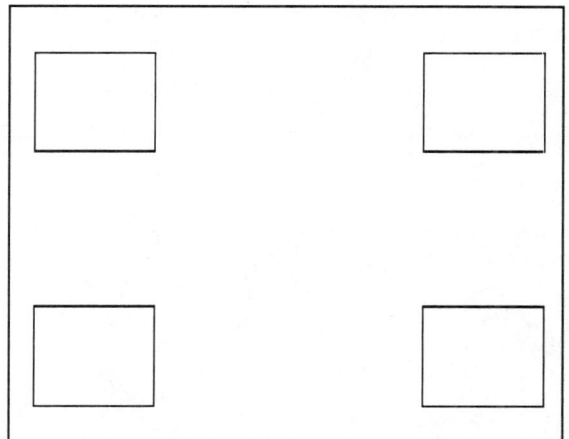

Small Corners

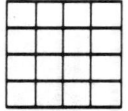

Layouts/FOR SIGN/WIDE AND CARD/TOP FOLD

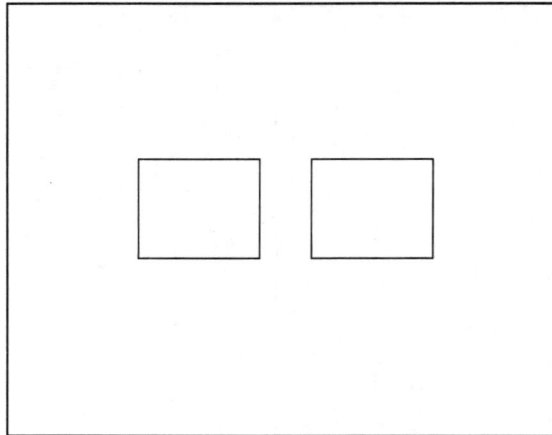

Small Pair

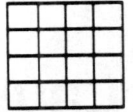

Layouts/FOR SIGN/TALL AND CARD/SIDE FOLD

Small Staggered

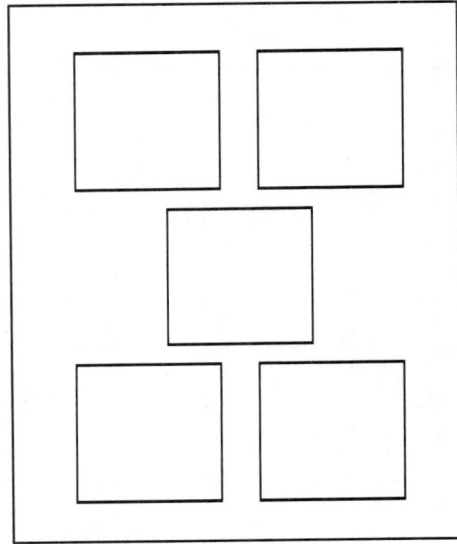

Medium Staggered

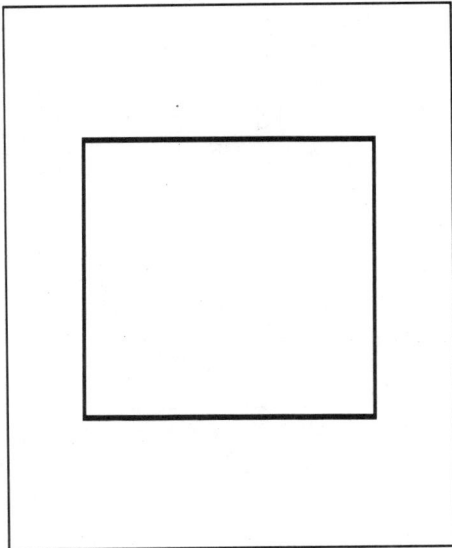

Large Center

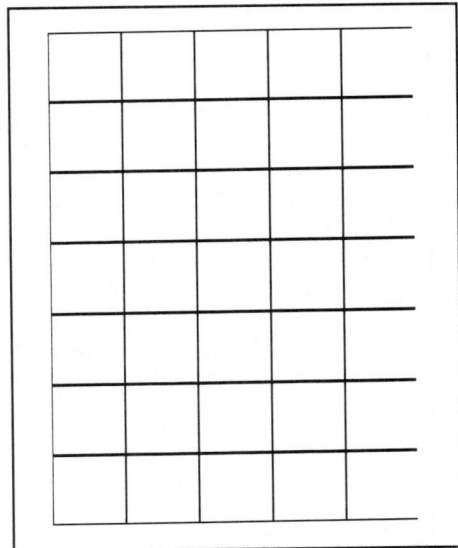

Small Tiled

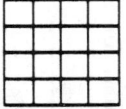

Layouts/FOR SIGN/TALL AND CARD/SIDE FOLD

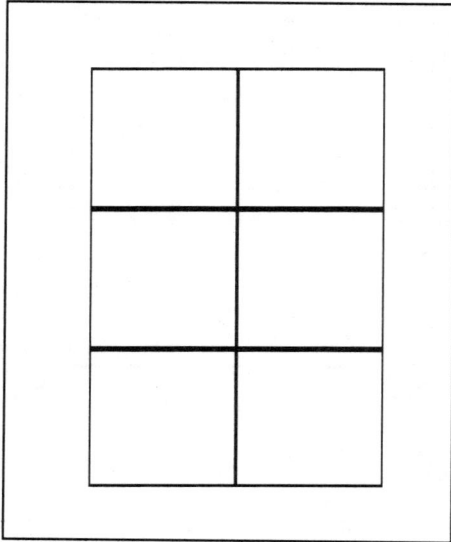

Medium Tiled

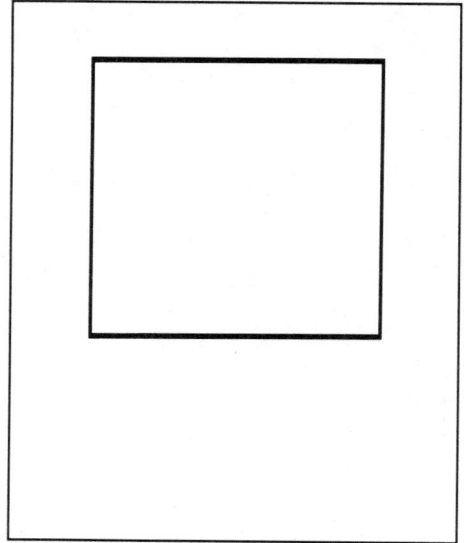

Large Top

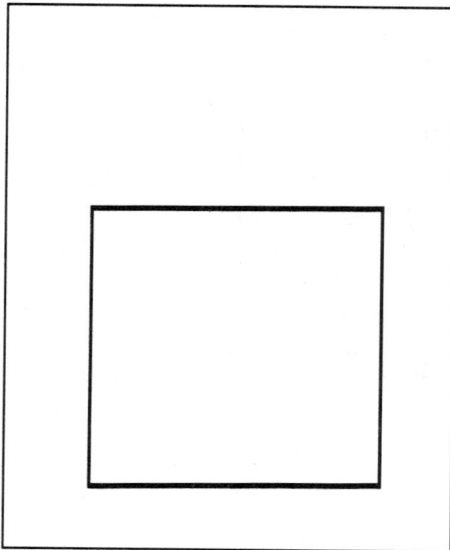

Large Bottom

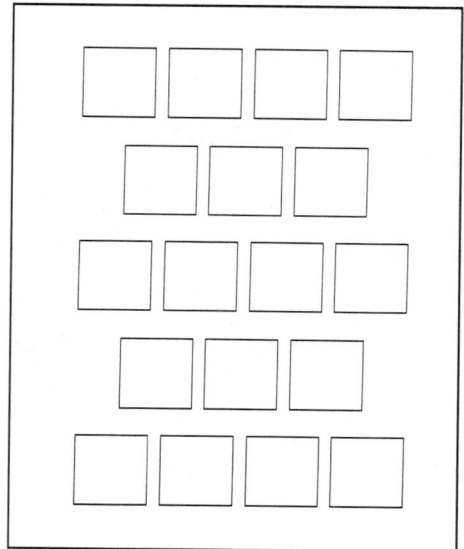

Small Staggered II

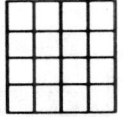

Layouts/FOR SIGN/TALL AND CARD/SIDE FOLD

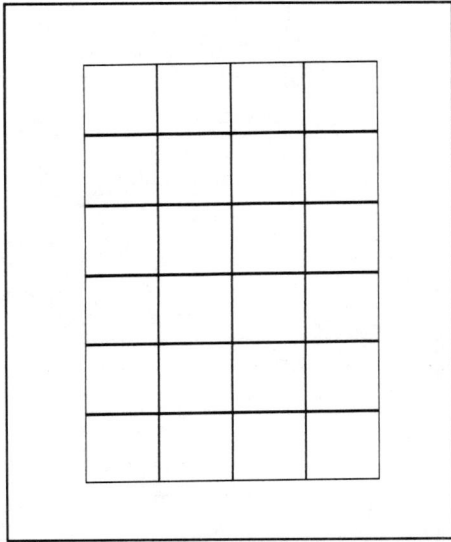

Small Tiled II

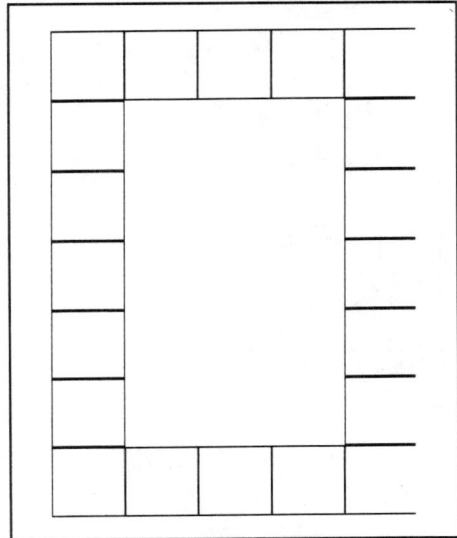

Small Frame

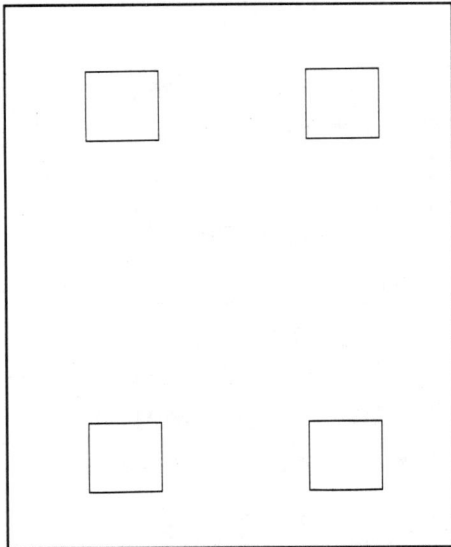

Small Corners

Small Pair

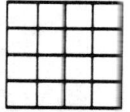

Layouts/FOR SIGN/TALL AND CARD/SIDE FOLD

Small Centered

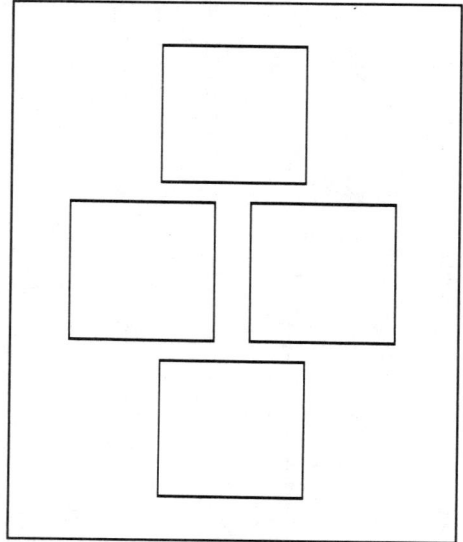

Medium Staggered II

Medium Tiled II

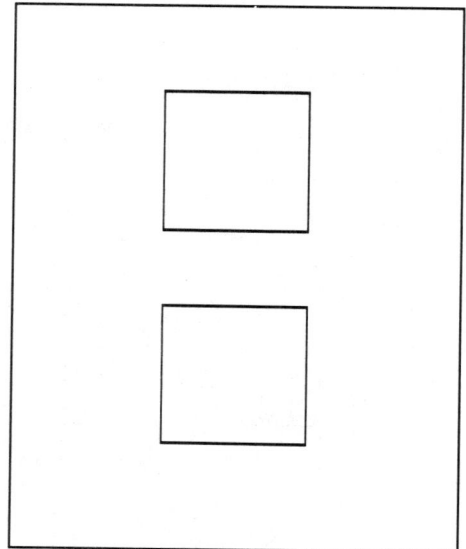

Medium Pair

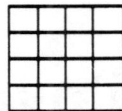

Layouts/FOR SIGN/TALL AND CARD/SIDE FOLD

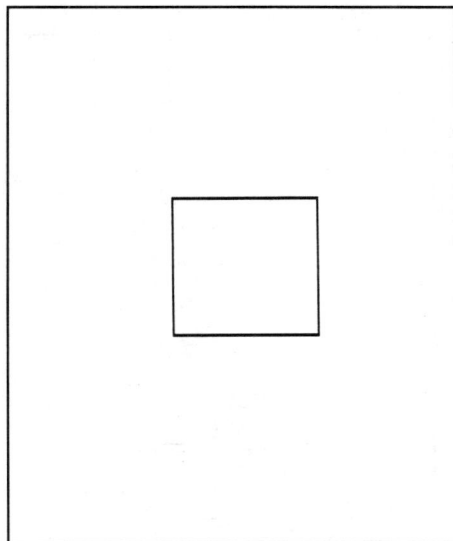

Medium Centered

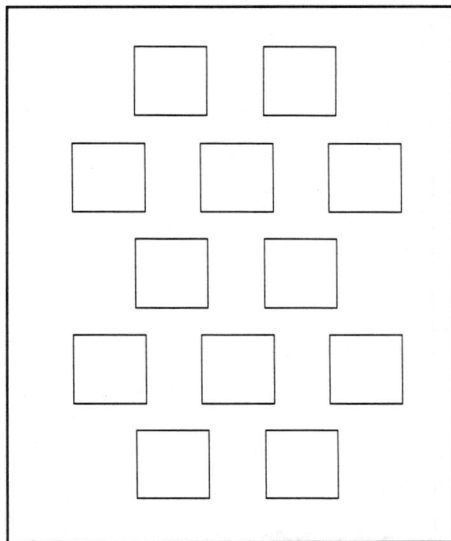

Small Staggered III

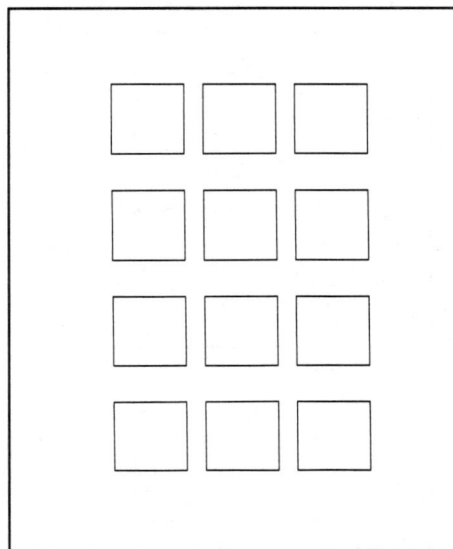

Matrix

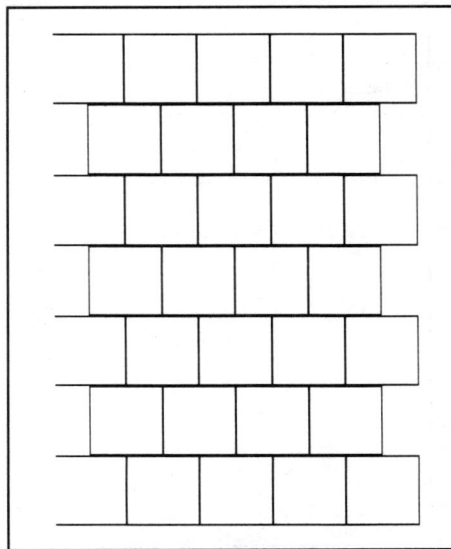

Bricks

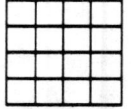

Layouts/ FOR SIGN/TALL AND CARD/SIDE FOLD

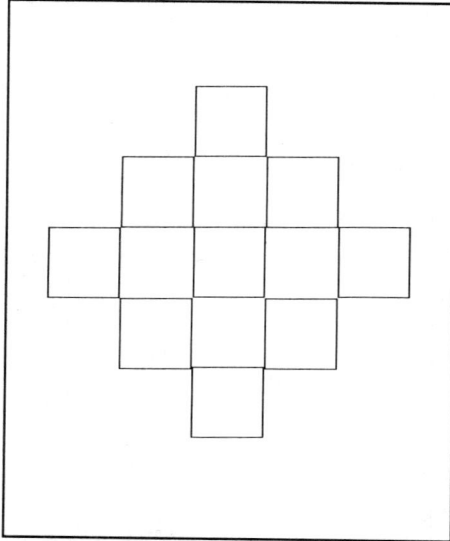

Small Diamond

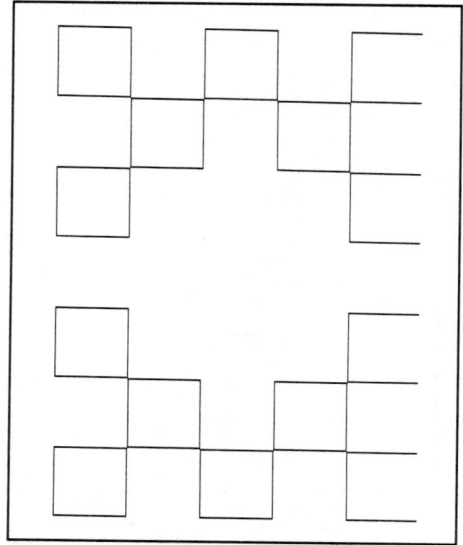

Reversed Diamond

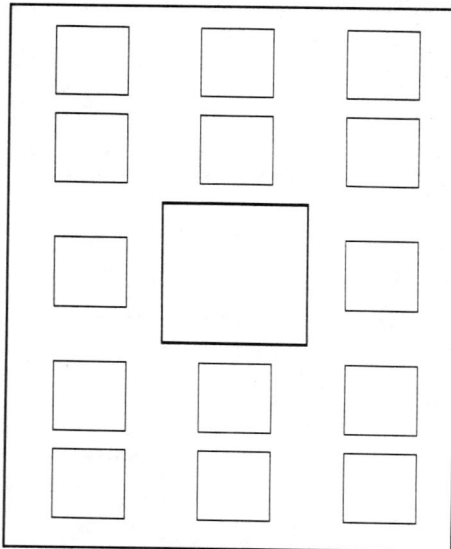

Medium Mix

Mixed Columns

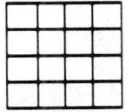

Layouts/FOR SIGN/TALL AND CARD/SIDE FOLD

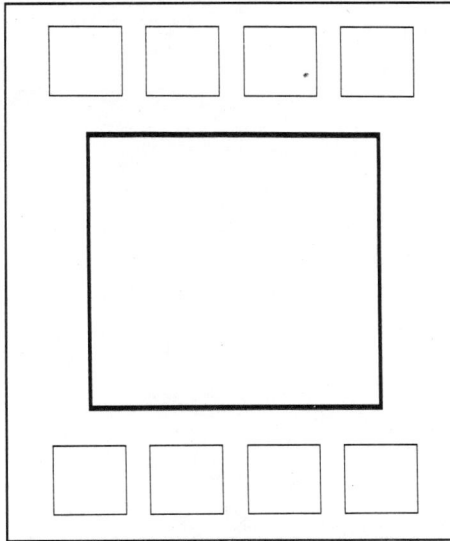

Mixed Rows

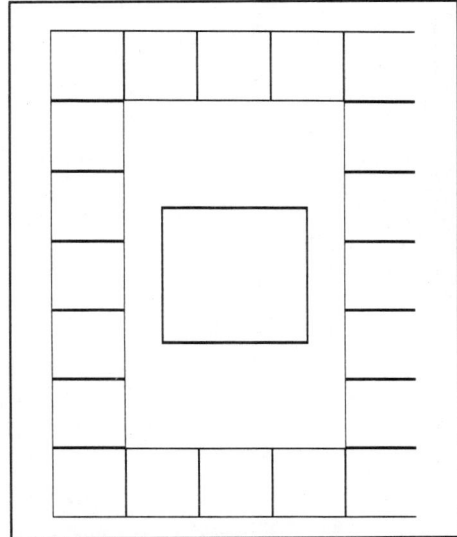

Medium Framed

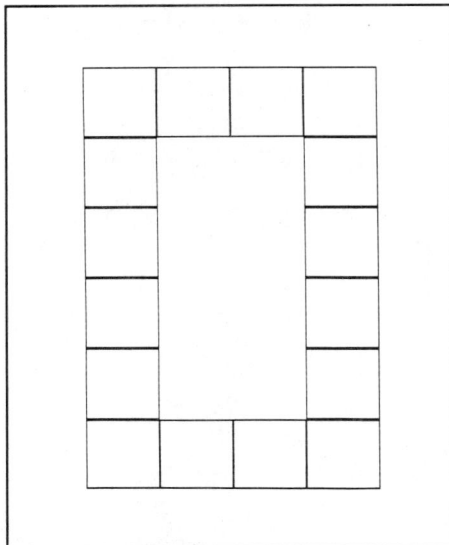

Small Frame II

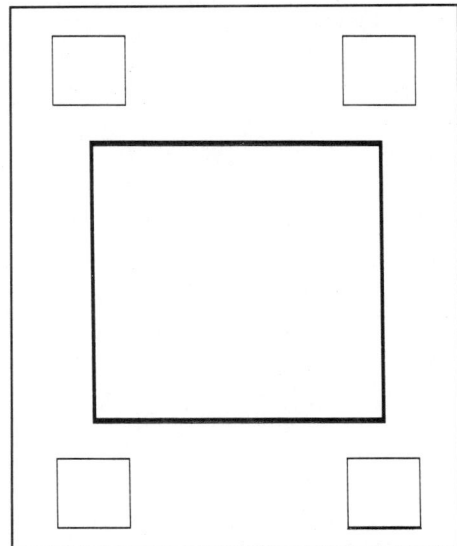

Large Cornered

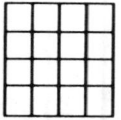

Layouts/FOR LETTERHEADS

Small Staggered

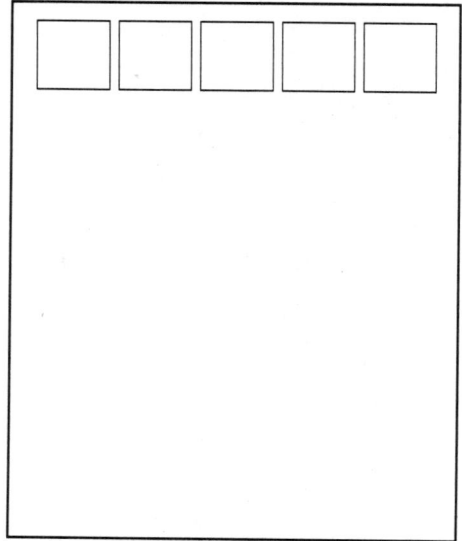

Medium Staggered

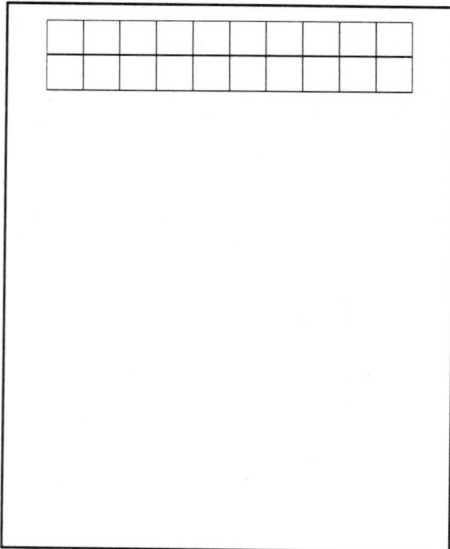

Small Tiled

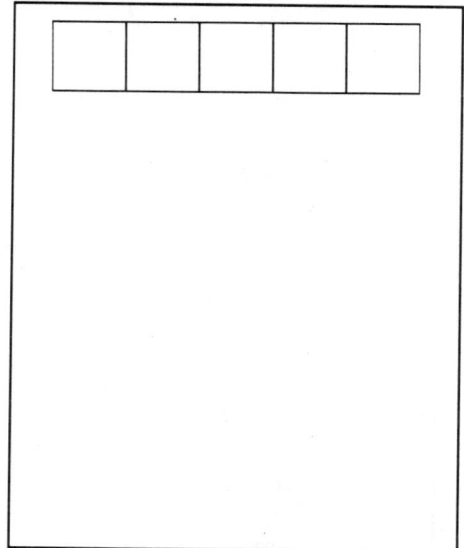

Medium Tiled

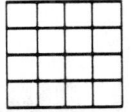

Layouts/FOR LETTERHEADS

Small Ends

Small Ends II

Small Ends III

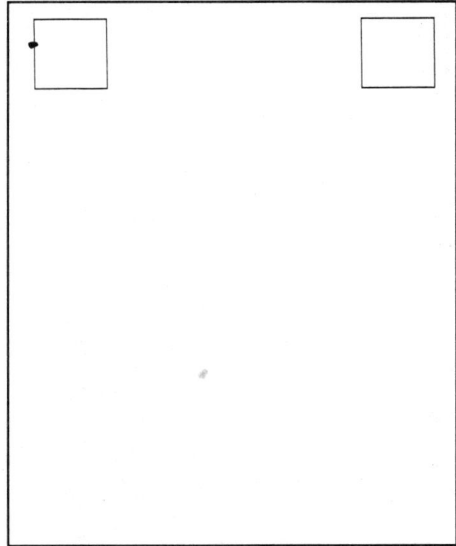

Medium Ends

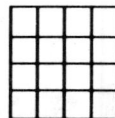

Layouts/FOR LETTERHEADS

Small Left

Medium Left

Small Right

Medium Right

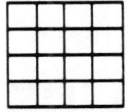

Layouts/FOR LETTERHEADS

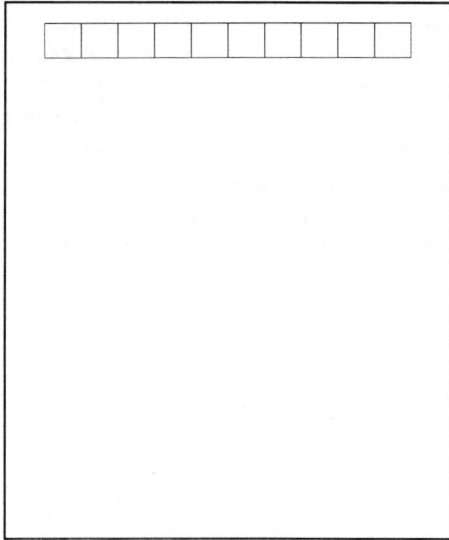

Small Center Row

Small Staggered II

Customize Features at a Glance

The New Print Shop lets you customize any design by manipulating graphics. Now you can move graphics to anywhere on the page. You can mix a variety of graphics and graphic sizes. You can stretch or shrink your pictures. Clone or flip your images. With the customize features at your fingertips, the design possibilities are endless.

Here, at a glance, is a "visual" overview of the customize features. Use this section to spark new ideas and expand the creative boundaries of your Print Shop designs.

Customize Features at a Glance

FEATURE	BEFORE	AFTER
MOVE	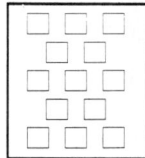	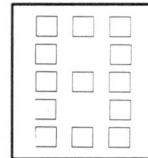
DELETE	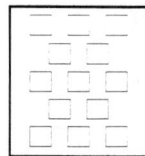	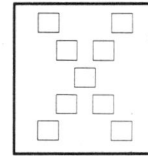
FLIP HORIZONTAL		
FLIP VERTICAL		
CLONE		
INSERT	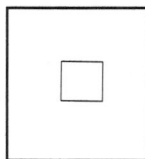	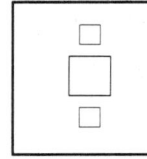

GRAPHIC STYLES

Solid

Outline

3-D

Raised

Shadow

STRETCH

SHRINK

IBM ONLY

ENLARGE

REDUCE

The Fonts

The New Print Shop program offers 12 different fonts. (For an overview, see page 269.) Each font, or text style, has a unique look and can accommodate a certain number of letters per line and a certain number of lines per page.

Turn to the font section when you're working on a new design and need to determine which text style best suits your message. The approximate number of letters that fit on a line (character count) and number of lines that fit on a page (line count) are indicated for all New Print Shop program fonts.

If you're working on an IBM or IBM-compatible system, use the printed font samples to see what each font looks like on the page and also to determine the character and line counts for the TALL sign and greeting card options. Use the chart at the left of each font to determine character and line counts for the WIDE options.

If you're working on an Apple II system, use the printed font samples to see what each font looks like on the page. Use the chart at the left of each font to determine the character and lines counts for both the TALL and WIDE sign and greeting card options.

It is important to note that the number of letters that fit on a line for each font will vary slightly depending on the width of the actual letters you select. For example, if your words have many narrow letters such as i's and l's, you may fit more letters on a line. If your words have many wide letters such as m's and w's, you may fit fewer on a line.

Use the font section to determine which font best suits your needs. Select a font that not only has the right look for your design but can accommodate all of your words. If you have a lot to say, try using a large, bold font for your headline and a small font for less important details. Remember—mixing fonts can help you get more mileage out of your design space.

The Fonts/AMADOR

TALL LAYOUT

Font Size	Caps/ Lowercase (LC)	No. Lines/ Page	Approx. No. Charac./Line
Small	Caps	8	13
Small	LC	8	14
Large	Caps	4	6
Large	LC	4	6

WIDE LAYOUT

Font Size	Caps/ Lowercase (LC)	No. Lines/ Page	Approx. No. Charac./Line
Small	Caps	4	11
Small	LC	4	12
Large	Caps	2	5
Large	LC	2	5

The Fonts/AMADOR

Small

ABCDEFGHIJKLM
B
C
D
E
F
G
H

abcdefghijklmn
b
c
d
e
f
g
h

Large

ABCDEF
B
C
D

abcdef
b
c
d

The Fonts/IMPERIAL

TALL LAYOUT

Font Size	Caps/ Lowercase (LC)	No. Lines/ Page	Approx. No. Charac./Line
Small	Caps	9(IBM)/8(APP)	11
Small	LC	9(IBM/8(APP)	14
Large	Caps	4	5
Large	LC	4	7

WIDE LAYOUT

Font Size	Caps/ Lowercase (LC)	No. Lines/ Page	Approx. No. Charac./Line
Small	Caps	4	10
Small	LC	4	12
Large	Caps	2	4
Large	LC	2	6

The Fonts/IMPERIAL

Small

ABCDEFGHIJK
B
C
D
E
F
G
H
I

abcdefghijklmn
b
c
d
e
f
g
h
i

Large

ABCDE
B
C
D

abcdefg
b
c
d

THE FONTS/LASSEN

TALL LAYOUT

Font Size	Caps/Lowercase (LC)	No. Lines/Page	Approx. No. Charac./Line
Small	Caps	7	14
Small	LC	7	21
Large	Caps	4	6
Large	LC	4	11

WIDE LAYOUT

Font Size	Caps/Lowercase (LC)	No. Line/Page	Approx. No. Charac./Line
Small	Caps	4(IBM)/3(APP)	12
Small	LC	4(IBM)/3(APP)	17
Large	Caps	2	5
Large	LC	2	9

The Fonts/LASSEN

Small

ABCDEFGHIJKLMN
B
C
D
E
F
G

abcdefghijklmnopqrstu
b
c
d
e
f
g

Large

ABCDEF
B
C
D

abcdefghijk
b
c
d

The Fonts/MADERA

TALL LAYOUT

Font Size	Caps/ Lowercase (LC)	No. Lines/ Page	Approx. No. Charac./Line
Small	Caps	12	14
Small	LC	12	17
Large	Caps	6	6
Large	LC	6	8

WIDE LAYOUT

Font Size	Caps/ Lowercase (LC)	No. Line/ Page	Approx. No. Charac./Line
Small	Caps	6	11
Small	LC	6	14
Large	Caps	3	5
Large	LC	3	7

The Fonts/MADERA

Small

ABCDEFGHIJKLMN
B
C
D
E
F
G
H
I
J
K
L

abcdefghijklmnopq
b
c
d
e
f
g
h
i
j
k
l

Large

ABCDEF
B
C
D
E
F

abcdefgh
b
c
d
e
f

The Fonts/MARIN

TALL LAYOUT

Font Size	Caps/ Lowercase (LC)	No. Lines/ Page	Approx. No. Charac./Line
Small	Caps	8	12
Small	LC	8	13
Large	Caps	4	5
Large	LC	4	5

WIDE LAYOUT

Font Size	Caps/ Lowercase (LC)	No. Lines/ Page	Approx. No. Charac./Line
Small	Caps	4	9
Small	LC	4	11
Large	Caps	2	4
Large	LC	2	5

The Fonts/MARIN

Small

Large

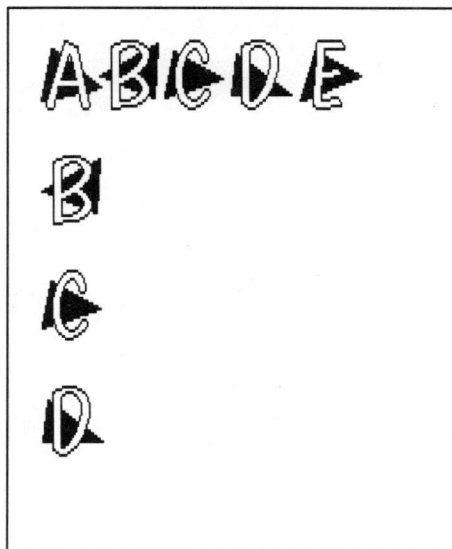

The Fonts/MERCED

TALL LAYOUT

Font Size	Caps/ Lowercase (LC)	No. Lines/ Page	Approx. No. Charac./Line
Small	Caps	8	12
Small	LC	8	18
Large	Caps	4	5
Large	LC	4	9

WIDE LAYOUT

Font Size	Caps/ Lowercase (LC)	No. Lines/ Page	Approx. No. Charac./Line
Small	Caps	4	8
Small	LC	4	15
Large	Caps	2	4
Large	LC	2	7

The Fonts/MERCED

Small

ABCDEFGHIJL
B
C
D
E
F
G
H

abcdefghijklmnopqr
b
c
d
e
f
g
h

Large

ABCDE
B
C
D

abcdefghi
b
c
d

The Fonts/SIERRA

TALL LAYOUT

Font Size	Caps/ Lowercase (LC)	No. Lines/ Page	Approx. No. Charac./Line
Small	Caps	13	14
Small	LC	13	18
Large	Caps	7	7
Large	LC	7	10

WIDE LAYOUT

Font Size	Caps/ Lowercase (LC)	No. Lines/ Page	Approx. No. Charac./Line
Small	Caps	7(IBM)/6(APP)	12
Small	LC	7(IBM)/6(APP)	15
Large	Caps	3	6
Large	LC	3	8

The Fonts/SIERRA

Small

ABCDEFGHIJKLMN
B
C
D
E
F
G
H
I
J
K
L
M

abcdefghijklmnopqr
b
c
d
e
f
g
h
i
j
k
l
m

Large

ABCDEFG
B
C
D
E
F
G

abcdefghij
b
c
d
e
f
g

The Fonts/SONOMA

TALL LAYOUT

Font Size	Caps/ Lowercase (LC)	No. Lines/ Page	Approx. No. Charac./Line
Small	Caps	12	15
Small	LC	12	18
Large	Caps	6	7
Large	LC	6	10

WIDE LAYOUT

Font Size	Caps/ Lowercase (LC)	No. Lines/ Page	Approx. No. Charac./Line
Small	Caps	6	13
Small	LC	6	15
Large	Caps	3	6
Large	LC	3	7

The Fonts/SONOMA

Small

ABCDEFGHIJKLMNO
B
C
D
E
F
G
H
I
J
K
L

abcdefghijklmnopqr
b
c
d
e
f
g
h
i
j
k
l

Large

ABCDEFG
B
C
D
E
F

abcdefghij
b
c
d
e
f

The Fonts/SUTTER

TALL LAYOUT

Font Size	Caps/ Lowercase (LC)	No. Lines/ Page	Approx. No. Charac./Line
Small	Caps	8	16
Small	LC	8	19
Large	Caps	4	7
Large	LC	4	10

WIDE LAYOUT

Font Size	Caps/ Lowercase (LC)	No. Lines/ Page	Approx. No. Charac./Line
Small	Caps	4	13
Small	LC	4	16
Large	Caps	2	6
Large	LC	2	7

The Fonts/SUTTER

Small

ABCDEFGHIJKLMNOP
B
C
D
E
F
G
H

abcdefghijklmnopqrs
b
c
d
e
f
g
h

Large

ABCDEFG
B
C
D

abcdefghij
b
c
d

The Fonts/VENTURA

TALL LAYOUT

Font Size	Caps/ Lowercase (LC)	No. Lines/ Page	Approx. No. Charac./Line
Small	Caps	9	13
Small	LC	9	17
Large	Caps	4	6
Large	LC	4	8

WIDE LAYOUT

Font Size	Caps/ Lowercase (LC)	No. Lines/ Page	Approx. No. Charac./Line
Small	Caps	4	11
Small	LC	4	14
Large	Caps	2	5
Large	LC	2	7

The Fonts/VENTURA

Small

ABCDEFGHIJKLM
B
C
D
E
F
G
H
I

abcdefghijklmnopq
b
c
d
e
f
g
h
i

Large

ABCDEF
B
C
D

abcdefgh
b
c
d

The Fonts/SMALL

TALL LAYOUT

Font Size	Caps/ Lowercase (LC)	No. Lines/ Page	Approx. No. Charac./Line
Small	Caps	20	29
Small	LC	20	31
Large	Caps	11	15
Large	LC	11	16

WIDE LAYOUT

Font Size	Caps/ Lowercase (LC)	No. Lines/ Page	Approx. No. Charac./Line
Small	Caps	10	25
Small	LC	10	27
Large	Caps	5	13
Large	LC	5	14

The Fonts/SMALL

Small

ABCDEFGHIJKLMNOPQRSTUVWXYZABC
B
C
D
E
F
G
H
I
J
K
L
M
N
O
P
Q
R
S
T

abcdefghijklmnopqrstuvwxyzaabbc
b
c
d
e
f
g
h
i
j
k
l
m
n
o
p
q
r
s
t

Large

ABCDEFGHIJKLMNO
B
C
D
E
F
G
H
I
J
K

abcdefghijklmnop
b
c
d
e
f
g
h
i
j
k

The Fonts/TINY

TALL LAYOUT

Font Size	Caps/ Lowercase (LC)	No. Lines/ Page	Approx. No. Charac./Line
Small	Caps	22(IBM)/24(APP)	40
Small	LC	22(IBM)/24(APP)	42
Large	Caps	16	20
Large	LC	16	21

WIDE LAYOUT

Font Size	Caps/ Lowercase (LC)	No. Lines/ Page	Approx. No. Charac./Line
Small	Caps	14(IBM)/13(APP)	33
Small	LC	14(IBM)/13(APP)	38
Large	Caps	8	17
Large	LC	8	18

The Fonts/TINY

Small

ABCDEFGHIJKLMNOPQRSTUVWXYZABCDEFGHIJKLMNO
B
C
D
E
F
G
H
I
J
K
L
M
N
O
P
Q
R
S
T
U
V

abcdefghijklmnopqrstuvwxyzaabbccddeeffgghh
b
c
d
e
f
g
h
i
j
k
l
m
n
o
p
q
r
s
t
u
v

Large

ABCDEFGHIJKLMNOPQRST
B
C
D
E
F
G
H
I
J
K
L
M
N
O
P

abcdefghijklmnopqrstu
b
c
d
e
f
g
h
i
j
k
l
m
n
o
p

The Graphics

- PROGRAM DISK

- SAMPLER EDITION

- SCHOOL & BUSINESS EDITION

- PARTY EDITION

Program Disk

FONTS: The fonts shown here come with upper and lowercase letters, numbers and punctuation. Each font can be printed in one of the seven colors supported by The New Print Shop.

AMADOR
ABCDEFGHIJKLMNOPQRSTUVWXYZ 1234567890
abcdefghijklmnopqrstuvwxyz

IMPERIAL
ABCDEFGHIJKLMNOPQRSTUVWXYZ 1234567890
abcdefghijklmnopqrstuvwxyz

LASSEN
ABCDEFGHIJKLMNOPQRSTUVWXYZ 1234567890
abcdefghijklmnopqrstuvwxyz

MADERA
ABCDEFGHIJKLMNOPQRSTUVWXYZ 1234567890
abcdefghijklmnopqrstuvwxyz

MARIN
ABCDEFGHIJKLMNOPQRSTUVWXYZ 1234567890
abcdefghijklmnopqrstuvwxyz

MERCED
ABCDEFGHIJKLMNOPQRSTUVWXYZ 1234567890
abcdefghijklmnopqrstuvwxyz

SIERRA
ABCDEFGHIJKLMNOPQRSTUVWXYZ 1234567890
abcdefghijklmnopqrstuvwxyz

SONOMA
ABCDEFGHIJKLMNOPQRSTUVWXYZ 1234567890
abcdefghijklmnopqrstuvwxyz

SUTTER
ABCDEFGHIJKLMNOPQRSTUVWXYZ 1234567890
abcdefghijklmnopqrstuvwxyz

VENTURA
ABCDEFGHIJKLMNOPQRSTUVWXYZ 1234567890
abcdefghijklmnopqrstuvwxyz

SINGLE COLOR GRAPHICS: The following graphics may be selected by picture or by number. When using a graphic "By Number," use the numbers listed on this card.

BALLOONS-1

BASEBALL-2

BASKETBALL-3

BOOKS-4

BUBBLY-5

CAKE SLICE-6

CASH BOX-7

CAUTION-8

CHANUKAH-9

COFFEE-10

COMPUTER-11

DAISIES-12

DESERT-13

EAGLE-14

FILE DRAWER-15

FOLDERS-16

FOOTBALL-17

ICE CREAM-18

IN BOX-19

INK BOTTLE-20

LETTER-21

MUSIC-22

NIGHT SKY-23

PARTY FAVOR-24

PENS-25
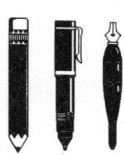

PIANO-26

PICNIC-27

PLAYTIME-28

POINSETTIA-29

PRINTER-30

PUSHPINS-31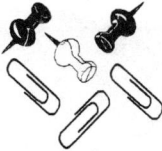

RIBBON-32

ROSEBUD-33

SOCCER-34

SUNSHINE-35

TEDDY BEAR-36

TELEPHONE-37

MULTICOLOR GRAPHICS: The following graphics are only available when using a color printer. They can also be converted to single color graphics by using the Convert program that comes with The New Print Shop.

BIRTHDAY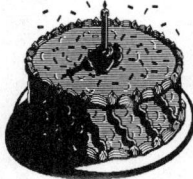

SALE SIGN

SANTA CLAUS

WIDE BORDERS: Wide borders can be used for Greeting Cards and Signs. They print in the seven colors supported by The New Print Shop.

BALLOONS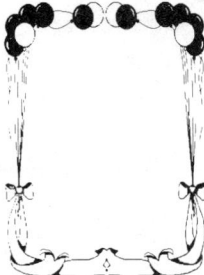

CLIPBOARD

COLUMNS

HOLLY

LILIES

HORIZONTAL FULL PANELS: The following designs can be used in topfold Greeting Cards, wide Signs, and horizontal Banners.

HEARTS

MEDALS

PARTY
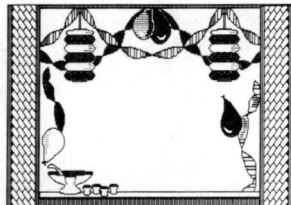

SALE TAG

SCREEN
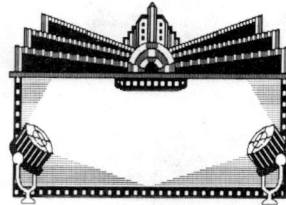

LETTERHEAD FULL PANELS: The following designs can be used in Letterheads and Cclendars.

FROM DESK

HOUSES
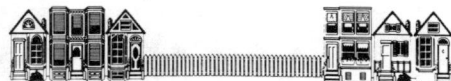

IRISES

LIBRARY

MEMO
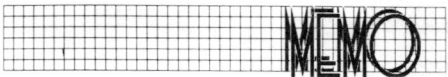

MENU

MIDNIGHT

NEW MEX

NEWS

SWEETS

THIN BORDERS: Thin borders can be used for Greeting Cards and Signs, and as trim for horizontal and vertical Banners. They print in the seven colors supported by The New Print Shop.

THIN LINE 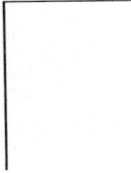   DOUBLE LINE    BLOCKS    DECO    FRILLY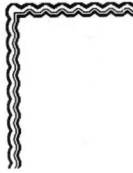

MAZE    NAVAJO    NEON    RIBBON    ROUNDED

APPLE THIN BORDERS

FRAME

LINES

CONFETTI

STRIPE

HOLLY

THICK

STARS

BOWS

WACKY

LADDER

SINGLE COLOR VERTICAL FULL PANELS: The following designs can be used in sidefold Greeting Cards, tall Signs, and vertical Banners.

CERTIF (CERTIFICATE)

FOOD

INVITE

JUKEBOX

OAK

OFFICE

ROBOT

SALE

SANTA

SCHOOL

MULTICOLOR VERTICAL FULL PANEL: This design is only available when using a color printer. It can also be converted to a single color full panel by using the Convert program that comes with The New Print Shop.

BIRTHDAY

PATTERNS: These graphics work well with tiled layouts.

LACE

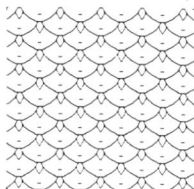

LEAVES

SHAPES

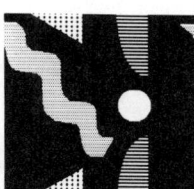

Apple Color Graphics

Sampler Edition

FONTS: The fonts shown here come with upper and lowercase letters, numbers and punctuation. Each font can be printed in one of the seven colors supported by The New Print Shop.

BRONTE
ABCDEFGHIJKLMNOPQRSTUVWXYZ 1234567890
abcdefghijklmnopqrstuvwxyz

ELIOT
ABCDEFGHIJKLMNOPQRSTUVWXYZ 1234567890
abcdefghijklmnopqrstuvwxyz

HARDY
ABCDEFGHIJKLMNOPQRSTUVWXYZ 1234567890
abcdefghijklmnopqrstuvwxyz

HUGO
ABCDEFGHIJKLMNOPQRSTUVWXYZ 1234567890
abcdefghijklmnopqrstuvwxyz

JOYCE
ABCDEFGHIJKLMNOPQRSTUVWXYZ 1234567890
abcdefghijklmnopqrstuvwxyz

POE
ABCDEFGHIJKLMNOPQRSTUVWXYZ 1234567890
abcdefghijklmnopqrstuvwxyz

SULLIVAN
ABCDEFGHIJKLMNOPQRSTUVWXYZ 1234567890
abcdefghijklmnopqrstuvwxyz

THOREAU
ABCDEFGHIJKLMNOPQRSTUVWXYZ 1234567890
abcdefghijklmnopqrstuvwxyz

TWAIN
ABCDEFGHIJKLMNOPQRSTUVWXYZ 1234567890
abcdefghijklmnopqrstuvwxyz

WILDE
ABCDEFGHIJKLMNOPQRSTUVWXYZ 1234567890
abcdefghijklmnopqrstuvwxyz

SINGLE COLOR GRAPHICS

AIRPLANE	BABY BOTTLE	BABY DINO	BICYCLE	BOWLING	BULL FROG

BURGER	CANDLESTICK	COCKATIEL	FIREPLACE	FLEUR	GALLEON

GARDENING	GIRAFFE	HIGH TOP	HOLLYWOOD	HORSE OPERA	HOT DOG

JOLLY ROGER	KITTY CAT	LIGHT BULB	MAN	MUSHROOMS	PIE SLICE

PIGGY BANK	PRESENT	RABBIT	RADIO DAYS	SCOTTIE	SKIER

TIME FLIES	TOOLS	VALLEY LILY	WEIGHTS	WOMAN

MULTICOLOR GRAPHICS: The following graphics are only available when using a color printer. They can also be converted to single color graphics by using the Convert program that comes with The New Print Shop.

BABY BLOCKS   BLOSSOM   BUTTERFLIES   CAROUSEL   CORNERPIECE

EASTER EGGS   FISH   FLAMINGO   GEESE   HONEY BEAR

ORCHID   ROSE   STOCKING   UP AND AWAY   WEDDING

PATTERNS: These graphics work well with tiled layouts.

AZTEC   FEATHER   FISH

GEOMETRIC   QUILT

SINGLE COLOR HORIZONTAL FULL PANELS: The following designs can be used in topfold Greeting Cards, wide Signs, and horizontal Banners.

FALLS

SCROLL

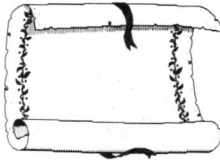

SODA SHOP

MULTICOLOR HORIZONTAL FULL PANELS: These designs are only available when using a color printer.

GLASS

POP ART

SINGLE COLOR VERTICAL FULL PANELS: The following designs can be used in sidefold Greeting Cards, tall Signs, and vertical Banners.

AUTUMN

DESERT

SPRING

SUMMER

MULTICOLOR VERTICAL FULL PANELS: These designs are only available when using a color printer.

WINTER

JAZZ

POW!

PRESENT

SINGLE COLOR LETTERHEAD FULL PANELS: The following designs can be used in Letterheads and Calendars.

DEAR

DINOSAUR

DROPLETS

SKYFLYER

SKYLINE

MULTICOLOR LETTERHEAD FULL PANELS: These designs are only available when using a color printer.

TUCSON

WINDOW

THIN BORDERS: Thin borders can be used for Greeting Cards and Signs, and as trim for horizontal and vertical Banners. They print in the seven colors supported by The New Print Shop.

CORNER

FLEUR

FLORAL

LINK

MULTI LINES

SINGLE COLOR WIDE BORDERS (IBM only): Wide borders can be used for Greeting Cards and Signs. They print in the seven colors supported by The New Print Shop.

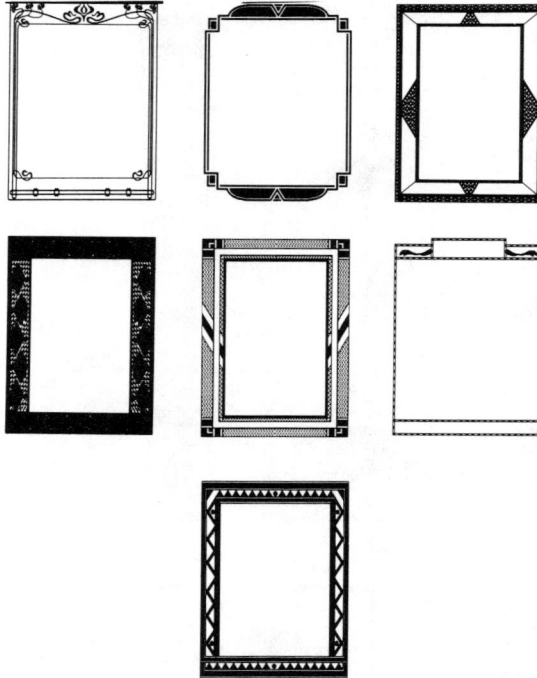

Apple Color Graphics

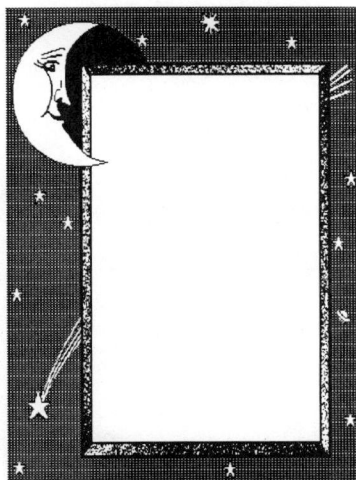

School & Business Edition

FONTS: The fonts shown here come with upper and lowercase letters, numbers and punctuation. Each font can be printed in one of the seven colors supported by The New Print Shop.

APPLE

BLIPPO
ABCDEFGHIJKLMNOPQRSTUVWXYZ 1234567890
abcdefghijklmnopqrstuvwxyz

CHILDREN
ABCDEFGHIJKLMNOPQRSTUVWXYZ   1234567890
abcdefghijklmnopqrstuvwxyz

CLASSIC
ABCDEFGHIJKLMNOPQRSTUVWXYZ 1234567890
abcdefghijklmnopqrstuvwxyz

COLORADO
ABCDEFGHIJKLMNOPQRSTUVWXYZ 1234567890
abcdefghijklmnopqrstuvwxyz

DIGITAL
ABCDEFGHIJKLMNOPQRSTUVWXYZ 1234567890
abcdefghijklmnopqrstuvwxyz

OCTOPUS
ABCDEFGHIJKLMNOPQRSTUVWXYZ 1234567890
abcdefghijklmnopqrstuvwxyz

PARISIAN
ABCDEFGHIJKLMNOPQRSTUVWXYZ 1234567890
abcdefghijklmnopqrstuvwxyz

RESUME
ABCDEFGHIJKLMNOPQRSTUVWXYZ 1234567890
abcdefghijklmnopqrstuvwxyz

STENCIL
ABCDEFGHIJKLMNOPQRSTUVWXYZ 1234567890
abcdefghijklmnopqrstuvwxyz

SINGLE COLOR GRAPHICS

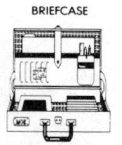

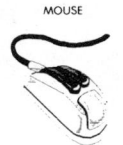

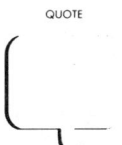

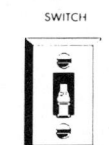

AIR MAIL	ART	BAND	BEAKER	BIOLOGY	BRIEFCASE

BUILDINGS	CALCULATOR	CHALKBOARD	CLOCK	DOLLARS	DRAFTING

DRAMA	ENGLISH	FLOPPY DISK	GEOGRAPHY	GLOBE	GYM CLASS

KEY	LUNCHTIME	MAGNIFIER	MATH	MOUSE	MOVING VAN

NO SMOKING	PC	POINTER	QUOTE	SCHOOL	STAMP

SWIMMING	SWITCH	TENNIS	TRACK	TROPHY

MULTICOLOR GRAPHICS: The following graphics are only available when using a color printer. They can also be converted to single color graphics by using the Convert program that comes with The New Print Shop.

APPLE

CHEERLEADER

FIFE & DRUM

FILM

FLAG

GRAPH

LEAVES

LUNCH PAIL

MONEY BAG

PAINT TUBE

POT O' GOLD

SAILBOAT

SCHOOL BUS

STOP LIGHT

TICKETS

PATTERNS: These graphics work well with tiled layouts.

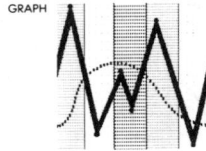

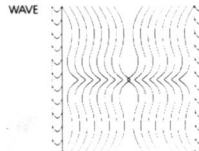

DIAGONAL

GRAPH

PENCIL

STATIONERY

WAVE

SINGLE COLOR HORIZONTAL FULL PANELS: The following designs can be used in topfold Greeting Cards, wide Signs, and horizontal Banners.

AWARD

DESKTOP

USA MAP

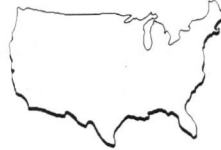

MULTICOLOR HORIZONTAL FULL PANELS: These designs are only available when using a color printer.

COAT ROOM

MEMO

SINGLE COLOR VERTICAL FULL PANELS: The following designs can be used in sidefold Greeting Cards, tall Signs, and vertical Banners.

CHALKBRD (CHALKBOARD)

EASEL

NOTEBOOK

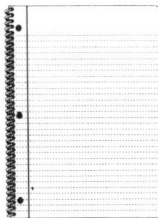

PROFITS

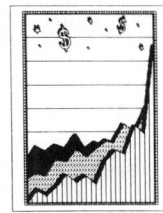

MULTICOLOR VERTICAL FULL PANELS: These designs are only available when using a color printer.

SCHOOLHS (SCHOOLHOUSE)

ARROW

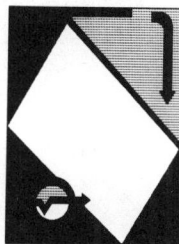

DINOSAUR

PEN & INK

SINGLE COLOR LETTERHEAD FULL PANELS: The following designs can be used in Letterheads and Calendars.

BUS

BUSINESS

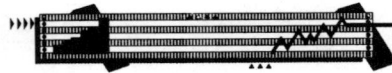

LEARNING

PRINTER

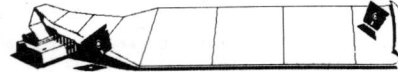

RECESS

MULTICOLOR LETTERHEAD FULL PANELS: These designs are only available when using a color printer.

SOARING

VILLAGE

THIN BORDERS: Thin borders can be used for Greeting Cards and Signs, and as trim for horizontal and vertical Banners. They print in the seven colors supported by The New Print Shop.

BOOKS   CAPS   CUT CORNERS   SCROLL   TWISTED

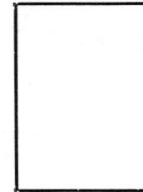

SINGLE COLOR WIDE BORDERS (IBM only): Wide borders can be used for Greeting Cards and Signs. They print in the seven colors supported by The New Print Shop.

Apple Color Graphics

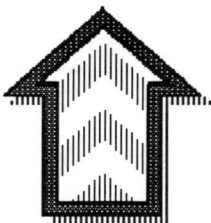

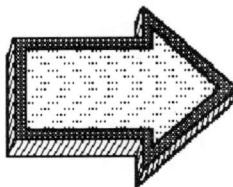

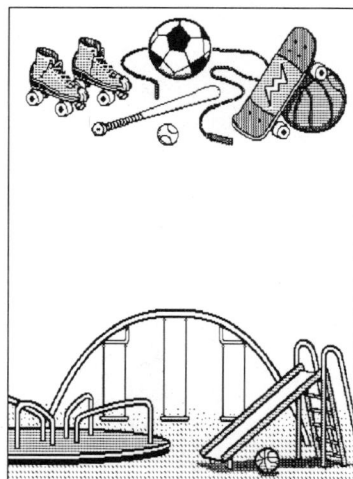

Party Edition

FONTS: The fonts shown here come with upper and lowercase letters, numbers and punctuation. Each font can be printed in one of the seven colors supported by The New Print Shop.

BALLOONS · ABCDEFGHIJKLMNOPQRSTUVWXYZ 1234567890
abcdefghijklmnopqrstuvwxyz

BRUSH · *ABCDEFGHIJKLMNOPQRSTUVWXYZ 1234567890*
abcdefghijklmnopqrstuvwxyz

CANDLES · ABCDEFGHIJKLMNOPQRSTUVWXYZ 1234567890
abcdefghijklmnopqrstuvwxyz

DOTS · ABCDEFGHIJKLMNOPQRSTUVWXYZ 1234567890
abcdefghijklmnopqrstuvwxyz

EASTERN · ABCDEFGHIJKLMNOPQRSTUVWXYZ 1234567890
abcdefghijklmnopqrstuvwxyz

FORMAL · *ABCDEFGHIJKLMNOPQRSTUVWXYZ 1234567890*
abcdefghijklmnopqrstuvwxyz

PARTY · **ABCDEFGHIJKLMNOPQRSTUVWXYZ 1234567890**

PRESENTS · ABCDEFGHIJKLMNOPQRSTUVWXYZ 1234567890
abcdefghijklmnopqrstuvwxyz

SHOWER · ABCDEFGHIJKLMNOPQRSTUVWXYZ 1234567890

WESTERN · ABCDEFGHIJKLMNOPQRSTUVWXYZ 1234567890
abcdefghijklmnopqrstuvwxyz

SINGLE COLOR GRAPHICS

BARBECUE	BAT	BIG TOP	BLACK CAT	BON VOYAGE	CAKE

COLLEGE	COOL DRINK	DINNER DATE	GINGERBREAD	GRADUATION	HOEDOWN

JAM SESSION	JUKEBOX	MAGIC	MASQUERADE	OPEN HOUSE	ORNAMENT

PARTY HAT	PENGUIN	PICNIC TIME	PIZZA	POKER	POPCORN

RATTLE	RINGS	SANDWICH	SIXTEEN	SLUMBER	SOCK HOP

ST. PATRICK	TEA PARTY	TRUMPETERS	TWENTY-FIVE	TWENTY-ONE

MULTICOLOR GRAPHICS: The following graphics are only available when using a color printer. They can also be converted to single color graphics by using the Convert program that comes with The New Print Shop.

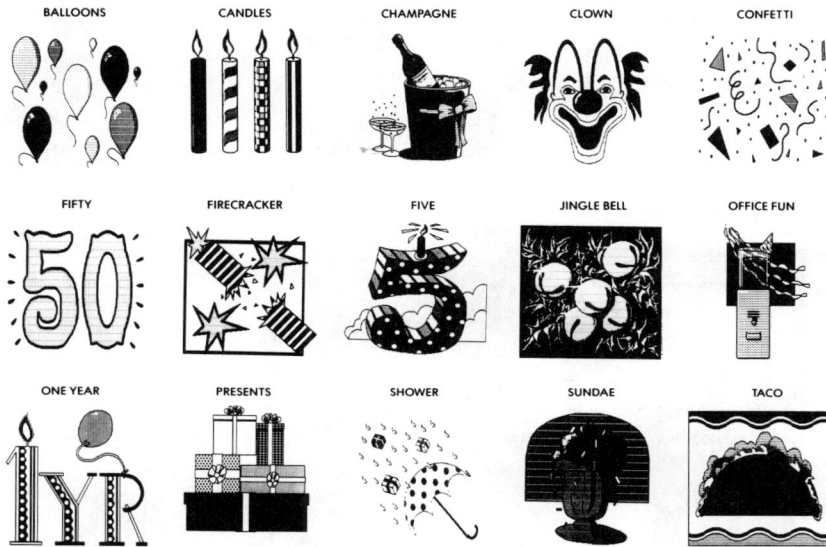

BALLOONS

CANDLES

CHAMPAGNE

CLOWN

CONFETTI

FIFTY

FIRECRACKER

FIVE

JINGLE BELL

OFFICE FUN

ONE YEAR

PRESENTS

SHOWER

SUNDAE

TACO

PATTERNS: These graphics work well with tiled layouts.

CHRISTMAS

FLOWER

HATS

SURPRISE

TRIANGLES

SINGLE COLOR HORIZONTAL FULL PANELS: The following designs can be used in topfold Greeting Cards, wide Signs, and horizontal Banners.

BARBECUE

CAKES

SURPRISE

MULTICOLOR HORIZONTAL FULL PANELS: These designs are only available when using a color printer.

CONFETTI

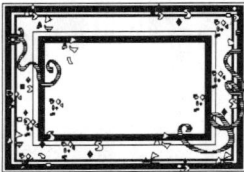

FIESTA

SINGLE COLOR VERTICAL FULL PANELS: The following designs can be used in sidefold Greeting Cards, tall Signs, and vertical Banners.

DANCERS

GAZEBO

HARVEST

NEW YEAR

MULTICOLOR VERTICAL FULL PANELS: These designs are only available when using a color printer.

RECORDS

CLOWN

HATS

SKATERS

SINGLE COLOR LETTERHEAD FULL PANELS: The following designs can be used in Letterheads and Calendars.

BOOGIE

HOAGIE

NAVIGATE

REUNION

SPORTS

MULTICOLOR LETTERHEAD FULL PANELS: These designs are only available when using a color printer.

PARADISE

PARTY

THIN BORDERS: Thin borders can be used for Greeting Cards and Signs, and as trim for horizontal and vertical Banners. They print in the seven colors supported by The New Print Shop.

BALLOONS

CAKES

CURVY
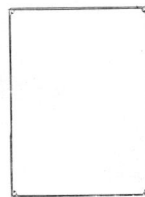

EVERGREENS

FIESTA

SINGLE COLOR WIDE BORDERS (IBM only): Wide borders can be used for Greeting Cards and Signs. They print in the seven colors supported by The New Print Shop.

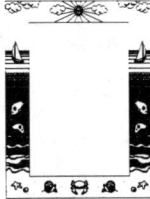

Apple Color Graphics

About the Art Grid

If you can't find a graphic that fits your design, why not draw your own? The art grid is the tool to use to create an original graphic. Just copy the grid onto a copying machine, grab a pencil, and you're ready to go!

Like graph paper, the art grid has many small boxes. Each box represents the position of a dot in the Graphic Editor drawing surface. Fill in the boxes on the art grid. When your drawing is exactly the way you want it, fill in the dots in the Graphic Editor in the exact same positions. Every tenth box on the art grid is highlighted to make it easier for you to identify its position. The position of every dot in the Graphic Editor is labeled on screen.

Copy your art grid drawing onto the Graphic Editor drawing surface and you'll have a new piece of art at your command. Save it to use or modify as often as you like.

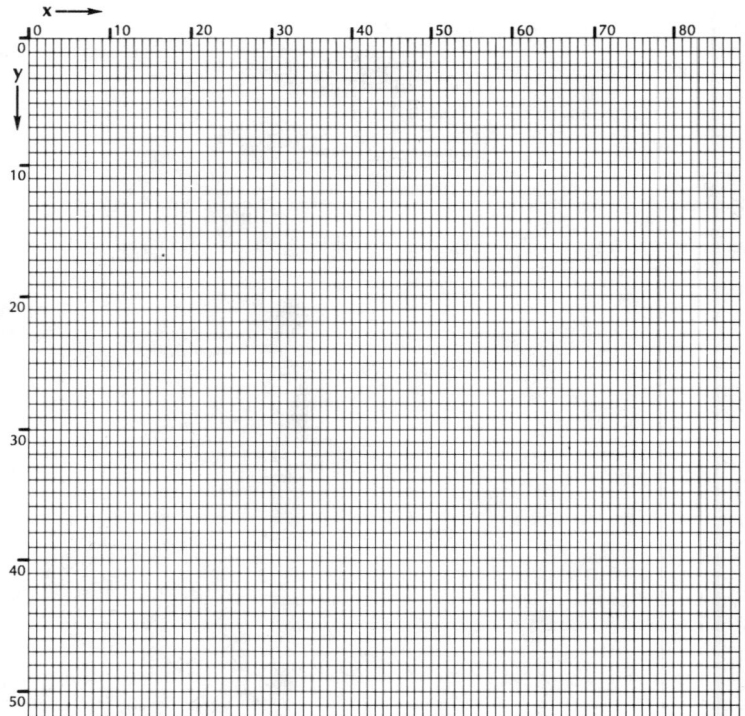

Four great ways to be even more creative with The New Print Shop!

You'll discover all kinds of exciting new possibilities when you add these all-new collections to your New Print Shop. Each New Print Shop Graphics Library® includes over 100 professionally created graphics, borders, and fonts! They give you the same improved resolution and quality as The New Print Shop — including multicolor designs and full panel graphics!

And if you have an IBM/Tandy computer, be sure to get The New Print Shop Companion. It lets you do things that have never been possible before!

◆ The New Print Shop Graphics Library: Sampler Edition

Here's a little bit of everything to add that extra something. From butterflies, bicycles and burgers to candlesticks, cocktails and carousels! Pie a la mode and pink flamingos! Covers popular themes like holidays, birthdays, school, sports and more.

◆ The New Print Shop Graphics Library: Party Edition

Create a total party environment. Make personalized invitations, signs, place cards, gift tags, banners, posters — even wrapping paper. Covers all kinds of celebrations, official and unofficial: holidays, anniversaries, birthdays, housewarmings, and beach parties, to name just a few.

◆ The New Print Shop Graphics Library: School and Business Edition

An absolute boon to students, teachers and business people. Reach out and grab someone with catchy communications: use it for signs, note pads, letterheads, folders, forms, schedules and more. From chalkboards and cheerleaders to floppy disks, calculators and "no smoking" signs.

◆ The New Print Shop Companion

Produce great-looking flyers and newsletters with *Page Publisher.* Design matching envelopes with *Envelope Maker.* Type personal or business letters with *Letter Writer*, using your New Print Shop letterheads. Create custom graphics, borders, and fonts, using easy-to-use editors. There's even a *Graphic Importer* for importing artwork from popular paint programs. Plus *Cataloger*, a special utility for cataloging all your graphics, borders and fonts. (IBM/Tandy only) **To order, please turn page.**

Special offer for owners of The Official New Print Shop Handbook:

Save 25% on the rest of The New Print Shop family!

As a "serious" user of The New Print Shop, you qualify for some serious savings: *25% off* the suggested retail price of The New Print Shop Graphics Libraries and The New Print Shop Companion. So you can increase your creativity ... while we decrease the price tag!

Use this handy order form or call 1-800-521-6263

For fastest delivery, credit card holders can call 1-800-521-6263, Monday through Friday, 8 a.m. to 5 p.m., Pacific Standard Time. To get the 25% discount, be sure to mention *The Official New Print Shop Handbook.*

OR, fill out the coupon and mail it with your payment or purchase order to Brøderbund Software-Direct®, P.O. Box 13717, San Rafael, CA 94913-3717.
Please include shipping and handling as indicated on the order form.

Allow 4 weeks for delivery.

NO RISK GUARANTEE
We stand by our products 100%. If, for any reason, you are not completely satisfied with a product you purchase from Brøderbund Software-Direct, return it within 10 days along with a copy of your invoice and the complete contents of the package. At your option, we will promptly exchange the program or refund your full purchase price.

( ) **YES! Send me the following New Print Shop Graphics Libraries for my IBM/Tandy or 100% compatible or Apple II series computer or The New Print Shop Companion (IBM/Tandy version only).**

Name_____

Address_____

City_____

State_____ Zip_____

Daytime Telephone_____
(required for credit card orders)

❏ Check/Money Order
❏ Purchase Order #_____
❏ VISA ❏ MasterCard ❏ American Express

Signature (required for credit card orders)

Account Number   Expiration

ITEM #	QTY	DESCRIPTION	PRICE	SALE	TOTAL
20610		Sampler Edition - IBM - 5.25"	$34.95	26.25	
20611		Sampler Edition - IBM - 3.5"	$34.95	26.25	
20650		Sampler Edition - Apple - 5.25"	$24.95	18.75	
20654		Sampler Edition - Apple - 3.5"	$24.95	18.75	
20710		Party Edition - IBM - 5.25"	$34.95	26.25	
20711		Party Edition - IBM - 3.5"	$34.95	26.25	
20750		Party Edition - Apple - 5.25"	$24.95	18.75	
20754		Party Edition - Apple - 3.5"	$24.95	18.75	
21210		School & Business Ed. -IBM- 5.25"	$34.95	26.25	
21211		School & Business Ed. -IBM- 3.5"	$34.95	26.25	
21250		School & Business Ed. -Apple- 5.25"	$24.95	18.75	
21254		School & Business Ed. -Apple- 3.5"	$24.95	18.75	
20412		Companion - IBM - 5.25"	$49.95	37.50	
20414		Companion - IBM - 3.5"	$49.95	37.50	

Sub-Total

Local sales tax must be included for the following states: CA, CO, GA, IL, MA, PA, TX, WA

Shipping & Handling Add $3.50 for one product and $1.00 for ea. additional product

GRAND TOTAL

92BPS